AMERICA'S COMMON BOND

Why English Should be the Official Language of the United States

AMERICA'S COMMON BOND

Why English Should be the Official Language of the United States

Saumyajit Ray

Reference Press

4831/24, Ansari Road, Darya Ganj,
New Delhi-110002
Tel. : 23260807, 41563444
Fax : 011-41563334
E-mail: info@essessreference.com
www.essessreference.com

Reference Press
4831/24, Ansari Road,
Darya Ganj,
New Delhi-110 002.

Tel.: 23260807, 41563444
Fax: 41563334
E-mail: info@essessreference.com
www.essessreference.com

Rs.875/-

First Published - 2010

ISBN: 978-81-8405-060-8

Cover Design by *Patch Creative Unit*

Published By Reference Press and printed at Salasar Imaging Systems

PRINTED IN INDIA

Dedicated to
MY PARENTS

Contents

Preface (*ix*)

1 The Search for the Language of America 1

(A) Behind language neutrality: Does constitutional silence make English official in America? 1

(B) E Pluribus Unum: American assimilationism in retrospect 16

2 The Melting Pot Boils Over 38

(A) Changing the face of America: The Immigration and Nationality Act of 1965 38

(B) From immigrants to ethnics: The judicial and statutory protection of minority language rights 54

3 Old Ties in the New World 89

(A) From "Know English" to "No English": The quagmire that is bilingual education 89

(B) Permanently alien residents: The baneful effects of bilingual education 109

4 The Surge for the Language of America 135

(A) Preserving America's common bond: The Official English movement 135

(B) Toward official monolingualism: H.R. 123 162

5 Nation versus Hyphenation 180

(A) A more perfect union: Official English Laws in the States 180

(B) From immigrants to Americans: The GOP and the Politics of Inclusion 210

6 A Nation of Immigrants, Not A Multilingual Boarding House 240

(A) Amero-conformity : Toward a New Theory of Assimilation 240

(B) One Culture, One Common Language : Official English and the Future of Assimilation 257

7 Postscript H.R. 4321 273

8 Suggested Readings 276

Index 300

Preface

In 1776, the United States emerged as the first English-speaking republic in the world. The majority of the population was of British descent, Thomas Jefferson wrote the *Declaration of Independence* in English, the deliberations at the Philadelphia Convention were conducted in English, the *Federalist Papers* were compiled in English, and so was the federal Constitution (1789). The Founding Fathers, though, did not designate English—or any other language, for that matter—as official; they did not feel the need to lay down in law what existed in fact. They had created a nation of immigrants, and their expectation from immigrants was that they would eventually assimilate into the culture and society of the United States, and that meant adopting the English language as well. But the Founding Fathers' action of maintaining a constitutional silence on the status of English denied that language an official recognition which it is yet to acquire.

The Official English movement—the movement to make English the official language of the United States through a federal constitutional amendment—was started formally in 1981 by Sen. S. I. Hayakawa (R-CA) when he moved an English Language Amendment (ELA) in the U.S.

Senate and launched an organization for the purpose named U.S.English. Since that time, many Republicans have moved ELAs in Congress, with little or no success. These ELAs not only aimed to declare English as the official language of U.S. government, but also wanted to put an end to bilingual education and multilingual ballots. Cultural pluralism—as did the governmental programs it inspired—was celebrating the "manyness" of the American people at the cost of national unity. A new phenomenon, something unheard of in American society till then, emerged: the reluctance of immigrants to assimilate, stemming from their refusal to learn and adopt the English language.

As the notion among the newest immigrants—especially those from Spanish-speaking backgrounds—that it was not necessary to learn English to live and work in America gained ground, it caused considerable alarm among mainstream (English-speaking) Americans. The result was that state after state started declaring English as their official language (30 states have done so till date). Since the legislatures in most of these states failed to muster courage in according cfficial status to English, the victory of Official English in these states came through popular initiatives. Hayakawa's U.S.English was in the forefront of these initiatives.

At the federal level, in August 1996, H.R. 123—the Bill Emerson English Language Empowerment Act—became the only ELA to be passed by the U.S. House of Representatives till date. Apart from proposing to amend the federal Constitution to make English the official language of U.S. government, H.R. 123 wanted to limit federal funding to *transitional* bilingual education only and abolish multilingual ballots and voter assistance.

The victory of Official English in the Republican-controlled U.S. House of Representatives in the 104th Congress is noteworthy. More so because the Republican Party had habitually maintained a silence on the issue of Official English despite the efforts of individual Republican Representatives and Senators. The Republican involvement in the Official English movement was all too evident.

On the contrary, the multiculturalist Democratic Party fiercely oppose the Official English movement, calling it nativist, anti-immigrant, and discriminatory. Democrats and their allies, usually a host of Hispanic organizations, accuse the GOP (Grand Old Party, that is, Republicans) of harboring nativist tendencies and of trying to wipe out the culture and language of non-English-speaking immigrants.

But, historically, Republicans had always associated with Americanization efforts, believing that immigrants should be swiftly assimilated into the American mainstream. They supported Theodore Roosevelt when he said that attachment to the native country, native culture, and native language was neither desired nor expected from immigrants and instead had to be substituted with loyalty to the United States and its political institutions, American culture, and the English language.

The Immigration and Nationality Act of 1965 opened the gates of America to immigrants from Asia and Latin America with little or no knowledge of English. The Democratic-controlled U.S. Congress passed the Bilingual Education Act in 1968 to enable language-minority students—children of these immigrants—learn both English and subject-matter courses in English. But *transitional* bilingual education, which involved teaching in the students' native language, degenerated into *maintenance* bilingual education through total native language instruction. Worse still, these students were taught to take pride in their native languages and cultures instead of the English language and American culture, with the result that language minority students started refusing to learn English and ended up dropping out of school and getting pushed into low-paid jobs. What is more, multilingual ballots and voter assistance—mandated by the 1975 amendments to the Voting Rights Act (1965)—prevented language-minority voters from participating meaningfully in the American political process.

Many mainstream Americans began feeling that bilingual education, multilingual ballots, and the absence of an official language of government at the federal level had become serious obstacles to the full assimilation of immigrants into American society. Cultural Pluralism as a political ideology also impeded assimilation and made immigrants reluctant to assimilate. A new Americanization effort was the need of the hour. Thus emerged the Official English movement.

This movement, which never sought a ban on the use of languages other than English in the United States, is deridingly referred to as the English *Only* movement. Apart from demanding that all governmental activities at all levels in the U.S. be conducted in English, it wants multilingual ballots to be scrapped and bilingual education to remain *transitional* only.

Just as the Teddy Roosevelt generation was alarmed by hyphenism among Americans, the present situation has given rise to a new and dangerous phenomenon in

American society: *ampersand* Americans. The *ampersand* idea insists on the retention of dual identities (for example, Mexican and American) and dual loyalties by immigrants, and encourages immigrants to change the society in which they have settled instead of assimilating into that society. The result has been disastrous: not only have many immigrants started treating the U.S. as a living space with no political loyalty or emotional attachment toward it, foreign language translations of public documents are made available at every level. A Texas border town, El Cenizo, even banned the public use of English and declared Spanish as its official language in August 1999.

This book argues that to prevent further calamities, English needs to be declared the official language of the United States. The movement for Official English is actually an attempt by mainstream Americans (not necessarily of Anglo-American descent) to reinforce America's assimilationist ideal and create an ethnically diverse but culturally united America, in line with the thinking of the Founding Fathers. That was the only way to strengthen and preserve America as a nation of immigrants. This book also introduces Amero-conformity, conforming to the culture of America as produced by the Melting Pot, as a new model of assimilation by pointing out the deficiencies in the earlier models and rejecting Cultural Pluralism as a model of assimilation in its own right.

This book is spread over six chapters.

The position of English in American society and polity as envisaged by the Founding Fathers and subsequent attempts to perpetuate it through collective action as the most effective tool for assimilating non-Anglophone immigrants are discussed in the introductory chapter, **The Search for the Language of America**.

How the Immigration and Nationality Act of 1965 started changing the face of American society forever and how bilingual education and multilingual ballots began a trend of unprecedented protection of and encouragement to minority languages (resulting in a kind of ethnic resurgence and revival unforeseen by the Founding Fathers) are looked at in the second chapter, **The Melting Pot Boils Over**.

The next chapter, **Old Ties in the New World**, focuses completely on the theoretical premises that gave birth to bilingual education in the United States and the consequences of such education on language-minority children.

The historical roots of the Official English movement, the activities of U.S. English, its partisan links with Republicans, its perception in the eyes of opponents, and its successes and failures are explored in the chapter titled **The Surge for the Language of America**.

In the chapter **Nation versus Hyphenation**, the Official English laws of all the thirty states are examined to see to what extent they have been able to incorporate the basic principles of the Official English movement. How the Republican ideology and politics of inclusion have served as breeding grounds for the Official English doctrine and how Republicans have sought to operate through this movement to expedite the acculturation and assimilation of immigrants into American society are also discussed.

The concluding chapter, **A Nation of Immigrants, Not a Multilingual Boarding House**, develops a new theory of assimilation—which I call Amero-conformity—in an attempt to overcome present difficulties in adopting earlier theories like Anglo-conformity and Melting Pot. It also rejects Cultural Pluralism as a theory of assimilation unsuitable for the American experience.

Author's Note

Working on the Official English movement is difficult. For two important reasons. One, I am based in India. And since I am, the paucity of research materials here has made me feel handicapped at every step. The internet cannot, and will never, be a substitute for books. More importantly, in an age where being politically correct is deemed fashionable, I was working on an issue that is regarded my many, in academic circles and outside, as being on the wrong side of the political debate.

I belong to a country where language is an emotive issue. The units of the Indian federation (though our Constitution does not describe it as one) are linguistic states. I was working on a country where the politics of language hardly ever takes centre-stage. But as I read more about it, I realized it was just beneath the surface. And something was always there in front of everyone's eyes, but hardly anyone took notice: the world's oldest democratic republic was without an official language. Worse, many believe and try to convince others that the United States was better off that way. Most of the literature I have come across till date are critical of any attempt to declare English—the language of America—as the official language of U.S. government. It has always been my conviction that political correctness must have its limits: if it threatens to alter society, government and politics beyond recognition, it deserves to be abandoned. Hence this book.

I am thankful to my professors at Jawaharlal Nehru University, Prof. (Dr.) Christopher S. Raj and Prof. (Dr.) Chintamani Mahapatra, for asking me to write this book in the first place. Without their help and encouragement, I doubt whether I would have taken up this project.

Thanks are also due to people who I have never met, but have always entertained my queries by promptly replying to my mails. They are eminent people, and I am grateful to them. One is former Governor Richard D. Lamm of Colorado, who may not agree with everything that I have written. The other is former Governor Michael Dukakis of Massachusetts, who may not agree with anything that I have written. The congressional staff of Rep. Steve King (R-IA), ranking member in the U.S. House Judiciary Committee's Immigration Subcommittee, also helped by providing answers and useful links.

James Crawford, whom I have more than once referred to as "that celebrated opponent of Official English", has been kind enough to reply to my queries too. I have also greatly benefited from his books which are compulsory readings for anyone who seeks to work on Official English.

On the home front, it is needless to say that my parents are happy. In India, it is unbecoming of a son to thank his parents; instead, it is to them that I dedicate this work. My beloved wife, who had been a student of mine at one point of time, was involved at every stage of writing this book; without her by my side, I would not have been able to overcome the moments of frustration and uncertainty that I encountered while working on it.

I am also hugely indebted to my publisher, Mr. Sumit Sethi of Reference Press, whose faith in me I hope I have been able to live up to.

While I was at the closing stages of proof-reading, interesting news came from America: the congressional Democratic majority has introduced legislation in the House (H.R.4321) that proposes to grant citizenship to about 12 million illegal immigrants. After that, certain portions of this book needed to be reworked, and a post-script included. Otherwise, it could have been released earlier.

My work may not be perfect, but with the limited resources at my disposal, I have tried to do my best. No doubt there is scope for improvement, and I take complete responsibility for any shortcomings that may become evident to a discerning reader. But then, if this book helps Indian students understand the politics and society of the United States better, or evokes the interest of Americans in an issue they seldom talk or think about, I will know that I did not labor in vain.

May God continue to bless America.

SAUMYAJIT RAY, PhD
Delhi, India

1

The Search for the Language of America

"Three hundred years of history had selected English as the language for Americans,... English has been central to American national identity."

- Samuel P. Huntington

(A) BEHIND LANGUAGE NEUTRALITY: DOES CONSTITUTIONAL SILENCE MAKE ENGLISH OFFICIAL IN AMERICA?

We,... the Representatives of the United States of America... solemnly publish and declare, that these United Colonies are, and of right ought to be Free and Independent States, that they are absolved from all allegiance to the British Crown, and that all political connection between them and the State of Great Britain, is and ought to be totally dissolved...

Wrote Thomas Jefferson in the *American Declaration of Independence*, adopted on July 4, 1776. The *Declaration* finally proclaimed to the world the freedom of the thirteen British colonies in North America from political control by the mother country. Jefferson's revolutionary document not only complimented the defeat of the British forces in the hands of General George Washington and his colonial army, it was also the first step toward creating a republic, albeit an English-speaking one. In 1789, when the Constitution of the United States was adopted, emerged the first English-speaking republic in the world.

The colonies, all thirteen of them, were either overwhelmingly or wholly British (only Pennsylvania had a sizeable German presence). The American War of Independence was no revolution of native peoples against a colonial power. The *Declaration* called the King of Great Britain a tyrant, accused him of bad governance, and charged him of being "unfit to be the ruler of a free people". The grievances of the people in the thirteen colonies against their king in faraway London was solely political; they had nothing to do with culture, religion or language. The British Empire in North America disintegrated, a victim of its own history of political mismanagement of its colonies. The revolution protested, and the *Declaration* corroborated the belief of the people in the thirteen colonies that they were free to determine their own political future, separate from that of the country they had left long back in search of a better life. An overwhelming majority of them shared the king's language and culture, if not his church; yet they repudiated his right to rule over them. The rejection of British monarchial authority by the thirteen North American colonies was in fact in pursuance of a political tradition very much British: the doctrine of the people's right to revolution, propounded by John Locke, which said that a government that failed to secure to its subjects the rights to life, liberty and property needed to be replaced by a new dispensation. This search for a new dispensation culminated in the establishment of the United States of America.

The Constitution of the United States, written in English, however did not designate English or any other language as the official language of the new republic. Many attempts have been made by opponents of Official English to explain this refusal of the Founding Fathers to canonize their native tongue for all official purposes. The most celebrated is the one by Shirley Brice Heath, professor of linguistics at Stanford University. Wrote Heath, exploring the reasons behind the absence of an official tongue:

> During the founding period of 1780-1820, the national elite recognized the plural nature of American society, as well as the need to strike a balance between the absence of restraint on the number and kind of languages to be spoken and the need and ability of the citizenry to belong to a common entity.[1]

That the nation was conceived in liberty there is no doubt about, and freedom of language choice indeed fell within its purview. But the fact remains that the overwhelming majority of the American population at the time of the writing of the Constitution—including all fifty-five delegates to the Constitutional Convention—spoke English. The framers did not think it expedient to lay down in law what existed in fact.

At the time of the American Revolution, the white American population was largely English and Protestant in origin, but they had already absorbed substantial groups of Germans and Scotch-Irish and smaller groups of French, Dutch, Swedes, Swiss, South Irish and Poles, and a handful of immigrants from other European nations. What Professor Heath meant was that the failure of the Founding Fathers to enact an official English language policy was actually a conscious decision on their part to support cultural pluralism. That the Founding Fathers were not cultural pluralists or their refusal to designate an official tongue was not intended to encourage the use of non-English languages in the new republic is borne out by the attitudes of George Washington and Thomas Jefferson toward the phenomenon of mass immigration to the United States. Wrote Washington in 1794 to John Adams, his successor as president:

> My opinion, with respect to immigration, is that ... there is no need of encouragement, while the policy or advantage of its taking place in a body (I mean the settling of them in a body) may be much questioned; for, by so doing, they retain the language, habits and principles (good or bad) which they bring with them.[2]

Thomas Jefferson was not only suspicious about mass immigration, but also wanted immigrants to assimilate as soon as possible:

> It is for the happiness of those united in society to harmonize as much as possible in matters which they must of necessity transact together... Every species of government has its specific principles. Ours... is a composition of the freest principles of the English constitution, with others derived from natural right and natural reason. To these nothing can be more opposed than the maxims of

> absolute monarchies. Yet from such we are to expect the greatest number of immigrants. They will bring with them the principles of the governments they leave... These principles, with their language, they will transmit to their children.[3]

There was as much derision for the monarchical political tradition, the culture, and language of the peoples of continental Europe in Jefferson's remarks as there was pride in English political culture and institutions. Yet there was a sense of resignation at the prospect of the immigration of such people to the United States, and at the inability to prevent such immigration. The solution lay in the assimilation of continental European immigrants into the English cultural tradition, political and otherwise. And, this could only be done by the maintenance of English institutions (as modified by the American Revolution), the English language, and English-oriented cultural patterns as dominant and standard in American life.

John Adams, on his part, proposed the setting up of a national language academy. In a "Letter to the President of Congress"—written while on a diplomatic mission to Europe during the Revolutionary War and posted from Amsterdam on September 5, 1780—the man who would be President wrote that since "republics have produced the greatest purity, copiousness, and perfection of language", it was necessary for Congress to set up a society under the name of "The American Academy for refining, improving and ascertaining the English language".[4] Adam's recommendations would have led to the creation of a national (if not official) language, an ultimate point of reference for proper grammar, spelling, and vocabulary for the entire United States. But the Continental Congress's—and then the Constitutional Convention's—failure to act on those recommendations has prompted Professor Heath to write:

> The Constitution of the USA contains no reference to choice of a national language. Early national leaders chose not to identify one language as the official or national standard... Some early national leaders, such as John Adams, proposed a national academy to regulate and standardize English, but these efforts were rejected as out of keeping with the spirit of liberty in the United States... The legacy of the language situation in the United States, therefore, is the rejection of an official choice of a national language or national institutions to regulate language decisions relating to spelling, pronunciation, technical vocabulary, or grammar.[5]

The reality, though, is that the legacy of the language situation in the United States is not a rejection of a proposal for an official language or a national language academy, but a silence on the issue. That the question of a standardized official language was sidestepped by the Founding Fathers could have been deliberate, or arising out of a British legal and constitutional tradition of not designating any language as official for the reason that it was a foregone conclusion, but it would be distorting facts to say that they did so to uphold the spirit of liberty in the United States; both Jefferson and Adams were proud of their English lineage, political traditions and, of course, language, and intended to establish and perpetuate them in the new republic they founded.

Americans were aware of the fact that their English was different from that used in England, if only because they were placed in a different situation. The British derided Americans on these differences, pointing out the innovations that had crept into the colonial tongue and for preserving language forms long abandoned in the mother-country.[6] But Americans were far from being apologetic about these differences. In fact, anti-British sentiment after the Revolutionary War was so high that there were suggestions that the new nation speak a language other than English. Proposals to rename colonial English as "American" came from many, including one Noah Webster. Webster, who compiled the *American Dictionary of the English Language* in 1828, was not only a pioneering lexicographer, he identified a positive role of language in nation-building. Acknowledging that the English language was the inheritance which Americans had received from their "British parents", Webster, nevertheless, said:

> Whatever predilection Americans may have for their native European tongues, and particularly the British descendants for English, yet several circumstances render a future separation of the American tongue from the English, necessary and unavoidable.[7]

Webster hoped that intercourse among the learned of the different states in the US would gradually erase the differences in dialect brought to the New World from Europe and that assimilation would produce a language in North America different from all other languages on the other side of the Atlantic.[8] He linked language to national identity: "As an independent nation, our honour requires us to have a system of our own, in language as well as government."[9] More importantly, he stressed the role of a single national language in the achievement of national unity: "Our political harmony is therefore concerned in a uniformity of language".[10] Webster, thus, believed that assimilation of peoples in the United States would produce a new distinct language as much as he understood that a common language could aid the process of assimilation itself.

Years later, in 1908, Israel Zangwill wrote his drama, *The Melting Pot*, but Webster seems to be the first scholar to talk about language-aided assimilation, something that would turn America into the melting pot that it was, a land where biological merger of the Anglo-Saxon peoples with other immigrant groups and a blending of their respective cultures would lead to the birth of a new indigenous American type of individual and culture. Webster's declaration of linguistic independence, which he believed should accompany and reinforce political independence, was echoed by Representative Washington J. McCormick (R-MT) who, in 1923, proposed the replacement of English with the term "American". McCormick, though, chided Webster for compiling the *American Dictionary of the English Language*, and not a "Dictionary of the American Language". But despite acknowledging the assimilative capacity of the English language, none of the three—Jefferson, Adams, and Webster—wanted to constitutionally designate English as the official language of the United States.

Adams' proposal for an American language academy was not only aimed at standardizing the English language in America; he understood that language and the form of government could influence each other.[11] In this, Adams had drawn from a very British tradition, that of Thomas Hobbes who clearly saw the connection between an ordered language and an ordered state. For Hobbes, language was a major organizing principle in human experience, for without it "there had been amongst men, neither commonwealth, nor society, nor contract, nor peace, no more than amongst Lyons, Bears and Wolves".[12] But implicit in Adams' statement is the idea that a free government can be best enjoyed and sustained by a people with a single common language, which in turn is left free to innovation by that government. English, at the time of the revolutionary war and also at the time of writing the federal Constitution, was the language of the people. So the Founding Fathers made every effort to preserve and popularize it as a way to preserving the liberty of the people in America and that of their government. The *Declaration of Independence* was written in English, the debates in the Continental Congress and the Constitutional Convention were conducted in English and most importantly, the Constitution of the United States was drafted in English. There was no fight with the parent culture but with the unjust government of the king. To highlight this, and to uphold the principle of liberty in thought and action, the Founding Fathers never considered seriously the suggestions to adopt Hebrew or Greek as the language of the people of America, or for that matter, Iroquois or Algonquin; for them, English was the language of freedom.

There was a time when Germans as a people and German as a language had raised the hackles of the Founding Fathers, especially of Benjamin Franklin of Philadelphia, the state which had the biggest German population of the time. Franklin, twenty-three years before the coming of political independence, was irked by the Germans' refusal to assimilate and their insistence on preserving their language and culture, and warned in no uncertain terms about their adverse impact on English society, English language, and the free government about to come.[13]

But Franklin's fears about German intrusion proved unfounded as on January 13, 1795, the US House of Representatives defeated a bill to print 3000 sets of the federal laws in German "for the accommodation of such German citizens of the United States, as do not understand the English language".[14] The decisive vote against bilingual publication was cast by Frederick Augustus Muhlenberg, first Speaker of the House.[15] Interestingly, Muhlenberg, a German American, hailed from Pennsylvania. This close congressional vote became, subsequently, the source of myths that German failed to become the official language of the United States by one vote. Two years later, Congress turned down a similar request. And, every year between 1843 and 1847, Congress voted against printing copies of the president's annual message in Low German, German or French.[16] Thus American government has traditionally operated in English. Noticeably, after the Constitution was adopted in 1789, there was not a single instance of Congress approving multilingual or bilingual publications during the time of the Founding Fathers; English has always been the language of the federal government.

In 1811, James Madison, the fourth president, signed the Louisiana Enabling Act, establishing the conditions under which Louisiana could join the United States; it required the laws, records and written proceedings of the new state to be in English. The Act actually mandated English as the language of the government of Louisiana, a state with a substantial French-speaking population. Incidentally, James Madison was the co-author of the *Federalist Papers* (1787-88) with Alexander Hamilton and John Jay, out of which grew the federal Constitution and the present system of government of the United States. The approval of this Act by President Madison was aimed at assimilation of the French-speaking in Louisiana for the purpose of a more perfect union of the former French colony with the rest of the United States. Language was seen from the beginning as "a potential element in constituting a political and cultural unity among the citizens of the new republic".[17]

Yet there was a period in American history when neither political parties nor interest groups, but churches took up the cudgels on behalf of the English language, making it the language of America:

> Taken together, these five English-speaking denominations—Congregationalists, Presbyterians, Baptists, Anglicans, and Quakers—embraced 85% of all the Protestant congregations at the time of the American Revolution... As the English language became the common language of all the colonists and as German and Dutch colonists joined with others in the American Revolution to defend their rights as Englishmen, so English patterns of church life tended to penetrate the churches of Continental origin. Gilbert Tennent, a Presbyterian, preached in Dutch Reformed pulpits. The early Swedish Lutherans along the Delaware and the French Reformed group in South Carolina both were absorbed into the Church of England, the German Lutherans—after an initial resistance led by Henry M. Muhlenberg—were to varying degrees Anglicized and Americanized.[18]

Samuel P. Huntington identifies British Protestantism—with the English language as its most important component—as constituting America's *core culture*:

> America... has had a mainstream Anglo-Protestant culture in which most of its people, whatever their subcultures, have shared. For almost four centuries this culture of the founding settlers has been the central and the lasting component of American identity... Would America be the America it is today if... it had been settled not by British Protestants but by French, Spanish, or Portuguese Catholics? The answer is no. It would not be America; it would be Quebec, Mexico, or Brazil.
>
> America's Anglo-Protestant culture has combined political and social institutions and practices inherited from England, including most notably the English language, together with the concepts and values of dissenting Protestantism, which faded in England but which the settlers brought with them and which took on new life on the new continent.[19]

Non-Anglo-Protestant immigrants to the United States had also traditionally assimilated into American society by adopting the Anglo-Protestant culture:

> Throughout American history, people who were not white Anglo-Saxon Protestants have become Americans by adopting America's Anglo-Protestant culture and political values... Millions of immigrants and their children achieved wealth, power, and status in American society precisely because they assimilated themselves into the prevailing American culture... . The core of their

> identity is the culture that the settlers created, which generations of immigrants have absorbed, and which gave birth to the American Creed. At the heart of that culture has been Protestantism.[20]

Even though the Constitution of the United States does not stipulate English as the nation's official language of government, thirty states till date have declared English as their official language.[21] But then there is New Mexico, America's only bilingual state. In March 1989, the New Mexico state legislature adopted House Joint Resolution 16 to "support language rights in the United States". That was seventy-seven years after it joined the Union as a full fledged state. The resolution noted:

> Whereas the people of New Mexico acknowledge that "English plus" best serves the national interest since it promotes the concept that all members of our society have full access to opportunities to effectively learn English plus develop proficiency in a second or multiple languages, and Whereas the people of New Mexico recognize that the position of English in the United States needs no official legislation to support it;...
>
> The... legislature of the state of New Mexico hereby reaffirms its advocacy of the teaching of other languages in the United States and its belief that the position of English is not threatened... proficiency in English plus other languages should be encouraged throughout the state.[22]

The New Mexico state legislature may believe that the position of English was not threatened in any way in the United States, but it is such resolutions that actually threaten the position of English as the single common language of the American people.

In a rare show of political and legal audacity, the south Texas town of El Cenizo (population 7800, overwhelmingly Spanish-speaking) declared on August 5, 1999 that all city government business would thenceforth be conducted in Spanish only.[23] Mayor Rafael Rodriguez, an illegal immigrant himself who spoke no English and flew the Mexican flag in City Hall, announced that any American who came to El Cenizo would need to learn Spanish.

There is no doubt that New Mexico's "English Plus" resolution and El Cenizo's Spanish-only measure are divisive, with the potential to create ethnic hatred between people belonging to different language groups throughout the United States or within a part of the country. Worse, the Constitution of the United States is not equipped to prevent the outbreak of such hatred or control the consequences if there was any. But it is emphatic about its supremacy:

> This Constitution, and the Laws of the United States which shall be made in pursuance thereof... shall be the supreme Law of the Land; and the Judges in every State shall be bound thereby, any Thing in the Constitution or Laws of any State to the Contrary notwithstanding. (Article VI).

Clearly, the effects of New Mexico's "English Plus" resolution and El Cenizo's audacious Spanish-only measure could have been nullified if English was constitutionally designated as the official language of government of the United States. In the absence of such a constitutional stipulation, an English Language Amendment (ELA) to the Constitution would have helped. If English would have been made the official language of America, either in the original Constitution or through an amendment, it would have been uniformly applicable throughout the United States by virtue of Article VI; there would have been no way to implement New Mexico's "English Plus" resolution or El Cenizo's Spanish-only measure. What is more, even state judiciaries would have been under no obligation to uphold such directives; in fact, they could have been struck down as *ultra vires* to the Constitution of the United States.

All said and done, constitutional silence does not make English the official language of the United States; to be "official" there must be a constitutional stipulation. Even though 329 languages are spoken in the United States, and 14% of Americans speak a language other than English at home, the fact remains that 98% of all Americans speak English "very well" or "well".[24] Immigrants also overwhelmingly believe both in learning English, and in English as the official language. But all these make English the single common national language of the people of the United States, but not the official language. It is truly the language of government of the United States and of the government of the various states—with or without Official English laws, not to mention New Mexico—but yet it does not make English the official language. States with Official English laws are constitutionally bound to implement the Bilingual Education Act (1968) and the 1975 amendments to the 1965 Voting Rights Act that mandated the provision of multilingual ballots in non-English-speaking jurisdictions. As English is not constitutionally designated as the official language of the United States, Article VI of the US Constitution has actually, in practice, reduced the Official English laws of the states to ceremonial value.

Amendment X (ratified December 15, 1791) to the US Constitution says: "The powers not delegated to the United States by the Constitution, nor prohibited by it to the States, are reserved to the States respectively, or to the people". The states have accrued to themselves, by virtue of this particular amendment, the power to designate an official language; thirty states have done that. New Mexico has also done the same with its "English Plus" resolution. If there was a constitutionally ordained official language (English, that is) there would have been no need for the thirty states to pass Official English laws. On the other hand, New Mexico could not have passed its "English Plus" resolution nor would El Cenizo been able to have its Spanish-only measure. If states or local bodies wanted separate declarations of official language, it had to be English; any other choice, by constitutional mandate, would have been *ultra vires* to the US Constitution.

(B) *E PLURIBUS UNUM*: AMERICAN ASSIMILATIONISM IN RETROSPECT

One of the complaints against King George III, expressed in the *American Declaration of Independence*, was that he had tried to thwart immigration to the colonies:

> He has endeavored to prevent the population of these states, for that purpose obstructing the laws for Naturalization of Foreigners; refusing to pass others to encourage their migrations hither.

It seems that the Founding Fathers did not want the

King to meddle in matters relating to immigration ; that they too were opposed to unbridled immigration, once the new republic came into existence, is borne out by their statements and testimonies quoted in the preceding section. As Milton M. Gordon has suggested, there is no reason to believe that the Founding Fathers looked upon the newly created United States as an impartial melting pot for the merging of the various cultures of Europe, or as a new "nation of nations", or as anything but a society in which Anglo-Saxon speech and institutional forms would be standard.[25]

The Founding Fathers' idea of assimilation, of the right of the English-speaking to inculcate non-English speakers with English culture and language, was best expressed by Benjamin Franklin in a passage in 1751, a quarter of a century before independence:

> Why should the Palatine Boors (Germans) be suffered to swarm into our settlements and, by herding together, establish their language and matters to the exclusion of ours? Why should Pennsylvania, founded by the English, become a colony of aliens, who will shortly be so numerous as to Germanize us instead of our Anglifying them?[26]

Though Germans were the largest language minority during the revolutionary years and even after independence and though the contribution of the German-American community to the revolutionary war and the subsequent building of the new republic was enormous, any encouragement to German language and culture was seen by the Founding Fathers as a step toward creating social and political divisions. Instead, Germans were expected to adopt the language and culture of the majority English-speaking population, with national unity as the ultimate goal. The same was expected of the French, the Dutch, the Spanish, the Portuguese, the Swedish and other language groups.

The idea that non-English speaking immigrants should adjust themselves to the culture, institutions, and language of the United States continued well into the 19th century; what is more, suggestions were even made that they should leave America if they failed to reconcile themselves to the new situation and still continued or insisted on continuing with the language and culture of the old country. John Quincy Adams, son of the second president, wrote in a letter to Baron von Füstenwaerther in 1818:

> They (immigrants) come to a life of independence, but to a life of labor – and, if they cannot accommodate themselves to the character, moral, political and physical, of this country with all its compensating balances of good and evil, the Atlantic is always open to them to return to the land of their nativity and their fathers. To one thing they must make up their minds, or they will be disappointed in easy expectation of happiness as Americans. They must cast off their European skin, never to resume it.[27]

The message was loud and clear: if immigrants failed to abandon their native culture and loyalties, they were unwelcome to the United States. The junior Adams, who was to become president himself seven years later, was then Secretary of State under James Monroe. His views acquire added significance, coming from the highest diplomatic officer of the United States.

Not only government officials and political figures, but even the American intelligentsia of those times professed similar assimilationist beliefs. Wrote Jesse Pickering, thirty years after the publication of Secretary of State Adams' letter:

> The people of the United States, considered as a whole, are composed of immigrants and their descendants from almost every country. The principal portion of them, however, derived their origin from the British nation, comprehending by this term the English, the Scotch and the Irish. The English language is almost wholly used; the English manners, modified to be sure, predominate and the spirit of English liberty and enterprise animates the energies of the whole people. English laws and institutions, adapted to the circumstances of the country, have been adopted here ... the tendency of things is to mould the whole into one people, whose leading characteristics are English, formed on American soil.[28]

Thus, assimilation of immigrants remained the over-riding concern of politicians and intellectuals alike. It was very important to ensure that non-English-speaking immigrants adopted the English language and imbibed English manners (as modified in America).

Despite these concerns, however, immigration to the United States continued. In fact, few restrictions were imposed on immigration in the decades following the revolution, and during most of the 19th century. The result:

immigrants from all over Europe flocked to the United States.

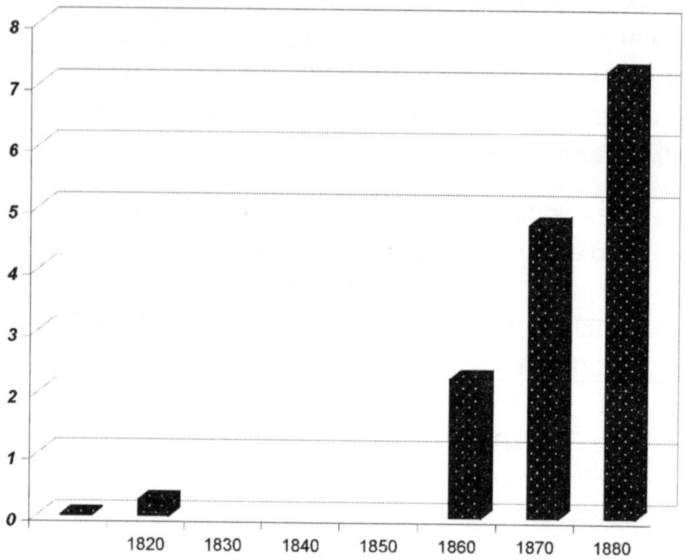

[DATA: Bill Piatt, *¿ Only English? Law and Language Policy in the United States* (See text)]

Fig. 1. Immigrants Entering The United States, 1820-1880 (In Millions)

That immigration continued unabated during the 19th century (Median immigration: 3.5 million) there is no doubt about. Another five million immigrants reached American shores during the 1880s, taking the total upto 19.5 million (Median immigration: 4.75 million, period ending 1890). A majority of these immigrants were Irish and German Roman Catholics, evoking in a big way anti-Catholic hatred in an unofficially Protestant nation. Anglo-Americans had traditionally regarded Roman Catholics as morally and intellectually dependent—even degenerate—and the Catholic immigrants of the Atlantic migration of the 1830s and 1840s, all impoverished and underemployed, were seen as the embodiment of dependence in all its dimensions. Coupled with their so-called extra-territorial loyalty to the papacy, Catholics came to be regarded by loyal citizens of the United States as unassimilable. This mass migration of Roman Catholics, especially Irish Roman Catholics, thus provided the context for the emergence of a powerful nativist movement with emphasis on the preservation of the nation's ethnic purity. Though anti-Catholicism provided the basis for the birth of American nativism, for the first time a movement emerged on the political spectrum of the United States seeking to proclaim and champion American national identity.

New York City proved to be the hub of nativist political activity in the 1830s. The Democratic Party thrived on the support of immigrant voters—especially Irish immigrants—and earned for itself the sobriquet of the "party of immigrants", much to the chagrin of Protestants within party ranks who sincerely believed that immigrants were not only corrupting the political system, but politicians' "aggressive solicitousness" for the interests of the foreign-born was at the root of the subversion of the American system of governance in every which way. Such Democratic Party regulars, led by Samuel F.B. Morse, organized the New York Native American Democratic Association (NADA) in March, 1835.[29] The organization drew its membership from shopkeepers, petty professionals, master craftsmen and journeymen, people who understood that their political voice was being weakened by the parties' (especially the Democrats') eagerness to garner immigrant votes. The purging of Revolutionary War veterans from public posts in New York by Democratic city administrators and their replacement by Irish Roman Catholics and more importantly, the appointment of a Roman Catholic—Roger Taney of Maryland—as the Chief Justice of the US Supreme Court by the Democratic administration of President Andrew Jackson in July 1835 convinced NADA activists that the Democratic Party—and its administrations at the federal, state and local levels—were more interested in the votes of immigrants than in preserving the sanctity of American republican institutions. Not only Democrats, but Whigs were also guilty of pandering to immigrant interests. When Massachusetts' Whig Governor Edward Everett chartered a Boston militia unit—the Montgomery Guards—composed of Irish immigrants and the sons of immigrants at the beginning of 1837, NADA denounced it as a shameless bid for Irish Roman Catholic political support.[30]

The threat to American republicanism was also seen in the Roman Catholics' attempt to capture the public schools—with their overt Protestant tenor and their use of the King James Bible—and in their objection to the way public education was managed in New York City (Catholics alleged it was associated with institutional Protestantism). Not only NADA regulars, but various self-described "producing classes" of artisans, neighborhood merchants, aspirant entrepreneurs, and petty professionals rose to defend the public education system, believing as they did that loss of political effectiveness that accompanied economic marginalization would certainly lead to a loss of republican citizenship and consequently, of nationality itself;[31] it was public education—and the Protestant ethic of economic independence it ingrained—that was at the root of American culture.

NADA's electoral success was limited. Nativist political activity surrounding the public school controversy acquired a more militant character with the formation in February 1844 of the American Republican Party by dissident Protestant Whigs and Democrats in Philadelphia. They had spectacular electoral successes in local elections and their candidates got elected as congressmen, state senators and representatives, and mayors, among others. Citing the public school controversy and the May 1844 Irish-NADA riots as evidences of a concerted effort to politically marginalize and neutralize committed republican citizens, American Republicans in Philadelphia appealed for a radical reform of the electoral process to protect and preserve the political interests of the native-born.[32] In November 1844, in Baltimore, Maryland, was organized another American Republican party with a similar demand for municipal reform and "purification" of the electoral process through extension of the prenaturalization probation for immigrants and keeping the foreign-born out of political offices.[33]

American Republicans, and other nativist fraternities like the Order of United American Mechanics (launched in Philadelphia in 1845) and its female wing, the Patriotic Daughters of America (also started in 1845), stood for an American "national character" based on economic self-determination and political independence—as distinct from the immigrants' perpetually parasitic character—and spread the idea that the foreign-born threatened American republicanism by not only contributing to the economic and political marginalization of native-born Americans but also by failing to display the economic and political independence required to make them reliable republican citizens themselves. In other words, nativists accused immigrants (mostly Irish Roman Catholics) of refusing to assimilate into the American "national character" and the established political parties (Whigs and Democrats) of encouraging that immigrant tendency in their eagerness for immigrant electoral and political support. The need for a new political party began to be increasingly felt.

In December 1844, the launching of the Order of United Americans (OUA) in New York City with Mayor James Harper's brother, John, as its first grand sachem, kept alive nativist enthusiasm. This, despite the fact that American Republicans failed as administrators and began to lose one election after another. The OUA rose in stature after Thomas Richard Whitney, a publisher (he published the OUA official organ, the *Republic*) and nativist ideologue, took over as its third grand sachem in 1846. Calling itself a "patriotic", benevolent and fraternal organization and drawing its membership from the ranks of petty professionals, neighborhood retailers, and craftsmen, the OUA had made clear its political position in 1846 itself when it opposed certain clauses of the proposed new Constitution of New York state, among which was the permission to naturalized citizens to be candidates for governor. Though Whitney called OUA "the oldest of all the American organizations", in 1856 the political field was teeming with a plethora of *fraternal* (those emphasizing organization and networking) and *political* (those who set up candidates for elections) nativist organizations. The OUA was joined by the Order of the Star-Spangled Banner (OSSB, started in 1850), the United American Mechanics, the United Sons of America (formed in 1852), and the United Daughters of America, among others. These "American" organizations together came to be called as "Know Nothings" (because supposed members, when questioned, professed to know nothing about any such organization), a term used for the first time by Horace Greeley of the *New York Tribune* in November 1853.[34]

The Know Nothing, or "American" party, though not yet formally organized, received spectacular electoral success in the New York state elections in 1854, capturing the office of the governor and all other statewide offices on the ballot, every state senate seat, and a majority of seats in the lower chamber, in addition to all the eleven congressional seats.[35] Spurred by this electoral success, the Know Nothing party quickly opened units in Pennsylvania, Ohio, North Carolina, Mississippi, Missouri, Alabama, Tennessee, Louisiana, Kentucky, and even in faraway California. Taking a principled and united stand against the "Intemperance, Pauperism and Crime" that characterized the foreign-born, the Know Nothings emerged as an effective third party in all the states where they spread. Interestingly, they came out strongly against the system of nominating party candidates through caucuses (where party "bosses" usually dominated), a tradition within the existing Democratic and Whig party organizations. Incidentally, it was through the caucuses that Irish Roman Catholic immigrants had come to–wield enormous political power within the Democratic Party.

The first time that the Know Nothing party put up a united show was during the presidential elections of November, 1856. Incidentally, it was the first and the last race for the office of the President of the United States that the Know Nothings ever took part in. Dedicating itself to the restriction of immigration, opposition to the "foreign" Roman Catholic Church and the promotion of public policies that would secure the political, economic and cultural interests of the native-born, the American or Know Nothing party nominated former President Millard Fillmore for president and Andrew Jackson Donelson of Tennessee for vice president. Though Fillmore lost to the Democrats' James Buchanan of Pennsylvania, polling

873,053 popular votes and only 8 electoral votes,[36] the Know Nothing platform of 1856 was the most anti-immigrant ever published by a leading political party in the United States.

The platform advocated nativist pre-eminence in American political life, with native born citizens selected for all state, federal, or municipal offices of government employment in preference to immigrants, so that "Americans" (and not immigrants) got to rule America.[37] The Roman Catholics' recognition of papal supremacy and their religious allegiance to the Vatican also came under attack:

> No person should be selected for political station (whether of native or foreign birth), who recognizes any alliance or obligation of any description to any foreign prince, potentate or power, who refuses to recognize the federal and state constitutions (each within its won sphere), as paramount to all other laws, as rules of particular action.[38]

Know Nothings held the political rights of the native-born to frame their constitution and laws to be most sacred. Voting rights were sacred too, and necessitated the shutting out of the foreign born.

But it would be wrong to say that nativists were allergic to immigrants or were exclusionists; what they actually did not like was the immigrants' refusal to assimilate.[39] Nativists frequently charged that the main problem with mass immigration was that it worked to prevent the assimilation of immigrants with Americans and more importantly, to preserve and perpetuate the habits, customs, peculiarities, and distinct characteristics of the immigrants. That nativists supported assimilation there is no doubt about, but they wanted assimilation to be the result of a sustained effort. The Know Nothing platform of 1856 proposed a continued residence of twenty-one years as a pre-requisite for bestowing citizenship on immigrants.[40]

Incidentally, the last presidential election that the Know Nothings fought was also the first for the Republican Party, formed July 6, 1854 at Jackson, Michigan.[41] This new party, born in opposition to the expansion of slavery to the territories, nominated former Senator John C. Fremont for president in 1856. It was Fremont (with 1,342,345 popular votes and 114 electoral votes[42]) who Buchanan beat in the race for the presidency. For the first time in US presidential elections, an established party was challenged by third parties (Fillmore ran on a combined Know Nothing and Whig ticket). But with Fillmore's disastrous defeat, the Know Nothings not only lost its position as a viable third party, Republicans emerged as the other major party in American politics. The Know Nothing party made an abrupt exit from national politics, as soon as it had emerged. There were a host of reasons for its demise, the chief being the failure to take a principled and unequivocal stand on the issue of slavery. In 1856, slavery, and not immigration, was the issue that rocked America. Nevertheless, even a pluralist of Michael Walzer's eminence has admitted the contribution of Know Nothings to American political thinking: "The logic of their position... pressed toward the creation of a politics independent of all the ethnicities and religions of civil society."[43]

Countries of Southern and Eastern Europe began to be represented significantly for the first time in the immigration of the 1880s. In the next decade immigrants from these sources became numerically dominant, and Italians, Jews and Slavs began to outnumber the English, Irish, Germans and Scandinavians. The new immigrants were poor, worked in lowly paid industrial jobs and lived in urban slums. The nativist scorn for them began to border on racism: a doctrine arose that the English, Germans, and others of the "old immigration" constituted a superior race of tall, blonde, blue-eyed Nordics or "Aryans", whereas the people of Eastern and Southern Europe made up the darker Alpines or Mediterraneans – both inferior races whose presence in America threatened the traditional American racial stock and superior culture. But alongside such racism, realization also dawned that the "new immigration" was irreversible, and that the new immigrants were in America to stay. The only way to deal with the problem, then, was to assimilate them.

Just before the outbreak of World War I, a movement—better known as the Americanization movement—started in the United States to make the immigrant forget his native culture and attachments and mold him into an American along Anglo-Saxon lines. And since all this was to be accomplished as rapidly as possible, a conscious and deliberate drive to hasten the assimilative process emerged. Americanization, thus, was an organized and articulate movement.

As one educator wrote in 1909:

> Everywhere these people (new immigrants) tend to settle in groups or settlements, and to set up here their national manners, customs and observances. Our task is to break up these groups or settlements, to assimilate and

> amalgamate these people as a part of our American race, and to implant in their children... the Anglo-Saxon conception of righteousness, law and order, and popular government, and to awaken in them a reverence for our democratic institutions and for those things in our national life which we as a people hold to be of abiding worth.[44]

Thus the Americanization campaign made the same assumption as the earlier nativist movement: that there was a core culture—largely Protestant and Anglo-American—on which the successful operation of republican government must be based. But Americanization also believed that most immigrants and their children could become part of that core if their environment was properly arranged through education, training, and supervision. Even President Woodrow Wilson believed that "hyphenism" kept Americans segregated; the need of the hour was to give up ethnic identities: "You cannot become Americans if you think of yourselves as groups. America does not consist of groups".[45]

Suspicion regarding the intent of the large German-American population produced in the minds of many American citizens of that period the menace of "hyphenated Americans". Accordingly, hatred of German cultural manifestations and persecution of Germans in the United States began to rise. This suspicion grew into a general concern for assuring the loyalty of all those who had come recently from other lands. Not only did the Americanization movement foster a militant nationalism, Americanizers generated the current of "100% Americanism".[46] As John Higham said:

> By threat and rhetoric 100 percent Americanizers opened a frontal assault on foreign influence in American life. They set about to stampede immigrants into citizenship, into adoption of the English language, and into unquestioning reverence for existing American institutions. They made them abandon entirely their Old World loyalties, customs, and memories.[47]

Americanization, as a movement and as a practical program to assimilate immigrants, was pursued by a partnership of public agencies and private organizations. The emphasis was on instruction in the use of the English language, cultural indoctrination, elementary American history and "patriotic" political science (the nature of the American system of government). The assumption underlying all these was that such domestic cultural missionary activity would transform immigrants into Americans and preserve the national character. The Committee for Immigrants in America, which grew out of the North American Civic League, in its journal *Immigrants in America Review*, spoke of a "conscious effort to forge the people of this country into an American race that will stand together for America in time of peace and war".[48] Thus, federal agencies like the Bureau of Education, the Bureau of Naturalization, and the Committee on Public Information, state governments, municipalities and a host of private organizations like the Daughters of the American Revolution, the Young Men's Christian Association, the National Americanization Committee, and Henry Ford's Ford English School joined the effort to persuade immigrants to learn English, take out naturalization papers, buy war bonds, forget their former origins, and join the nationalist wave that was generated in the wake of the great war.

Since Americanization, as a movement to further ethnic unity, initially relied on the common school as the most potent medium during the war years and after, state governments centered their principal effort on immigrant education. More than twenty states passed laws authorizing night school classes in English for immigrants. Idaho and Utah made laws requiring non-English speaking "aliens" to attend Americanization classes. The governor of Iowa issued a proclamation banning all non-English languages in schools, church services, and conversations in public places or over the telephone. In 1919, fifteen states enacted laws to the effect that English must be the sole language of instruction in all primary schools, public and private. Nebraska stipulated that all meetings of a public nature, except religious or lodge meetings, be conducted in English. Oregon required that all foreign language publications display prominently a literal English translation of all their contents.[49]

Americanizers were harried when the Bolsheviks came to power in Russia in 1917 after a protracted civil war. Socialism and communism were regarded as corrupting foreign ideologies from which Americans had to be insulated at all costs. Lenin's open letter *To the American Workers* was regarded as a direct appeal to unassimilated and under-assimilated ethnic Americans of East European descent. Any sympathy for socialism was treated as an example of incomplete Americanization. But as World War I came to an end, the Big Red Scare also passed with it. An economic depression also set in that forbade the business classes from funding the Americanization effort. The crusade for Americanization suddenly lost all urgency. Americanization had taken permanent root as a workday endeavor to teach English and political science to immigrants in the public evening schools, and it endured. But as a major expression of militant American nationalism, Americanization swiftly faded during the later half of 1920 and 1921.[50]

Since the struggle to culturally transform the foreign-born was now deemed not worthy of the time, energy and expenses that it required, attention turned to keeping the immigrants out of American shores. In the place of indoctrination of immigrants which Americanization championed, there arose a new wave of restrictionist sentiment, a demand for restriction of the influx of new immigrants. Based on the assumption that the inherent inferiority of East and South Europeans made them unassimilable, the goal of the restrictionists was not only to affect a decrease in the total number of immigrants to the United States, but to set up a formula that would favor and enhance the entry of immigrants from Northern and Western Europe (who were considered culturally superior and perfectly assimilable). Beginning 1921, a series of immigration laws passed by Congress set out to do just that.

Assimilationists were also convinced of the cultural superiority of Anglo-Saxon institutions as developed in the United States. Those among them who did not harbor such prejudices believed simply that since English culture has constituted the dominant framework for the development of American institutions, immigrants should adjust accordingly. Assimilationists demanded that immigrants to America abandon the cultural forms of their native lands and adopt the behavior and attitudes of the dominant Anglo-Saxon mold of their new country. As the Superintendent of the New York public schools stated in 1918:

> Broadly speaking, we mean ... (by Americanization) an appreciation of the institutions of this country, (and) absolute forgetfulness of all obligations or connections with other countries because of descent or birth.[51]

The maintenance and continuation of ethnic identities were construed as a threat to American national unity. The fact that America was a nation of immigrants kept the suspicion alive in the minds of assimilationists that persistence of "hyphenism" was proof of extra-territorial loyalties of the new immigrants, be it support of the Irish Roman Catholics for a "Free Ireland", or that of other immigrants of East and South European descent for the nationalist aspirations of peoples in their homelands. What assimilationists wanted was "America first": assimilation was the way to a socially and politically united America.

For Huntington, Americanization was the other name of assimilation in America: "Historically America has thus been a nation of immigration *and* assimilation, and assimilation has meant Americanization."[52]

He has identified certain factors that had facilitated assimilation of immigrants into American society, namely, most immigrants were from European societies with cultures similar to or compatible with American culture, immigrants wanted to be Americans, immigrants came from many countries with no single country or language predominant at any time, immigrants dispersed to ethnic neighborhoods throughout the United States with no single group of immigrants forming a majority of population in any region or major city, immigration was not a continuous process, and immigrants died in American wars and shared a common concept of American identity.[53]

Huntington also points to certain ideas and influences that have disrupted the process of Americanization, and hence assimilation.[54] The first was the idea that immigrants may assimilate into American society and yet not assimilate America's core culture. The other idea, says Huntington, was that Americanization was unnecessary. The third disruptive belief, according to Huntington—and this was comparatively new historically and ideologically—was that Americanization was undesirable and un-American, floated by theorists like Michael Walzer. Wrote Walzer not very long ago: "A radical program of Americanization would really be un-American… America has no singular national destiny."[55]

Because of these ideas, concludes Huntington, assimilation was no longer synonymous with Americanization by the end of the twentieth century but had taken several forms like *segmented assimilation* (assimilation not into mainstream American society but into a marginal segment of that society), *nonassimilation* (the perpetuation in the United States of the culture and social institutions the immigrants had brought with them), and the *ampersand* phenomenon (dual citizenship, dual nationality, dual allegiance).[56]

On the ground, this meant 21 million immigrants in 2000 said they did not speak English very well.[57]

REFERENCES

1 Shirley Brice Heath, "A National Language Academy? Debate in the New Nation", *International Journal of The Sociology of Language 11*, (1976), pp. 9-43

2 *The Writings of George Washington,* Collected and edited by W.C. Ford (New York, NY, 1889), vol. XII, p.489. Quoted in Milton M. Gordon, *Assimilation in American*

Life: The Role of Race, Religion, and National Origins (New York, NY, 1964), p. 90

3 Thomas Jefferson, *Notes on Virginia, Query 8*. Quoted in Gordon, ibid., p. 91

4 *The Works of John Adams*, ed. Charles Francis Adams (Boston, MA, 1852), pp. 249-51

5 Shirley, Brice Heath, "English in our language heritage", in Charles A. Ferguson and Shirley B. Heath (eds.), *Language in the USA*, (Cambridge, 1981), p. 6

6 Dennis Baron, *The English-Only Question: An Official Language for Americans?* (New Haven, CT, 1990), p. 41

7 Noah Webster, *Dissertation on the English Language; With Notes, Historical and Critical*, (Meniston, England, 1967), pp. 35-36

8 ibid.

9 ibid.

10 ibid.

11 Adams, op.cit.

12 Thomas Hobbes, *Leviathan* (London, rep. 1973), part I, Ch.4, p.12. Quoted in David Simpson, *The Politics of American English, 1776-1850*. (New York, NY, 1986), p.33

13 Benjamin Franklin, *Papers*, Leonard W. Laboree (New Haven, CT, 1961), Vol. 4, p. 234

14 *Annals of the Congress of the United States*, Vol. 4, (Washington, DC), p. 1082

15 Baron, op cit., pp. 88-9

16 ibid., p.91

17 Simpson, op cit., p. 30

18 Winthrop S. Hudson, *American Protestantism* (Chicago, IL, 1961), p. 22

19 Samuel P. Huntington, *Who Are We? America's Great Debate* (London, 2004), p. 59

20 ibid., pp. 61-2

21 For a more detailed discussion, see Chapter 5 (A) of this book.

22 James Crawford (ed.,), *Language Loyalties: A Source Book on the Official English Controversy* (Chicago, IL, 1992), p. 154

23 For a more detailed discussion, see Chapter 2 (B), of this book.

24 "Demographics", *National Journal*, May 1, 1993, p.1058

25 Gordon, op cit., p. 90

26 Quoted in Bill Piat, *¿Only English? Law and Language Policy in the United States* (Albuquerque, NM, 1990), p. 7

27 *Nile's Weekly Register*, vol. XVII, April 29, 1820, pp. 157-8. Quoted in Gordon, op cit., p. 94.

28 Jesse Pickering, *Immigration into the United States* (Boston, MA, 1848), pp. 79-80. Quoted in Gordon, ibid., p. 95

29 Dale T. Knobel, *America for the Americans: The Nativist Movement in the United States* (New York, NY, 1996), p. 23

30 ibid, p. 54

31 ibid, pp. 56-7

32 ibid, p. 63

33 ibid., p. 87

34 ibid., pp. 88-92

35 ibid., pp. 93-4

36 Donald Bruce Johnson (Compiled), *National Party Platforms, Vol. I, 1840-1956* (Urbana, IL, 1978), p. 22

37 ibid.

38 ibid.

39 *Jersey City Daily Sentinel and Advertiser* (1954), quoted in Knobel, op cit., p. 136

40 Johnson, op cit., p. 23

41 Malcolm Moos, *The Republicans: A History of Their Party* (New York, NY, 1956), p. 9

42 Johnson, op cit., p. 22

43 Michael Walzer, *What it means to be an American: Essays*

on the American Experience (New York, NY, 1992), p. 34

44 Ellwood P. Cubberly, *Changing Conceptions of Education* (Boston, MA, 1909), p.15-16, pp. 15-16, Quoted in Gordon, op cit., p. 98

45 Quoted in Knobel, op cit., p. 244

46 John Higham, *Strangers in the Land: Patterns of American Nativism, 1860-1925*, 2nd Ed., (New Brunswick, NJ, 1988), p. 245-7

47 ibid, p. 247

48 Quoted in Knobel, op cit., p. 245

49 Higham, op cit., p. 251

50 ibid, p. 260

51 *The Evening Post*, 9 August, 1918. Quoted in Gordon, op cit., p.101

52 Huntington, op. cit., p.184

53 ibid., p.185

54 ibid.

55 Walzer, op cit., p. 49

56 Huntington, op cit., p. 220

57 ibid., p. 201

2

The Melting Pot Boils Over

"My opinion, with respect to immigration, is that... there is no need of encouragement, while the policy or advantage of its taking place in a body (I mean the settling of them in a body) may be much questioned; for, by so doing, they retain the language, habits and principles which they bring with them."

- George Washington

(A) CHANGING THE FACE OF AMERICA: THE IMMIGRATION AND NATIONALITY ACT OF 1965

"Keep, ancient lands, your storied pomp", cries she With silent lips. "Give me your tired, your poor, your huddled masses yearning to breathe free.

The wretched refuse of your teeming shore, Send these, the homeless, the tempest-tosst to me, I lift my lamp beside the golden door!"[1]

Says the inscription at the base of the Statue of Liberty, from the poem by Emma Lazarus. Since 1776 and throughout the 19th century, millions with neither education nor money to speak of—the "tired", the "poor", the "huddled masses", and the "homeless" from "ancient lands"—flocked to American shores every decade. Irish, Germans, Scandinavians, Italians, Greeks, Armenians, Poles, Hungarians, East European Jews, French Canadians, Japanese, and Chinese flooded America during the century of immigration from 1820 and 1924. Between 1900 and 1914 alone, 13 million people entered the United States, raising concerns about "unsuitable classes" immigrants.[2]

By the turn of the century, though, the phenomenal rise in both the number of immigrants and the array of immigrating nationalities had begun to encourage legislation supporting restrictions to entry. The report of the United States Immigration Commission (1909-11)—headed by Senator William P. Dillingham (R-VT)—reaffirmed the popular belief that certain immigrants from northwestern Europe were more "desirable" than those from southern or eastern Europe.[3] In the Far West, the Japanese were prohibited by law from buying or leasing land in California and Texas. During World War I, immigrants from the Orient (notably alien seamen and aliens considered subversive) were barred from entering America. Not only the government, but public opinion had also turned against the changing face of America. If national security was the concern behind keeping out the German and the Japanese, ethnic prejudices fueled the ire against the Irish, Italians, Poles, Hungarians, and Greeks. Let alone assimilating them into American society, the very desirability and wisdom of allowing them entry into the United States were questioned. Suddenly, the harbor light that had guided millions to the liberty available on its shores was being switched off; the nation of immigrants was closing its door to immigrants.

The first congressional measure restricting immigration, however, was an 1862 law that forbade American vessels from transporting Chinese immigrants to the United States. Twenty years later, a bipartisan majority in Congress overwhelmingly passed the Chinese Exclusion Act. Designed to protect the economic interests of White workingmen in California and elsewhere in the West, the Act stopped Chinese laborers from immigrating to the United States for ten years. Senator George Frisbee Hoar (R-MA), in the anti-racist spirit that his party represented, held that excluding the Chinese amounted to legalization of racial discrimination.[4]

An 1891 statute, seeking to keep out "all idiots, insane persons, paupers or persons likely to become a public charge, persons suffering from a loathsome or contagious disease, persons who have been convicted of a felony or other infamous crime or misdemeanor involving moral turpitude",[5] displayed the first congressional concern with the physical and mental health and character of prospective immigrants. Continuing with this tradition, the Immigration Act of March 3, 1903 (32 Statutes-at-Large 1213) added polygamists and political radicals to the exclusion list.[6]

Knowledge of English was made a basic requirement for naturalization for the first time by the Naturalization Act of June 29, 1906.[7] It was meant to slam the door on both East Europeans and Asians (Chinese and Japanese), the former because they threatened American culture and society, the latter because they sought to displace

American labor. What the Act of 1906 (34 Statues-at-Large 596) tried to achieve was what the Immigration Restriction League—formed by a group of Harvard graduates arguing for a fundamental change in American immigration policy—wanted way back in 1894. Once of its founders, Prescott F. Hall, said that the issue for Americans was to decide whether they wanted their country to be peopled by the "historically free, energetic, (and) progressive" British, Germans and Scandinavians, or by the "historically down-trodden, atavistic and stagnant" Slav, Latin and Asiatic races.[8]

The Immigration Act of February 20, 1907 (34 Statutes-at-Large 898)—better known as the Gentleman's Agreement—sought to restrict Japanese immigration to America. This diplomatic agreement between the United States and Japan provided that the Japanese government would not issue passports to Japanese laborers intending to enter the United States. As a result of this ban on the entry of Japanese workingmen to the US, nearly twenty thousand adult Japanese women migrated to the United States between the Act's adoption in 1907 and its abrogation by Congress in 1924: most of them newly married to Japanese immigrants already in America, and some of them wives of male relatives of Japanese Americans. Nevertheless, Japanese immigration was restricted to a considerable extent.[9] The Act of 1907 also added people with physical and mental infirmities, or with tuberculosis, and children unaccompanied by parents to the exclusion list. On its part, the Immigration Act of February 5, 1917 (39 Statutes-at-Large 874) banned illiterates, persons of psychopathic inferiority, men as well as women entering for immoral purposes, alcoholics, stowaways, vagrants, anarchists, and subversives from American shores.[10]

The Act of 1917 also sought to impose a *literacy* test, the crusade for which had begun in Congress from 1895. One of the principal demands of the Know Nothing party and the Immigration Restriction League and vetoed by Presidents Grover Cleveland, William Howard Taft and Woodrow Wilson after passing Congress in 1897, 1913, and 1915 on various grounds, the literacy test nevertheless failed to check immigration to the desired levels because first, literacy was defined as the ability to read and write in any recognized language (and not only in English) and, more importantly, because of the rising standards of literacy in Europe.[11] The Act of 1917 also created an Asiatic Barred Zone to keep out Asians. In its last year of operation, between July 1920 and June 1921, more than 800,000 immigrants entered the United States.[12]

In 1921, Congress passed its first Quota Act—authored by the Dillingham Commission and signed into law by President Warren Harding—not only to restrict overall immigration but also to limit immigration from certain areas. The Quota Act of May 19, 1921 (42 Statutes-at-Large 5) limited the total number of immigrants to be admitted in any one year and assigned percentages of that total to particular nationalities on the basis of the number of people from that nation already in the United States. In effect, the number of aliens of any nationality admitted to the United States in a year could not exceed 3 per cent of the number of foreign-born residents of that nationality living in the United States in 1910. There was no quota for Canada, Mexico, or any other New World nation, Asians were kept out, and the bulk of the European quota went to the British, Germans, and Scandinavians.[13] It was the first attempt to base immigration on national origins.

In 1924, Congress passed the first permanent

limitation on immigration—the Immigration Act of May 26, 1924 (43 Statues-at-Large 153)—establishing the National Origins Quota System. Quotas were based on the presumed desirability of various nationalities; immigrants from northern and western Europe were considered more sought after than those from southern and eastern Europe. The root of this presumption was the intellectual conviction of the times that since Anglo-Saxons and Nordics had superior innate characteristics and were the only ones who could sustain democratic political institutions, they should be encouraged to migrate to the United States. On the other hand, since South and East Europeans had no democratic tradition of their own and could not thus be expected to participate effectively in democratic discourse and political exercises associated with it, they must be barred from entering America.

The Quota Act of 1924 not only placed limits on overall immigration to the United States, but also set up quotas on immigration from Central Europe, Eastern Europe, and Asia. The National Origins Quota system imposed country-by-country quotas to control immigrations to the United States annually from all countries outside the Western hemisphere, each country's quota being based on the number of persons of that national origin who were already in the United States in 1920. Because the ethnic composition of America in 1920 was primarily British, Irish, and German, use of the 1920 origins basis in assigning quotas heavily favored immigration of persons born in the British Isles, Ireland, and Germany, while sharply limiting immigration from the rest of Europe, Africa, and Asia.[14] For sponsors of the legislation, apart from their superior innate characteristics and capability in sustaining democratic political institutions, the desirability of north and west Europeans as immigrants had one more important reason. In fact it was the most important of them all: people from those areas were easier to assimilate into American society than those from other parts of Europe and the world. The two biggest opponents of this measure were Presidents Harry S. Truman and John F. Kennedy.

The repeal of the Chinese Exclusion Act in 1943 and the grant of a small quota to the Chinese marked the beginning of the end of the highly discriminatory National Origins system, purportedly based on national prejudice. In 1946, Congress allowed two other Asian groups—the Filipinos and "natives of Indian Origin"—entry into America. But it still treated other Asians—Koreans, Japanese, Southeast, and Southwest Asians—as aliens ineligible for citizenship.

This situation continued for another six years when in 1952 Congress passed, overriding President Truman's veto, the McCarran Walter Act that ended the total exclusion of certain racial and ethnic groups from naturalization and immigration. The Act of 1952 rid naturalization laws of whatever racial prejudice they might have been based on. As leader of the Free World, the United States could no longer afford to blatantly exclude so many people from different parts of the word from admission into its territory.[15] But despite this, the McCarran Walter Act continued with most of the discriminatory policies of the Act of 1924 and essentially preserved the National Origins system; in effect, the National Origins system remained the basic immigration law of the land till 1965. This explains President Truman's veto; taking strong exception to discriminatory policies persistent within the McCarran-Walter Act, the President of the 'Fair Deal' wrote that it "deliberately and intentionally" discriminated against many of the peoples of the world. The purpose behind it was to cut down and virtually eliminate immigration to this country from Southern and Eastern Europe.[16] Though Senator Patrick A. McCarran (R-NV) contended that "the Act does not contain one iota of racial or religious discrimination,"[17] there is no denying that the president most accurately pointed out the measure's most serious drawback. The Democratic Party was trying to reassert itself as the "party of immigrants" in the aftermath of the Second World War.

The biggest beneficiaries of the McCarran-Walter Act—in spite of its discriminatory policies—were Hispanics and Asians. Latin American immigration jumped from a mere 7% in 1920 to more than 20% in the 1950s and 40% in the 1960s. Asian immigration rose from a miniscule 3% in the 1940s through 6% in the 1950s to 12% in the 1960s.

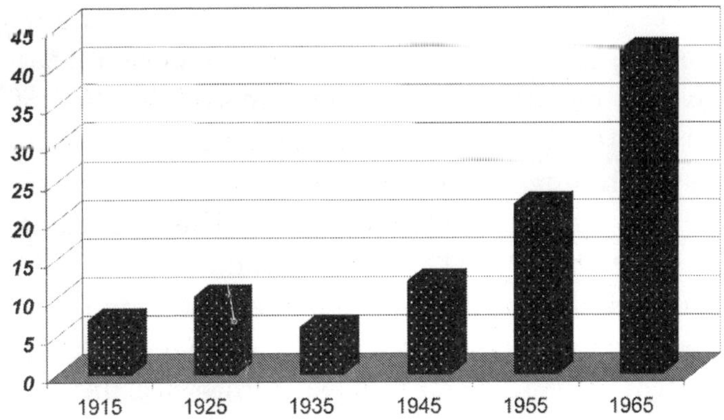

[DATA: Roger Daniels, *Coming to America*.]

Fig. 2. Latin American Immigration To The U.S. 1915-1965

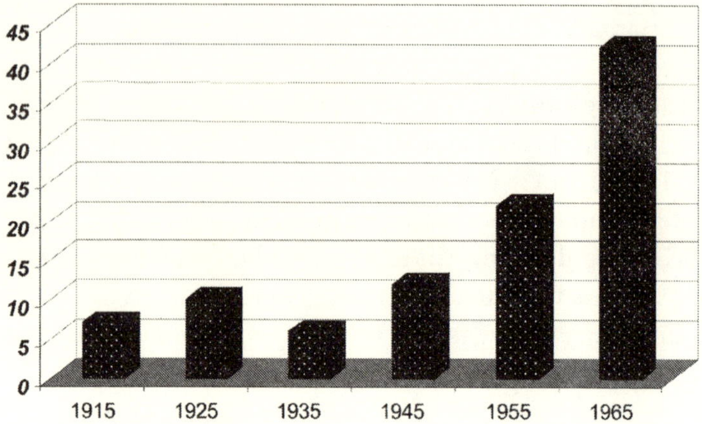

[DATA: Roger Daniels, *Coming to America.*]

Fig. 3. Asian Immigration to the United States 1915-65

John F. Kennedy, 35th president of the United States, took the first meaningful steps toward immigration reform when in 1963—months before his assassination in Dallas, Texas—he sent a proposal for immigration reform to Congress with three major provisions: That the Quota system be phased out over a five-year period; that the natives of no one country receive more than 10% of the newly authorized quota numbers; and, that a seven-member immigration board be set up to advise the president on immigration issues. The president, on receiving the board's recommendations, would be authorized to reserve up to 50% of the unallocated numbers for persons disadvantaged by the change in the Quota system and up to 20% for refugees. Otherwise, immigrants should be selected on a first-come, first-served basis, depending on registration at American consulates, subject to the proposed 10% ceiling.[18]

JFK's unfinished presidency left the task of

immigration reform to his Vice President, Lyndon B. Johnson of Texas, who took over as president hours after Kennedy succumbed to bullet injuries sustained in a motorcade in downtown Dallas, on November 22, 1963. As U.S. Senator, LBJ had voted to override President Truman's veto of the McCarran-Walter Act in 1952, but as president, in his first State of the Union message in 1964, he not only endorsed his slain predecessor's proposals for immigration reform, but also called for scrapping the National Origins Quota system.

After he won in 1964 in the biggest landslide in the history of American presidential elections, trouncing conservative Sen. Barry M. Goldwater (R-AZ), LBJ kept pressing the 89th Congress for repeal of the National Origins Quota Act of 1924. The McCarran Walter Act—co-sponsored by Senator Patrick A. McCarran (R-NV) and Representative Francis E. Walter (D-PA)—was a bipartisan law. The proposed new legislation on immigration, as LBJ wanted it, was to be an out-and-out Democratic affair. The president told U.S. House Speaker John McCormack that no legislation before Congress "in terms of decency and equity is more demanding of passage than the Immigration Bill,"[19] and insisted that it "not be changed by one comma"[20]; he wanted immigration reform to be part of his Great Society. This, in spite of the fact that a third of the country wanted continuance of the National Origins Quota system and another 17% chose to be indifferent in a nationwide poll.[21]

The Immigration Bill (H.R. 2580) passed the U.S. House of Representatives August 25, 1965 by an overwhelming 318-95 roll-call vote and the U.S. Senate September[22] by another landslide 76-18 roll-call.[22] Both chambers adopted the conference report on the bill

September 30. President Johnson signed the new Immigration and Nationality Act (PL 89-236) October 3, 1965 in a ceremony held in Liberty Island in New York Harbor, describing the passage of the legislation as rectifying "a very deep and painful flaw in the fabric of American justice."[23]

But H.R. 2580 had its share of opponents. In the Senate, conservative Sam Ervin (D-NC) opposed the impending legislation on the ground that the Mc Carran-Walter Act (1952) was based on the recognition of "the obvious and natural fact that those immigrants can best be assimilated into our society who have relatives, friends, or others of similar background already here."[24] Among those who opposed the new immigration measure outside Congress were the highly conservative Liberty Lobby (formed 1955) and the American Committee on Immigration Policies (formed 1964); both supported the principles of the 1952 Act.[25]

A host of groups fervently lobbied for the bill's passage. Among them were the American Immigration and Citizenship Conference (formed 1960) of New York City headed by former Senator Kenneth B. Keating (R-NY), and the National Committee for Immigration Reform (formed 1965). Ethnic lobbying groups representing Italian Americans (the American Committee for Italian Migration), Greek Americans (American-Hellenic Educational Progressive Association), Japanese Americans (Japanese-American Citizens League), and Jews (National Council of Jewish Women) also got actively involved in support of H.R. 2580. Not to be left behind, religious groups like the National Catholic Welfare Conference, the National Council of Churches of Christ, and the Lutheran Immigration Service provided strong and active support to the bill. The United Steelworkers of America (affiliated to the AFL-CIO) and the AFL-CIO's Industrial Union Department lobbied both in Washington, DC and all over the country for immigration reform supporting H.R. 2580 as a matter of priority.[26]

The Act of 1965 passed for a number of reasons. For one, there was relatively strong support from the Johnson Administration for the bill. Both chambers of Congress had overwhelming Democratic majorities which were ready to go all the way with LBJ on immigration reform. Not only that, Representative Michael A. Feighan (D-OH), Chairman of the House Judiciary Committee's Immigration and Nationality subcommittee—which prepared the bill—was all for the repeal of the National Origins Quota system at the earliest. Most importantly, the threat of "invasion" by "undesirable" immigrant ethnic and racial groups was not as great as in the past, marking a sea-change in American attitudes toward race and national origins.

PL 89-236 abolished the National Origins Quota system and set up a new system to become fully operational after June 30, 1968 following a three-year transition period.

Instead of country-by-country quotas, an overall ceiling of 170,000 annual immigrants from outside the Western Hemisphere was to be permitted, no more than 20,000 from one country. The new law established an admission system in this order: persons whose special skills would be "especially advantageous to the United States"; unmarried adult (over 21 years of age) children of American citizens; spouses and unmarried children of aliens living permanently in the United States; other relatives of persons living in the United States and workers with "lesser skills", who could fill special labor needs.[27] Family reunification and the need for special skills were the primary motives behind this provision.

For the Western Hemisphere, an overall ceiling of 120,000 immigrants a year from all countries combined was to be established, to be filled on a first-come, first-served basis, without country-by-country quotas, preferences or limits on how many persons could enter from any one country (subject to the overall 120,000 hemispheric limitation).[28]

Immediate relatives were not to be subject either to the 170,000 non-Western hemispheric limitation or to the 120,000 Western hemispheric limitation.[29] The 1952 Act's specification that an individual's country of birth, rather than his place of residence or citizenship (if different) be considered for the application of hemispheric rules was retained, though the "Asia-Pacific Triangle", applied to persons of non-White Asian origin by taking into account their racial ancestry and not their country of birth in ascertaining their "national origins", was repealed.[30]

The Immigration and Nationality Act of 1965 thus greatly increased immigration from southern Europe and Asia, which had a huge backlog of applicants. Growing numbers of Asians had been entering the United States since 1943 and many other skilled Asians qualified for immigration under the various preference provisions of the 1965 Act. Once an Asian came to America as a permanent resident alien, a whole lot of other persons became eligible to enter the country as third-preference immigrants. And as soon as the original immigrant was administered the oath of citizenship of the United States, more persons became eligible as second-preference immigrants. Those brought in as preference immigrants could start the same procedure all over again. This chain migration of relatives has been one of the major consequences of the 1965 Act.

Since 1965, the major source of immigration shifted to Latin America and Asia, reversing the trend since the founding of the nation.

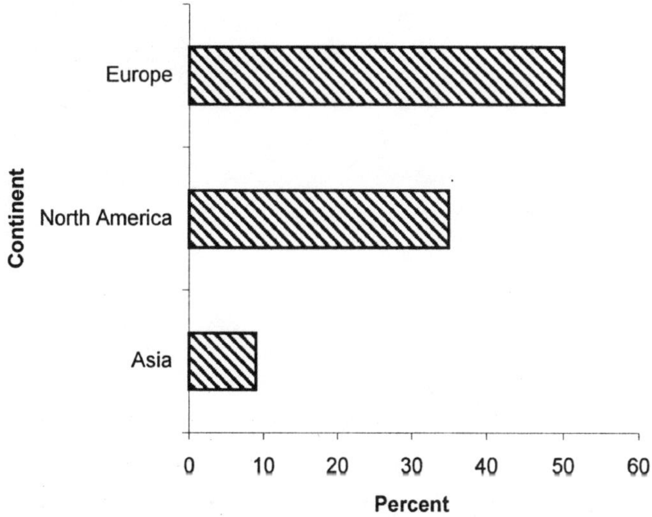

[DATA : *FAIR*, 3/96]

Fig. 4. Percentage Immigration to the U.S. 1955-64

Evidently, entries from West Europe dropped as a result of the 1965 Act. But for the first time in history, a person from an Asian or African nation received the same consideration as a person from France or Germany. As President Johnson said after signing H.R. 2580 into PL 89-236, "We can now believe that it (The National Origins Quota system) will never again shadow the gate to the American nation with the twin barriers of prejudice and privilege."[31] The effects of the Act of 1965 can be felt till today: between 1991 and 2000, only 1100 immigrants of

European origin entered the United States, whereas 3800 immigrants came from the Americas and 2200 immigrants came from Asia during the same period.[32]

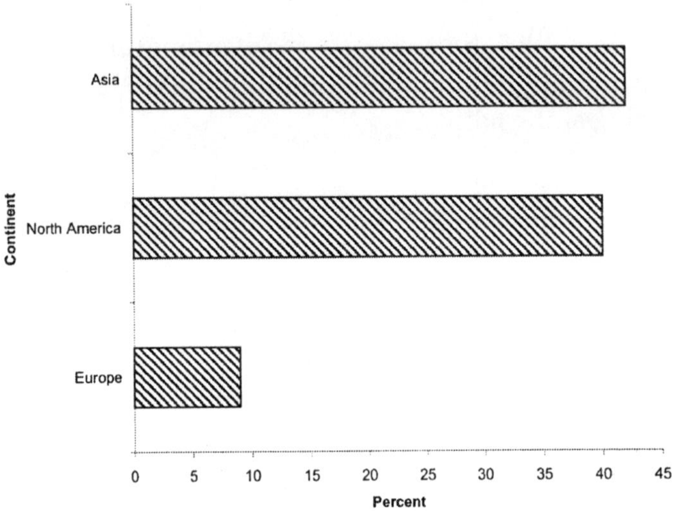

[DATA: *FAIR*, 3/96]

Fig. 5. Percentage Immigration to the U.S. 1965-88

The post-1960 influx, generated by the Act of 1965, left its impact on all aspects of American life: it increased population growth and influenced politics, education, and religion, and changed American music, food-habits and dress-habits; the diversity it created also altered the nation's racial and ethnic makeup and, most importantly, its perception of itself.[33]

The fundamental reason behind this new rush of immigrants were the same socio-economic forces that had led to mass migration from Europe in the 19th century—the pressure of rising population and the transformation of the old economic order—that now made their appearance in the Third World and effectively set people in motion. Not only that, the image of the United States as a land of abundance and opportunity created by mass media, books, magazines, radio and television programs, American movies and music videos and also by private remittances and letters sent by friends and relatives settled in the United States stimulated a growing eagerness among the peoples of the Third World countries to seek a share of the American Dream.[34] Consequently, the proportion of the foreign born population rose dramatically.

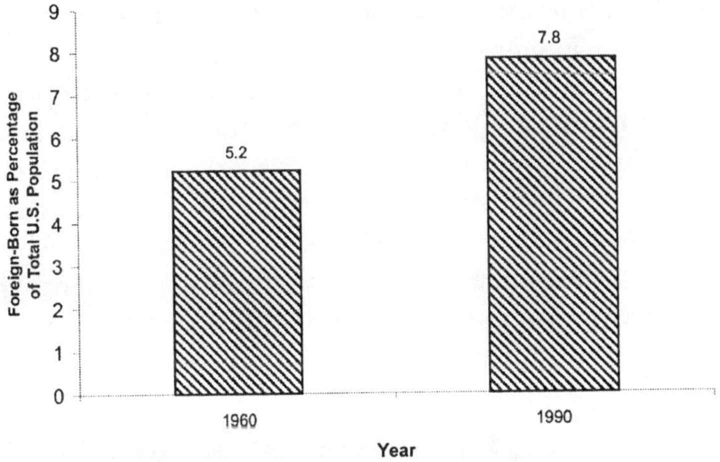

[DATA: Jones, *American Immigration*]

Fig. 6. Rise in the Proportion of the Foreign-born as Part of U.S. Population, 1960 & 1990

This new influx, however, raised a plethora of questions, all regarding the future of the United States and the uncertainty that the surge of aliens created: how many immigrants and of what kind, did the country actually need, and how many was it capable of absorbing? Could millions of people from such a variety of races, languages, and cultures be assimilated into American society? Was it desirable that they should be?

All these questions could open the possibilities of a new nativism in the United States, more so when the biggest casualty of the 1965 Act was English proficiency. Many countries of Asia and Africa—former colonies of Great Britain—had eliminated the use of English after the coming of political independence. Immigrants from those countries had little or no English proficiency. On the other hand, English proficiency of immigrants from countries that had continued with the use of English even after political liberation—in the form of an associate official language and/or as a second language in schools, like India—was high. But Asian Indians were an exception. The Chinese, Japanese, Koreans, Vietnamese, Cambodians, and Laotians could neither read, write or converse in English fluently. Added to Asians were Latin Americans—Mexicans, Cubans, Salvadorans—for whom English was an alien tongue. But English was the language of America. A new problem arose for the United States, and for the new immigrants: the problem of language.

(B) FROM IMMIGRANTS TO ETHNICS: THE JUDICIAL AND STATUTORY PROTECTION OF MINORITY LANGUAGE RIGHTS

Wide open and unguarded stand our gates,
And through them passes a wild motly throng,
Men from the Volga and Tartar steppes,
Featureless figures from the Hoang-Ho,
Malayan, Scythian, Teuton, Kelt and Slav,
Flying the Old World's poverty and scorn;
These bringing with them unknown gods and rites,
Those tiger passions here to stretch their claws,
In street and alley what strange tongues are

these,
Accents of menace in our ear
Voices that once the Tower of Babel knew.[35]

Wrote poet and novelist Thomas Bailey Aldrich (1836-1907), expressing the dismay of Americans toward the end of the 19th century not only at the volume of immigration and the type of immigrants admitted to the United States, but also at the wide variety of alien languages they spoke. Neither the aliens nor their languages were welcome; in fact, they were despised. A similar situation arose again after 1968, when the United States threw open its gates to the world, replacing the restrictive and discriminatory National Origins Quota system with a more liberal and equitable Hemispheric Quota system in the Immigration and Nationality Act of 1965.

For the new immigrants, the melting process was not always smooth. A majority of these newest arrivals were Latin Americans and Asians. In fact, Latinos, or Hispanics—Mexicans, Cubans, Salvadorans, Puerto Ricans, Dominicans, Ecuadorians, Colombians—are the largest immigrant group and ethnic community in the United States. They are drawn from twenty-three different nationalities, but speak a common language: Spanish. Their numerical strength has made the United States the fourth-largest Spanish-speaking nation in the world.[36] And Hispanics are determined to preserve their culture, especially their language. Today, according to the U.S. Census Bureau (2000 report), among those who spoke a language other than English at home, 59.6% spoke Spanish, rising from 54.5% a decade earlier.[37]

If Hispanics are zealously clinging to their native

language and are consequently unwilling to learn English, Asians harbor no such prejudice; it is only that they find language a great barrier because English is vastly different from their native speech. The countries they come from either do not encourage the use of English or, even if they do, the immigrants' families in their native lands could not afford to send them to expensive English-medium schools. Accordingly, barring Asian Indians, all Asians—Chinese, Koreans, Filipinos, Japanese, Vietnamese, Laotians, Cambodians, Pakistanis, and Bangladeshis—find it difficult to learn English. Most of them do not understand English when they arrive, and the continued use of native languages at home further discourages the acquiring of English. This, despite being aware that English was the language of America. But immigrants themselves are not solely responsible for their limited proficiency in the English language. The federal government of the United States, believing as it does that a child can be best educated in his/her native language—even if it was not English—and a citizen's constitutional right to vote can be best exercised if he/she was supplied with voting materials in the native tongue, has contributed largely to this minority language maintenance and limited English proficiency of non-English speaking immigrants, keeping them from assimilating into the greater American society.

But governments in the United States had not always encouraged the persistence of non-English native tongues. Since the literacy and language requirements in the immigration laws existing at the turn of the century were not sufficiently reducing the linguistic and cultural differences within the American population, a new proposal to limit immigration based on the national origin of immigrants was mooted. The federal government (in effect, the U.S. Congress) responded by enacting the National Origins Quota Act in 1924 in order to limit immigration from countries which did not share America's language, traditions and political system.

Even former president Theodore Roosevelt came out strongly against the persistence of non-English native tongues and any attempt to use them to thwart the process of assimilation of immigrants. In an appeal drafted in September 1917 at the height of World War I—entitled the 'Children of the Crucible" and signed by thirty-eight other prominent citizens, including several from non-English backgrounds, Roosevelt said:

> We Americans are the children of the crucible.... Out of the crucible, the melting pot of life in this free land, all the men and women of all the nations who come hither emerge as Americans and as nothing else.... The crucible must melt all who are cast in it; it must turn them out in one American mold, and this must be the mold shaped 140 years ago by the men who under Washington founded this as a free nation, separate from all others... Even at that time true Americans were of many different race strains;... But the majority of leaders and of their followers were of English blood... We must have but one flag. We must also have but one language. That must be the language of the Declaration of Independence, of Washington's Farewell Address, of Lincoln's Gettysburg speech and second inaugural... We have room for but one language here and that is the English language, for we intend to see that the crucible turns our people out as Americans, of American nationality, and not as dwellers in a

> polyglot boarding house... We cannot tolerate any attempt to oppose or supplant the language and culture that has come down to us from the builders of this Republic with the language and culture of any European country. The greatness of this nation depends on the swift assimilation of the aliens she welcomes to her shores. Any force which attempts to retard that assimilative process is a force hostile to the highest interest of our country.[38]

Ironically, President Barack Obama, who during his highly divisive 2008 campaign for the White House had declared that it was more important for English-speaking Americans to learn Spanish than to insist that Spanish-speakers learnt English, recently stated that America's 12 million mostly Hispanic undocumented workers needed to learn English before they could even be considered for citizenship.[39] Coming from a Democrat, this is revolutionary. Obama is the first Democratic president in the bilingual education era to make the acquisition of English a pre-condition for being considered for U.S. citizenship, a far cry from his fellow Democrats in the U.S. Congress and outside who famously insist that it was not necessary for Hispanics to learn English at all even after acquiring citizenship of this country.

Going back to Roosevelt, the former president cautioned German-Americans against any attempt to extend support to Germany during World War I. He urged Americans of German descent to oppose Germany in the same manner that Washington and his associates rose against Great Britain in spite of their own British ancestry; otherwise they (Germans) would be regarded as traitors to America.[40]

By 1918, a groundswell of wartime anti-German sentiment forced twenty-five states to remove German from their curricula.[41] In 1921, Nebraska passed a comprehensive law making English the state's official language, prohibiting foreign language instruction before the ninth grade, and protecting the use of English in all public gatherings. Violators were subject to fines ranging from twenty-five to one hundred dollars, and up to thirty days in prison.[42] But before that, Nebraska had passed a statute—the Nebraska Sessions Laws of 1919—prohibiting the teaching of any foreign language to any student in any private, denominational, parochial or public school or teach any subject in any language other than English before the completion of the eighth grade.[43] Unfortunately, it was in Nebraska that a controversy erupted that altered forever the terms of the debate regarding the right to use and teach in minority languages.

Meyer v. Nebraska (1923)

Robert T. Meyer, a teacher at the Lutheran Zion Parochial School in Hamilton County, Nebraska, was charged with violation of the statute of 1919 when he taught German to ten-year old Raymond Papart "between the hour of 1 and 1.30 on May 25, 1920." Papart, the student, had not passed the eighth grade and thus attracted provisions of the statue. Meyer, accordingly, was tried and convicted for unlawfully teaching in a non-English language. His offense consisted in the reading of German biblical stories and he claimed he was giving religious instruction to his student in a parochial school outside normal school hours.[44] The Nebraska Supreme Court upheld Meyer's conviction on the ground of "direct and intentional teaching of the German language"[45] in clear violation of the 1919 statute. Meyer had appealed to the Nebraska apex court arguing that the statute forbidding the teaching of German violated his right to choose and pursue a profession, guaranteed by the Fourteenth Amendment to the U.S. Constitution, and the right of parents to decide what their children should be taught. The Nebraska Supreme Court determined that the obvious purpose of the statue was to make English the native language of all children reared in the state and, accordingly, concluded that rather than being an infringement of Meyer's due process rights, the application of the statute was well within the police power of the state of Nebraska. The court observed that the result of permitting foreigners, "who had taken residence in this country" and to rear and educate their children in "the language of their native land" was found "to be inimical to our own safety," and upheld the constitutionality of the 1919 statute as well, along with Meyer's conviction.[46]

The Supreme Court of the United States rejected this reasoning of the Nebraska apex court in a seven-to-two verdict. The Nebraska Sessions Law (1919), under which Meyer had been charged, and similar statutes in Iowa and Ohio prohibiting teaching of any foreign language before the eighth grade were struck down as unconstitutional. Since there was no clearly defined "right to language" in the United States, in *Meyer V Nebraska* (1923), the U.S. Supreme Court was for the first time applying the Fourteenth Amendment to a case relating to the right to use, teach, and learn a language, more so when the federal Constitution neither stipulated any language as official nor declared the use of any language as unlawful.

Delivering the majority opinion on June 24, 1923, U.S. Supreme Court Justice James C. McReynolds said that the important question here was to determine whether the statute (Nebraska Sessions Law, 1919) infringed the liberty guaranteed by the Fourteenth Amendment.[47]

The judge then defined the extent of liberty guaranteed by the Fourteenth Amendment as denoting

> not merely freedom from bodily restraint but also the right of the individual to contract, to engage in any of the common occupations of life, to acquire useful knowledge, to marry, establish a home and bring up children, to worship God according to the dictates of his conscience, and generally to enjoy those privileges long recognized at common law as essential to the orderly pursuit of happiness by free men.... (T)his liberty may not be interfered with, under the guise of protecting the public interest, by legislative action which is arbitrary or without reasonable relation to some purpose within the competency of the state...[48]

Accordingly, the court upheld Meyer's right to teach and the right of parents to engage him (or any other teacher, for that matter) to instruct their children as guaranteed liberties of the Fourteenth Amendment, rebuking the Nebraska legislature for attempting to violate them.[49]

Then the court turned to the issue of language rights. Recognizing that the states could indeed "go very far" in order to improve the quality of its citizens, the court said that such responsibility of the state was incumbent on the protection of certain fundamental rights of individuals, not only of "those born with English on the tongue" but also of "those who speak other languages."[50] The court accepted the desirability of having a common language—English—

throughout the country but cautioned lawmakers against trying to impose it by violating the fundamental rights of individuals.[51]

The court concluded its verdict by holding that it did not question the state's power to require that its schools gave instructions in English. At the same time it reminded the state of Nebraska that there was no such great emergency that could justify prohibition of a child's knowledge of languages other than English on the ground that it could be harmful "with the consequent infringement of rights long freely enjoyed."[52]

Though the U.S. Supreme Court's verdict in *Meyer V. Nebraska* (1923) accepts the pre-eminent position of the English language in America, it is nevertheless construed as a landmark in ensuring minority language rights.

Forty-five years later, minority language rights emerged as a national issue because of public concern regarding the educational handicaps of children, especially Hispanic children, considered to be Limited English Proficient (LEP). Proponents of bilingual programs argued that such programs would overcome these handicaps by facilitating the acquisition of basic skills in the language the child used at home. As pointed out earlier, language minority groups in the United States, especially Hispanics, continued using their native languages for domestic purposes.

The bilingual movement received its driving force as well as its ideology from its reaction against and rejection of the Melting Pot ideal and its goal of cultural unity.[53] The ideological inspiration behind this movement was a certain Horace Kallen, a Harvard-educated American Jewish philosopher who, in a series of two articles entitled

"Democracy *Versus* the Melting Pot" published in *The Nation* in 1915 developed his theory—known as Cultural Pluralism—that ethnic groups in America, while learning English as the general language of communication and participating in the overall economic and political life of the nation, were actually free to preserve their own language, religion, communal institutions, and ancient culture.[54] Far from being a melting pot, said Kallen, America was more like a salad bowl where the ingredients did not melt but maintained distinct identities in a whole, complementing each other in the process. Applying to language minorities the argument that forced assimilation could be psychologically damaging, ethnic (or cultural) pluralists sought to use the schools for the purpose of heightening consciousness of the ethnic heritage of immigrant (mostly language minority) children. The Bilingual Education Act (1968), which started funding programs designed to meet the needs of LEP children, raised the fundamental question of whether bilingual education should be a means of rapid transition to English [*Transitional* Bilingual Education (TBE)] or a way to perpetuate cultural differences [*Maintenance* Bilingual Education (MBE)]. In actuality, though, as bilingual programs proliferated, they increasingly became a vehicle for cultural maintenance.[55]

The Bilingual Education Act (1968)

Senator Ralph Yarborough (D-TX), while attending one of the conferences of the National Education Association (NEA) in 1966, was attracted to the idea of instructing children in their native language while they were learning English. The idea of bilingual education was floated by the NEA after a survey it conducted in 1965-66—the Tucson Survey—convinced it of the plight of Mexican American schoolchildren in the Southwest because of their language barrier. Senator Yarborough, whose Texas had a huge population of Mexican American Limited English Speaking Ability (LESA) students, introduced legislation in the U.S. Senate on January 17, 1967 by the name Bilingual American Education Act. He worded it thus:

> In recognition of the special educational needs of the large numbers of students in the United States whose mother tongue is Spanish and to whom English is foreign language, Congress hereby declares it to be the policy of the United States to provide financial assistance to local educational agencies to develop and carry out new and imaginative elementary and secondary school programs designed to meet these educational needs.[56]

Among such programs, Yarborough suggested, would be the teaching of Spanish as the native language and English as a second language, and programs designed to impart to Spanish-speaking students knowledge of their ancestral culture and language and foster in them a pride in their native linguistic and cultural heritage.[57]

According to Yarborough, such programs were needed because

> Mexican Americans have been the victims of the cruelest form of discrimination. Little children, many of whom enter school knowing no English and speaking only Spanish are denied the use of their language. Spanish is forbidden to them, and they are required to struggle along as best as they can in English, a language understood dimly by most and not at all by many. Thus the Mexican

> American child is wrongly led to believe from his first day of school that there is something wrong with him, because of his language. This misbelief soon spreads to the image he has of his culture, of the history of his people, and of his people themselves. This is a subtle and cruel form of discrimination because it indelibly imprints upon the consciousness of young children an attitude which they will carry with them all the days of their lives.[58]

Although Yarborough's bill was limited to Spanish-speaking students, it led to the introduction of 37 other bills which were merged into a single piece of legislation known as Title VII of the Elementary and Secondary School Education Act (ESEA) or the Bilingual Education Act, 1968 (PL 90-247).[59] Senator Yarborough's fellow Texan and fellow Democrat, President Lyndon Baines Johnson, beleaguered by the Vietnam War, signed it on January 2, 1968. Title VII was the first federal recognition that LESA students—subsequently redefined as Limited English Proficient (LEP) students—had special educational needs and that in the interest of equal educational opportunity, bilingual programs that addressed these needs should be federally funded.[60] Initially, though, Title VII was seen largely as a remedy for civil rights violations. However, it also began the process of formally recognizing that ethnic minorities could seek differentiated services for reasons other than segregation or racial discrimination, like discrimination on the basis of language. More significantly, it encouraged instruction in a language other than English as well as ethnic cultural awareness.[61] This went a long way in fostering ethnic segregation and hampering the process of assimilation.[62]

There were reauthorizations of the Bilingual Education Act in 1974, 1978, 1984, and 1988.

Lau v. Nichols (1974)

Hispanic children, it seems, were not the only ones having difficulty in learning and effectively communicating in the English language. Chinese American students in California encountered a similar difficulty when they found themselves failing school examinations because they did not know English.

The guardian of Kinney Kinmon Lau of San Francisco, one of the students who failed, filed a class action suit at the United States Supreme Court on behalf of more than 1800 Chinese American students—all English-deficient—of the San Francisco Unified School District (SFUSD), alleging violation of the students' rights under the Fourteenth Amendment. The students, according to the suit, were being denied an equal education because of their limited English skills.

Although California had a policy to ensure that all students learn English which was required for high school graduation, these students were not receiving any supplemental English instruction; though they were attending school, they were not being given any education at all. Despite the lower federal courts' assertion that equal education was not being denied, the U.S. Supreme Court overruled the lower courts, arguing that the same facilities, textbooks, teachers, and curricula do not constitute equal education.[63] Since the issue was whether school administrators had already fulfilled their obligation to provide equal educational opportunities merely by treating all students the same, or whether they must offer special help to students unable to understand English, the U.S. Supreme Court held that SFUSD could not sidestep its responsibility of rectifying minority children's language deficiency. Justice William O. Douglas delivered the judgment on January 21, 1974, six years after the signing of the Bilingual Education Act (1968).

In 1970, the Department of Health, Education and Welfare (H.E.W.) issued a regulation which held that ignoring the needs of non-English-speaking groups was a form of national origin discrimination and ordered school districts receiving federal funds to rectify the language deficiencies of students speaking little or no English by taking "affirmative action".[64] Clearly, the administration of President Richard M. Nixon had done its bit in promoting assimilation through the English language.

In *Lau v. Nichols*, the U.S. Supreme Court found that the provisions of this law had not been upheld by SFUSD; in fact, it (the school district) had violated the 1970 HEW regulations and, consequently, denied Chinese-speaking students "a meaningful opportunity to participate in the educational program".[65] Accordingly, the U.S. Supreme Court ordered SFUSD to mend its ways and put an end to the discrimination it practiced.[66] But the court did not prescribe any specific remedies for San Francisco schools to adopt. However, it listed two possible options: either the teaching of English to these Chinese students, or direct instruction in Chinese. The Court also accepted the possibility of other acceptable solutions.

In *Lau v. Nichols*, thus, the U.S. Supreme Court did not create any specific language rights for the Chinese-speaking students, proposing native language instruction as one of the possible remedies. But this 1974 decision of the U.S. Supreme Court has remained the major precedent regarding the educational rights of language minorities and opened the door to the so-called *Lau Remedies*, a requirement that elementary school children belonging to language minority groups be instructed in their native language until they were able to participate in English-only classrooms. Congress codified these guidelines later that year.

The Equal Education Opportunity Act (1974)

Since the Bilingual Education Act of 1968 did not explicitly require bilingual instruction or the use of the student's native language for educational purposes, encouraging "innovative programs designed to teach LESA students English" instead, and since participation in bilingual programs under the Act was voluntary, Congress amended the Act of 1968 for the first time in 1974 to clarify the intent and design of programs for LESA students. Title II of the Educational Amendments Act of 1974 (better known as the Equal Educational Opportunity Act)[67] affected the education of LESA students by specifically mentioning that language barriers were to be overcome by instructional programs; it barred states from denying equal educational opportunity to individuals on account of race, color, sex, or national origin and specifically due to the failure of an educational agency to take appropriate action to overcome language barriers.[68]

The most important contribution of the Act of 1974, however, was the definition of a bilingual education program. The Act defined a bilingual education program as one that provided instruction in English and in the native language of the student to progress effectively through the educational system. English as a Second Language (ESL) programs alone were considered insufficient. The goal of a bilingual education program, according to the Act, was to prepare LESA students to participate effectively in the regular classroom as quickly as possible.[69] But the Act of 1974 reasserted that the maintenance of the native language and culture of LESA students was a worthwhile and desirable objective.

Castañeda v. Pickard (1981)

However, the 1974 Act failed to clarify the meaning of "appropriate action" to overcome language barriers of LESA students. That was left for the 5th U.S. Circuit Court of Appeals to do in *Castañeda v. Pickard* in 1981. *Castañeda* was another class action law suit filed by Mexican American school children and their parents against the Raymondville (Texas) school system charging, among other things, that it (the school system) failed to implement an adequate bilingual education program to overcome linguistic barriers.[70]

The 5th Circuit Court developed an analytical framework to determine whether a school district had met the 1974 Act's requirement of "appropriate action" to overcome language barriers, testing it on theory, implementation, and results. First, was the district "pursuing a program informed by an educational theory recognized as sound by some experts in the field"? Second, was this program "reasonably calculated to implement effectively the educational theory adopted by the school"? Third, and most important, has the program "produced results indicating that the language barriers confronting students are actually being overcome"? If not, even a program based on a legitimate theory and properly implemented over a period of time "no longer constitute appropriate action."[71]

The revolutionary amendments of 1978

A heavily Democratic Congress and a Democrat in the White House were not really the kind of setting for attempts to make bilingual education programs purely transitional and put an end to native language instruction. But that is exactly what happened when Congress amended the Bilingual Education Act of 1968 for the second time by way of the Education Amendment Act of 1978 (PL 95-561).[72]

The Act of 1978 specified the goals of *transitional* bilingual programs. Such programs were to prepare "limited English proficient" (LEP) students to enter the regular classroom as quickly as possible. The native language was to be used only to the extent necessary for students to become proficient in English. Programs designed only to maintain the native language were excluded from funding. Reading and writing skills were added to the program goals to further enable LEP students to become proficient in English.[73]

The 1978 Act also expanded the eligibility for bilingual programs from those who were students of "limited English-speaking ability" (LESA) to those who were of "limited English proficiency" (LEP), defining the new category as students with "sufficient difficulty speaking, reading, writing or understanding the English language as to deny such individuals the opportunity to learn successfully in classrooms where the language of instruction is English."[74]

1981: End of the *Lau Remedies*

The Office of Civil Rights of the Department of Health, Education and Welfare issued in 1975 a set of guidelines—collectively called the *Lau* Remedies—to enable school districts to comply with the *Lau v. Nichols* (1974) ruling of the U.S. Supreme Court that they guarantee "a meaningful opportunity to participate in school programs."[75] The guidelines had a two-fold purpose: to determine whether a school district complied with the law (and consequently upheld the civil rights of LEP students) and to provide guidance in the development of adequate educational plans aimed at rectifying civil rights violations.[76] Among the guidelines was a requirement that school districts develop and submit to the Office of Civil Rights specific voluntary compliance plans if they had 20 or more students of the same language group identified as having a "primary or home language other than English" (PHLOTE). Interestingly, these 20 students need not necessarily have to be of the LEP category. The guidelines, however, specifically prohibited segregation of LEP students in classes and schools so that large blocs of language minority students were not formed as a result of bilingual education programs, allowing upto 40% of the students in any given classroom to be English-speaking so long as the goal of the program was to improve English language skills. The *Lau Remedies*, nevertheless, continued to promote *maintenance* bilingual education as the bilingual programs they prescribed called for the use of native language instruction in most cases.[77]

But the *Lau Remedies* were never published in the *Federal Register* as regulations and, accordingly, lacked the legal authority of a federal regulatory document. In August 1980, three months before conservative former Governor Ronald Wilson Reagan of California was elected 40th president of the United States, the Department of Education published a proposed set of rules on bilingual education for public comment. This was to comply with a 1979 legal mandate issued in *Northwest Artic v. Department of Health, Education, and Welfare* committing both the OCR and the Department of Education to publish for public comment the *Lau Remedies*.[78]

The proposed set of rules wanted to have LEP students learn English as quickly as possible and to receive instruction in subject-matter courses in a language they could understand until they learned English. The debate in public hearings focused on three questions: first, who should control education: the federal government or the local governments? Second, who should pay for bilingual education programs: the federal government or local school districts? Third, and most important, should schools teach exclusively in English or allow the use of native languages?[79]

Ultimately, the proposed regulations were deemed neither cost-effective nor practicable. The newly installed Reagan Administration moved swiftly with regard to the problem: Secretary of Education T.H. Bell withdrew the proposed regulations. Subsequently, the *Lau Remedies* were scrapped. Even though bilingual education programs continued to be administered and funded by the federal government, the Reagan Administration declared a 25% reduction in funds allocated for them. The issue of the continued use of native language instruction was settled three years later.

The 1984 Bilingual Education Act

President Reagan's federalism was based on devolution of power to the states through a gradual dismantling of the federal Big Government. Accordingly, the Bilingual Education Act of 1984 provided more flexibility to state and local school districts in devising their own bilingual programs.

The most significant step taken by the Reagan Administration to put an end to bilingual education was to float the idea of "special alternative instructional programs" which did not require the native language to be used but consisted of English language instruction and special instructional services meant to facilitate the achievement of English competency. This was one of the major provisions of the Act of 1984 and 4% of overall funds for bilingual education was set aside for this purpose.[80] Modern-day assimilationists represented by U.S. English and a host of similar organizations agitating for making English the official language of the United States support "special alternative instructional programs" as the only way to put an end to *maintenance* bilingual education which *transitional* bilingual education has degenerated into.

The Act of 1984 also awarded grants for several special programs for LEP students. These included *transitional* bilingual education programs, in which structured English language instruction is combined with a native language component and upto 40% of the class may be non-LEP students; and *developmental* bilingual education programs, in which full-time instruction is given both in English and a second language with the goal of achieving competence in both English and the second language.[81]

Even though the Reagan Administration allocated 75% of funds to *transitional* bilingual education programs and the Act of 1984 did not provide for the total elimination of native language instruction, it was the first attempt to restructure *transitional* bilingual education as a means for the achievement of English proficiency by LEP students. This shift in emphasis from maintenance of native language and culture to achievement of competence in the English language for LEP language-minority school children was meant to facilitate a faster and smoother assimilation of such children into the American mainstream. Accordingly, parents and guardians were allowed the right to decline enrollment in any of the bilingual education classes and accept enrollment in mainstream classes for their wards.

Extensive parental involvement in the education of LEP students was also proposed by Secretary of Education William J. Bennett (himself a great opponent of bilingual education) by requiring that parents and guardians be placed on advisory councils of school districts. He also suggested that school districts determine the extent of native language instruction required for special programs for LEP students. Most importantly, Secretary Bennett proposed the removal of the 4 to 10% cap on the granting of funds for "special alternative instructional programs" and wanted that preference be given to those programs that quickly moved LEP students from native language to mainstream classes; he made it clear that the goal of programs for LEP students was the rapid acquisition of fluency in English.[82]

Secretary Bennett incorporated his proposals—collectively known as the *Bilingual Education Initiative* of 1985—into the Bilingual Education Act of 1988, also known as the Hawkins-Stafford Elementary and Secondary School Improvement Act (1988). He raised grants to "special alternative instructional programs" from

4 to 10% in earlier authorizations to 25% of the total allocation, keeping 75% for *transitional* bilingual education programs. Since there were a number of minority language school districts, states were given the freedom to choose the type of program needed, such as *transitional* bilingual education programs, *developmental* bilingual education programs, *special alternative* instructional programs, or other programs. Most importantly, a three-year limit—with an extension of upto a maximum of two years—for LEP students' participation in a *transitional* bilingual education program or a *special alternative* instructional program was provided for.[83] Secretary Bennett's heart lay in the phasing out of bilingual education itself. He acted accordingly.

The 1975 amendments to the Voting Rights Act of 1965

Minority language rights, the federal government decided in 1975, could not be given legal protection without extending them to the realm of voting. The right to vote in the United States was extended and expanded by several constitutional amendments since the early days of the republic so that universal adult franchise could be exercised by American citizens regardless of race and color (Fifteenth Amendment, 1870), sex (Nineteenth Amendment, 1920), tax status (Twenty-fourth Amendment, 1964), and age i.e. eighteen years (Twenty-sixth Amendment, 1971). The Voting Rights Act of 1965 temporarily suspended literacy tests required for voter registration, enfranchising large numbers of illiterate African Americans in the South. As a result, the New York State Constitution's English literacy requirement for voting got nullified under the Act, giving the right to vote to Puerto Ricans who were literate in Spanish but not in English.

But it was the first time that voting rights were sought to be expanded in the United States by effecting a fundamental change in voting practices. In 1975, Congress admitted that language minority citizens continued to be excluded from the electoral process through the use of English-only elections.[84] Accordingly, Congress held extensive hearings about voting discrimination suffered by Hispanics, Asian Americans and Native Americans because of English-only elections, and the 1975 Amendments to the Voting Rights Act (1965) added protections for minority-language citizens from voting discrimination.[85] The 1975 Amendments explicitly required that written voting materials and oral voter assistance be made available in languages other than English in jurisdictions where a single language minority group constituted more than 5% of its voting-age citizens and where the English literacy rate of such persons was below the national average. Also, such jurisdictions must have conducted the 1972 elections in English only and attracted the participation of fewer than 50% of potential voters. In such jurisdictions, state and local governments were required to provide voting materials in the voters' native or primary language.[86]

In 1980, 386 such jurisdictions—most of thesc are counties or towns—were set aside to meet the 5% figure. In 2002, 335 jurisdictions in thirty states were still providing written voting materials and oral voter assistance in languages other than English, out of which 220 were doing it in Spanish.[87] The multilingual voting system has brought about a significant increase in voter participation by non-English-speaking communities across the United

States and helped them to win public office as never before.

The peculiar case of EL CENIZO

"Spanish is the official language of one part of the American polity," wrote Nathan Glazer way back in 1966.[88] At that time, there was no Official English movement in the United States, and only three states—Louisiana, Nebraska and Illinois—had adopted English as their official language (Illinois had declared "American" to be its official language in 1923 which it changed to English in 1969). But more than three decades later, Spanish became the official language of a small town on the Mexican-American border, confirming the worst fears of Official English advocates about the future of English in America. The name of the town: El Cenizo.

A city council meeting held on August 5, 1999 passed an ordinance declaring that all city meetings and functions and all city government business in El Cenizo, a ramshackle blue-collar town of 7800 residents (90% of whom spoke Spanish only) just 15 miles downriver from Laredo along the Rio Grande in south Texas, would be conducted in Spanish. There was little discussion and no dissension as the city council voted to make Spanish official.[89] The council's decision also made El Cenizo the first in the country to declare a language other than English as official.

Another ordinance declaring El Cenizo as a "safe haven" for undocumented immigrants was also passed. This Safe Haven Ordinance forbade city employees and officials to ask residents whether they were illegal immigrants or citizens or to help an agency like the dreaded Border Patrol, the *La Migra*, and the Immigration and Naturalization Service apprehend illegal entrants; city employees who violated the ordinance were to be fired.[90]

Mayor Rafael Rodriguez, who spoke Spanish only like most of the town's residents, had reportedly illegally crossed over from Mexico in 1979 and had become a U.S. citizen only in 1995.[91] Worse still, Rodriguez flew the flag of Mexico over City Hall along with the Stars and Stripes.[92] Elected as mayor along with two city commissioners in November 1998, Rodriguez declared that Americans who came to his town would need to learn Spanish. But he refused to tread a path of confrontation with anyone, least of all the federal government. His only intention, as he put it, was to make Spanish-speaking people participate meaningfully in city council meetings.[93] City Commissioner Flora Burton said that for several years, meetings of the city council have been bilingual since residents regularly asked commissioners to explain things in Spanish; some Spanish-speaking residents even stopped attending the council's meetings because of the language barrier. The Spanish-only measure, said Burton, was meant to ensure popular participation in city business.[94] The other commissioner, Gloria Romo, reasserted her colleagues' stand that it was aimed at making people more comfortable and enhancing their participation and cooperation in running El Cenizo's affairs.[95]

James Crawford, a celebrated opponent of Official English, could not have agreed more. But with one important difference: he accused "Right-wingers" (read Republicans and Official English advocates) of making a hue and cry out of a non-issue. In a personal communication with this author, Crawford wrote:

> This (El Cenizo) is a small town on the Mexican

> border, where a high percentage of residents speak only or mostly Spanish. What local officials did was to add Spanish as an official language – certainly not to ban English. A great national controversy was stirred up, however, by right-wing talk radio programs, which spread lots of misinformation. El Cenizo's bilingual approach was motivated primarily by a desire to provide access to government services for local Spanish speakers rather than any movement for cultural or linguistic nationalism.[96]

Crawford's ardent and spirited multiculturalism may not have allowed him to see any wrong in El Cenizo's Spanish-only ordinance, but the fact remains that the town's officials did not "add Spanish as an official language"; they *made* Spanish the official language of El Cenizo. More importantly, El Cenizo's was not a "bilingual approach": it wanted to make the town Spanish monolingual. Even though the ordinance had made a provision that English translations of council proceedings would be made available if a request was made 48 hours in advance, the fact that the residents were overwhelmingly Spanish-speaking meant that such a request was seldom going to be made, thus making the provision meaningless and the town officially Spanish monolingual.

Surprisingly, though the federal government led by the multiculturist President Bill Clinton maintained absolute silence over the development—as did the then Texas governor, Republican George W. Bush—many federal officials heartily endorsed El Cenizo's Spanish-only policy, among them Israel M. Reyna of the federally funded Texas Rural Legal Aid who curiously called America a "developing democracy" where it was important to get people involved.[97] But he conveniently overlooked the fact that the United States was a developed democracy, and immigrants—especially from undemocratic nations or developing democracies—were expected to be able to read and understand the laws and the Constitution of the United States in the language in which they were written if they wanted to fully and meaningfully participate in the political process.

Not only was El Cenizo precariously close to the Mexican border, the fact that the Safe Haven Ordinance had made scouting for illegal immigrants itself illegal in the eyes of local law would definitely encourage illegal immigration from Mexico. That would not only mean continuation of El Cenizo's Spanish-only policy but also trigger a demand for a similar policy for other Hispanic-majority border towns and pockets with large Russian, Cambodian, Korean, and Arabian populations. Jim Boulet, executive director of the Virginia-based advocacy group, English First, echoed such a fear. Calling El Cenizo America's "very own Quebec", Boulet said that its Spanish-only policy would encourage a separatist attitude among non-English speakers:

> In a nation of immigrants, we have to be able to communicate with each other... (W)e are either going to speak in one language in this nation of immigrants or we are going to be speaking in many. El Cenizo is the canary in the mine. This is a wake-up call, first to George W. Bush, who seems to think that being against English-only will get him Hispanic votes but who doesn't mind this, and then to our own federal government, because if we're not going to insist on a common language, we can expect more like this one... Language

> divisions rather quickly lead to other divisions. It proves we really need a national language policy sooner rather than later.[98]

Mauro E. Mujica, Chairman and CEO of U.S. English—who himself migrated from Chile in 1965—expressed similar fears, pointing out that it was the Mexican Americans' refusal to assimilate that was behind El Cenizo's Spanish-only ordinance:

> This type of separatism is exactly what U.S. English has been warning about for 15 years. But I fear that this is no isolated incident. Unlike earlier generations of immigrants, who understood their responsibility to become Americans, many new immigrants from south of the border refuse to adopt an American identity and refuse to speak our common language...This is what happens when the federal government refuses to patrol the border and politicians pander for the so-called Hispanic vote. Let me be blunt: it is simply un-American for an American town to declare a Mexican identity. This small town has national implications. If Governor Bush doesn't deal with this appropriately, he risks losing the support of millions of Americans who rightly view this separatism as a bad sign for the future unity of America.[99]

Governor Bush refused to intervene, calling El Cenizo's Spanish-only ordinance a local matter. The result: he won a huge chunk of the Hispanic vote in the 2000 presidential elections. By passing Executive order 2417 in 2001, which required federal agencies to produce all public documents in both English and Spanish by 2005 and directed federal employees to undergo mandatory Spanish language training,[100] he was hoping to improve his Hispanic vote-share during his re-election bid in 2004.

A U.S. English official, in a personal communication with this author, asserted that if English was declared the official language of the United States, it would prevent Spanish-only laws from being passed at the local level:

> To ensure there is not another El Cenizo, U.S. English has a bill in the U.S. House of Representatives, H.R. 997. This bill would make English the official language of the United States government. H.R. 997, when passed, will thus negate any local level language laws.[101]

Clearly, till the time English becomes the official language of the United States, the danger of local level non-English language laws would remain.

This danger is a real one: the danger of linguistic separatism that can plunge the United States into a turmoil unprecedented in its history, seriously undermining American identity and the unity of the country. A nation of immigrants like the United States cannot afford to be officially bilingual or multilingual. In the aforesaid personal communication, James Crawford wrote, "The claim that there are significant separatist tendencies among Latinos is laughable."[102] If El Cenizo's Spanish-only ordinance does not indicate a separatist tendency, what does?

In September 1995, nearly four years before El Cenizo passed its Spanish-only measure, Republican presidential candidate Robert J. "Bob" Dole had warned that "ethnic separatism" was a threat to national unity and called for making English the official language of the country.[103] Evidently, Dole was farsighted.

REFERENCES

1 Quoted in Gov. Richard D. Lamm and Gary Imhoff, *The Immigration Time Bomb: The Fragmenting of America* (New York, NY, 1985), p.4

2 Lisl Zach, "Legislative History of Immigration Restriction 1901 to the Present", May 6, 1998, p.1

3 ibid., Roger Daniels, *Coming to America: A History of Immigration and Ethnicity in American Life* (New York, NY, 1990), p. 280

4 Daniels, ibid, p. 271

5 ibid. p. 274

6 Zach, op.cit.

7 ibid.

8 Barbara Miller Solomon, *Ancestors and Immigrants* (Cambridge, MA, 1956). Quoted by Daniels, op.cit. p. 276

9 Daniels, ibid., p. 255

10 Zach, op. cit.

11 Daniels, op. cit., pp. 278-9

12 ibid.

13 ibid. p. 280

14 *Congress and the Nation, Vol. II, 1965-1984 A Review of Government and Politics* (Washington, DC, 1969), pp. 57-60

15 Daniels, op. cit., p. 329

16 Quoted in ibid., p. 332

17 Quoted in ibid. p. 333

18 ibid. pp. 338-9

19 Quoted in Robert Dallek, *Lyndon Johnson and His Times 1961-1973* (New York, NY, 1988), pp. 227-8

20 ibid.

21 ibid.

22 *Congress and the Nation,* op.cit., p. 60

23 Dallek, op.cit., p. 228

24 Quoted in Daniels, op.cit. p. 340

25 *Congress and the Nation,* op.cit. p. 58-59

26 ibid.

27 "Historical Overview of U.S. Immigration Policy: The Period of Reforms, 1965-1990", *www.fairus.org*. November 18, 1996. Adapted from M.E. Glade and J.R. Giese, *Immigration: Pluralism and National Identity* (Public Issues Series, Social Science Education Consortium, 1989)

28 *Congress and the Nation,* op.cit., p. 60

29 ibid.

30 ibid., p. 61

31 ibid.

32 Eric Foner, *Give Me Liberty! An American History* (New York, NY, 2005), p. A-42

33 Maldwyn Allen Jones, *American Immigration,* 2nd Ed. (Chicago, IL, 1992), p. 265

34 ibid. pp. 268-9

35 Thomas Bailey Aldrich, "The Unguarded Gates," *Atlantic Monthly,* June 1882. Quoted in Daniels, op.cit. p. 275-76

36 Judith Bentley, *American Immigration Today: Pressures, Problems, Policies* (New York, NY, 1981), p. 233-34

37 "U.S. Census Bureau Report", 2000. Quoted in *FAIR*, 4/03, *www.fairus.org*

38 Theodore Roosevelt et al., "The Children of the Crucible", September 1917. Reprinted in *Annals of America,* vol.14, 1916-28 (Chicago, IL, 1968), p. 129-31

39 "People can't be pouring over border: Obama", *Hindustan Times* (Delhi), March 20, 2009, p. 17

40 Roosevelt, op cit.

41 Report in *New York Times,* May 25, 1918, cited in Dennis Baron, *The English-Only Question: An Official Language for Americans?* (New Haven, CT, 1990), p. 109

42 ibid. p. 143

43 Quoted in ibid. p. 145

44 Bill Piatt, *¿Only English? Law and Language Policy in the United States* (Albuquerque, NM, 1990), p. 39; Baron, op.cit. p.145

45 *107 Neb. 657*, 1922

46 Piatt, op.cit. pp. 39-40

47 *Meyer V. Nebraska*, 262 U.S. 390, (1923)

48 ibid.

49 ibid.

50 ibid.

51 ibid.

52 ibid.

53 Jones, op.cit., p. 276

54 Milton M. Gordon, *Assimilation in American Life: The Role of Race, Religion, and National Origins* (New York, NY, 1964), pp. 141-42

55 For a detailed discussion, see Chapter 3 (A) of this book.

56 Senator Ralph Yarborough, "Introducing the Bilingual Education Act" in James Crawford, ed., *Language Loyalties: A Source Book on the Official English Controversy* (Chicago, IL, 1992), p. 324

57 ibid.

58 ibid., pp. 323-4

59 Gloria Stewner-Manzanares, "The Bilingual Education Act Twenty Years Later", *The National Clearinghouse for Bilingual Education,* Number 6, Fall 1988

60 Stewner-Manzanares, op. cit.

61 ibid.

62 For a detailed discussion, see Chapter 3 (A) of this book.

63 Stewner-Manzanares, op.cit. Also Baron, op. cit. p. 171.

64 *33 Fed. Reg. 4955; 35 Fed. Reg. 11595.*

65 *Lau V. Nichols*, 414 U.S. 563 (1974).

66 ibid.

67 *20 USC* § 1701-20

68 *20 USC* § 1703 (f)

69 Stewner-Manzanares, op.cit.

70 Martha Jimenez, "The Educational Rights of Language-Minority Children" in James Crawford, ed., *Languages Loyalties: A Source Book on the Official English Controversy* (Chicago, IL, 1992), pp. 247-74.

71 ibid. p. 248

72 Stewner-Manzanares, op.cit.

73 ibid. Also, Crawford, "Bilingual education: Language, learning, and politics", *Education Week*, April, 1987, pp. 19-50

74 PL 95-561. Quoted in Stewner-Manzanares, op. cit. Also in Diego Castellanos, *The best of two worlds: Bilingual-bicultural education in the U.S.* (Trenton, N.J., 1983), p. 179

75 *Lau V. Nichols* (1974), op.cit.

76 Stewner-Manzanares, op. cit.

77 ibid.

78 ibid.

79 ibid.

80 ibid.

81 ibid.

82 William J. Bennett, *The condition of bilingual education in the nation, 1988: A report to Congress and the President* (Washington, DC, 1988)

83 Enrique Cubillos, *The Bilingual Education Act: 1988 Legislation* (Wheaton, MD, 1988)

84 *S. Rep. No. 295,* 94th Congress, Ist Session, p. 28. Quoted

in " "Official English": Federal Limits of Efforts to Curtail Bilingual Services in the States", *Harvard Law Review* (Vol. 100, no. 6,), April 1987, p. 1351

85 "Introduction to Federal Voting Rights Law: The Voting Rights Act of 1965", United States Department of Justice, Civil Rights Division, Voting Section, *www.doj.gov.*

86 *42 USC,* § 1973 aa-Ia (b), 1982

87 Sandra Guerra, "Voting Rights and the Constitution: The Disenfranchisement of Non-English Speaking Citizens", *Yale Law Journal* (Vol. 97, no. 77), June 1988, p. 1423. Also Huntington, *Who are We? America's Great Debate* (London, 2004), p. 161

88 Nathan Glazer, "The Process and Problems of Language-Maintenance: An Integration Review" in Joshua A. Fishman et. al., *Language Loyalty in the United States: The Maintenance and Perpetuation of Non-English Mother Tongues by American Ethnic and Religious Groups.* (The Hague, 1966), p. 364

89 Lynda Gorov, "Texas town makes Spanish official, stirs war of words," *Boston Globe,* August 28, 1999, p. E08

90 Madeline Baro Diaz, "Border City Goes All-Spanish," *The Associated Press,* August 19, 1999

91 Gorov, op.cit. Also "Texas Town Adopts Spanish As Official Language", *Reuters,* August 6, 1999

92 Don Feder, "An un-American act in a Texas town", *Washington Times,* September 1, 1999

93 Gorov, op.cit, *Reuters,* op.cit.

94 Baro Diaz, op.cit.

95 Quoted in Gorov, op. cit.

96 James Crawford, personal correspondence through email with Saumyajit Ray, February 2, 2004.

97 Feder, op. cit.

98 Baro Diaz, op. cit.; Gorov, op.cit; *Reuters* op.cit.

99 "Texas Town Declared Itself America's First "Spanish

Only City", *U.S. English Press Release*, August 13, 1999; also Feder, op.cit.

100 "In Focus: Executive Order 2417", *www.whitehouse.gov.*

101 Chad Becker, Membership Coordinator, U.S. English Inc., personal correspondence through email with Saumyajit Ray, February 25, 2004.

102 Crawford, personal correspondence with Saumyajit Ray, op cit.

103 David S. Broder, "Dole Backs Official Language; English is Needed to Unify Nation, Presidential Hopeful Says," *The Washington Post,* September 5, 1995.

3

Old Ties in the New World

"The greatness of this nation depends on the swift assimilation of the aliens she welcomes to her shores. Any force which attempts to retard that assimilative process is a force hostile to the highest interest of our country.... A hyphenated American is not an American at all."
- Theodore Roosevelt

(A) FROM "KNOW ENGLISH" TO "NO ENGLISH": THE QUAGMIRE THAT IS BILINGUAL EDUCATION

Introducing S. 428, the American Bilingual Education Act, in the 90th Congress, Senator Ralph Yarborough (D-TX) said,

> It is not the purpose of this bill to create pockets of different languages throughout the country... not to stamp out the mother tongue and not to make their mother tongue the dominant

> language, but just to try to make these children fully literate in English, so that the children can move into the mainstream of American life.[1]

It is true that the Yarborough legislation, known as Title VII of the Elementary and Secondary Education Act (ESEA) or the Bilingual Education Act (P.L. 90-247), signed into law on January 2, 1968, did not explicitly require bilingual instruction or the use of the students' native language for educational purposes but encouraged "innovative programs" designed to teach English to Limited English Speaking Ability (LESA) students. For the first time, bilingual education, defined as a program that provided instruction in English and in the native language of the student to allow the student to progress effectively through the educational system, was introduced by the 1974 amendments to the Act of 1968. But evidence over the years has given reason to believe that the federal government's bilingual education policy, sought to be implemented through a technique known as *transitional* bilingual education (TBE)—helping limited English proficient (LEP) students keep up with reading, math, science and other subjects in their native tongues while they are taught enough English to transfer to regular English-only classrooms—has failed to solve the educational problems of such students, many of whom had fallen behind in school or dropped out altogether. What is more, Congress quickly moved to expand its commitment to bilingual education by including within its purview bicultural instruction, in which language-minority students were taught about their own ethnic groups. Worse, linguistic minorities saw in bilingual education an opportunity to maintain and revive cultural identities. Clearly, Senator Yarborough's objectives have not been fulfilled; the fears he tried to dispel have proved to be real.

William J. Bennett, President Reagan's Secretary of Education between 1985 and 1988, in an address to the Association for a Better New York delivered on September 26, 1985 in New York City, said that though each American was "justly proud" of his or her own ethnic heritage, as Americans they shared their pride in common.[2] He reminded his audience that it was necessary to share in something common as citizens: common principles, common memories, and a *common language* in which to discuss their common affairs. America's common language, asserted Secretary Bennett, was, of course, English. More importantly, the common task of Americans was to ensure that non-English-speaking children learnt this common language.[3]Also, he said that he expected the schools to help teach all students English.[4] It was a virtual admission that schools had failed to fulfill their obligation in that regard.

Creating one nation and one people, said Secretary Bennett, was the objective of bilingual education as he understood it, and English-language literacy was central to the achievement of that objective.[5] The secretary not only underlined the assimilationist capability of the English language in America but also spoke of the need to reorient educational policies to hasten and perpetuate such assimilation.[6] Not only was Secretary Bennett a truly assimilationist Republican, serving in the Cabinet of another assimilationist Republican, he posited English as the language of freedom: commitment to democratic ideals and the English language were the two commonalities shared by all Americans, and it was through the English language that such commitment was best expressed and fulfilled in America. This was over and above the secretary's belief that it was the mission of U.S. schools to nurture a common language—English—in order to foster a common national identity.

Non-English and bilingual education programs, however, were not unheard of in 18th and 19th century America. Before the Civil War, some Cincinnati (Ohio) schools taught in both English and German. German-English bilingual schools were also started in Indianapolis (Indiana), St. Louis (Missouri), Baltimore (Maryland) and other cities with large German communities. Apart from this, there were French-English educational programs in Louisiana, Spanish-English programs in the Territory of New Mexico and some Norwegian, Italian, Polish, and Dutch programs. Even Native Americans were engaged in bilingual education: by 1852, Cherokees in Oklahoma achieved 90% literacy in its native language and a literacy rate in English higher than White native speakers in either Texas or Arkansas.[7] But such bilingual schools started disappearing during the Americanization movement, and ultimately perished in the wake of resurgence in anti-German sentiment during World War I. As President Theodore Roosevelt, a leading cultural assimilationist of his time, wrote in *The Foes of Our Household* in 1917, eight years after he demitted office:

> There is no room in this country for hyphenated Americanism... Any man who comes here... must adopt the language which is now the native tongue of our people... It would not be merely a misfortune, but a crime to perpetuate differences of language in this country.[8]

This aversion toward non-English native languages was accompanied by a stern warning that those who insisted on perpetuating them could not be accommodated in America.[9]

Bilingual education made a comeback in 1963 when the Coral Way Elementary school in Dade Country (Miami, FL) introduced an experimental bilingual education program for children in its first three grades. Devised in the aftermath of Fidel Castro's rise to power in Cuba in 1959 and the subsequent Cuban influx to Florida, both Spanish and English-speaking children participated in the program, since its objective was to foster bilingualism among native speakers of both languages.[10] The popularity of the Coral Way experiment prompted other communities in the Southwest to emulate it, though with slight variations and by 1969 some 56 bilingual programs were already under way; all were Spanish-English except one in Navajo-English at Rough Rock, Arizona.[11]

The more than hundred witnesses who testified in support of S. 428 before the Special Subcommittee on Bilingual Education of the Senate Labor and Public Welfare Committee (to which S.428 was referred) broadly argued that bilingual education was necessary to prevent the academic retardation resulting from "sink-or-swim" monolingual English instruction to Spanish-speaking children who, though proficient in their native language, had little or no English proficiency; to minimize and ultimately stem the psychological damage caused to Spanish-speaking students when they entered the linguistically and culturally alien English-only schools; to prevent the loss the of the bilingual potential among Spanish-speaking students; to foster strong and effective home-school cooperation; and, to conserve the nation's language and cultural resources.[12]

José A Cardeñas, once director of the Intercultural Development Research Association, San Antanio (TX), identified three reasons for opting for bilingual education:

the need for continued learning as a non-English-speaking child moved from one language to another necessitated the use of the child's native language for instructional purposes while English was being learned; the need to reduce the alienation which minority-language children frequently faced when pushed into an unfamiliar language situation necessitated the use of the native language not only to moderate the trauma of transition but also to develop and maintain a positive concept of self (on the ground that a positive concept of self contributed to successful performance, which led to an improved self-concept and more successful performance); and, the use of the native language was imperative to the intellectual development of the child.[13]

Cardeñas' assumptions are highly questionable.[14] He regarded bilingual programs with native-language instruction as the "best option" for LEP children as they allowed for continued learning and the continued increase in the capacity for learning as the transition to a new language was being made. Not only that, he saw bilingual education as the best approach for teaching the English language without academic retardation, with the minimum development of negative concepts of self, and with the maximum development of the intellectual potential of the individual.[15] He steadfastly supported the continued use of native language instruction. Rejecting the recommendation of critics of bilingual education that the school should discontinue the use of the native language as soon as the child had a basic understanding of English, Cardeñas contended that a basic understanding of English—frequently determined by the child's ability to communicate in social situations—was far from the level of language proficiency needed for learning activities.[16] No doubt, then, that *transitional* bilingual education has degenerated into *maintenance* bilingual education wherein native language instruction is never discontinued for language-minority children during their years in school.

Gary Imhoff, a Washington-based writer on public policy issues and senior consultant to U.S. English, believe that the professional advocates of bilingual education based their arguments upon a particular educational theory. According to Imhoff, bilingual education theory rested upon four central premises: that second languages were best introduced to children only after they were thoroughly fluent in their first (or native) languages; that intensive instruction in a second language should be postponed until after first-language fluency was achieved; that achieving adequate academic fluency in a second language took many years of schooling after conversational fluency was achieved, a minimum of six years of schooling was required for the purpose; and that, subject-matter courses should be taught in the first language for several years while English was introduced slowly, and in small amounts.[17]

Cardeñas' cardinal beliefs testify for the accuracy of Imhoff's description. What is more astounding is his (Cardeñas') proposition that native language instruction actually enhanced the learning of English by preventing the loss of language and communication capability of the LEP child. In fact, Imhoff cites the example of two prominent proponents of bilingual education, Stephen Krashen and Douglas Biber, who had written in their *On Course: Bilingual Education's Success in California:* "Time spent in the first language building literacy and subject matter knowledge may be the best possible way of promoting English!"[18]

The flaw of Cardeñas' and his fellow travelers' proposition is too glaring, because the continued use of native language instruction not only retards English language acquisition but also ill-equips students (instructed in the native language in a K-12 school) to learn subject matter courses in English in college.

Krashen tries to explain his thesis by saying that language acquisition happened through *comprehensible input*. When a second-language acquirer understood the language of a subject-matter class in English, it was also a language lesson for him. Alternatively, subject-matter classes taught in the first language contributed directly but powerfully to the acquisition of English, because such classes resulted in knowledge that helped make English input more comprehensible.[19] But what Krashen proposes may be true for a small number of above-average intelligent students; for the vast majority of students who had received native language instruction in school, coping with subject-matter courses for higher degrees in English becomes almost impossible, reflected in falling grades and a progressively worse academic record. A child—whether born in an English-speaking or a language-minority home—is a *blank slate:* he will acquire, by way of both knowledge and language whatever he hears. He may use his native language at home and perform successfully in English-only classes right from infant school. This is the reality of students in India and other Asian nations going to "English-medium" schools, and of children from Indian American homes in the United States. This author has never conversed in anything but in his native Bengali at home, but that has never come in the way of acquiring fluency in reading, writing, and conversing in English outside.

So Krashen is right when he agrees with Dr. Jim Cummins that the use of first language at home by minority students did not prevent success in school.[20] Cummins, of the Ontario Institute for Studies in Education, makes the interesting observation that what was important was the quality of parent-child interaction, and not the actual language used at home; in fact, the use of the majority language (that is, English) at home may have a detrimental effect on the child's acquisition of that language, especially if parents were not conversant in English.[21]

A. Bruce Gaarder, Chief of the Modern Language Section of the U.S. Office of Education, testifying in support of S.428 before the Special Subcommittee on Bilingual Education of the Senate Committee on Labor and Public Welfare and defining bilingual education as "the use of both English and another language—usually the child's mother tongue—as mediums of instruction in the schools,"[22] cited five main reasons in favor of bilingual education, the first three pertaining to the child's years in elementary school, the rest applying when the bilingual child became an adult: the non-English-speaking children's conceptual development and acquisition of knowledge could proceed without retardation if the mother tongue were used as an alternative medium of instruction; the use of the child's mother tongue (which is used at home) by some of the teachers and as a school language is necessary to facilitate a strong, mutually reinforcing relationship between the home and the school; the rejection of the mother-tongue of an entire group of children by their school could seriously and adversely affect those children's concept of their parents, their homes, and themselves; if a minority language child grows up without achieving reasonable literacy in his mother tongue, it will rob him of a potential career advantage, his bilingualism; and, non-English languages in the United States could only be conserved through bilingualism.[23]

Gaarder suggested presenting English *as a second language* to children who spoke other languages, because the failure to do so helped produce what he called "functional illiteracy" among a majority of Spanish speakers in Texas. According to him, in a bilingual education program, English would be taught from the very beginning in school, but a language minority child's concept development and acquisition of knowledge—his total education, that is—would no longer depend on his imperfect knowledge of English.[24] In other words, Gaarder supported native language instruction for language minority students, and the teaching of English as just another academic discipline. The perfect recommendations for a culturally plural America.

James J. Lyons, former executive director of the National Association for Bilingual Education (NABE), denied that the goal of bilingual education was to ultimately promote English monolingualism; in fact, he regarded English monolingualism as a negative educational outcome of the American school system.[25] It is evident that he detests English monolingualism and holds *transitional* bilingual education responsible for the creation of English monolinguals out of minority language monolinguals. If Lyons is not for *transitional* bilingual education, then the only alternative to that is *maintenance* bilingual education which reinforces preservation of minority languages—and cultures—through continued use of native language instruction. LEP students in *maintenance* bilingual programs seldom become proficient in English[26]; they remain monolinguals in their native languages. Can such minority language monolingualism be regarded as a positive outcome of the bilingual education system or a desirable goal for bilingual education? Will it not lead to the creation of "pockets of different languages" throughout the Unites States, something that Senator Yarborough said was not the purpose of S.428 when he introduced it in the U.S. Senate on 17 January 1967?

The Bilingual Education Act of 1968, in fact, was the first federal incursion in the field of bilingual education. It was a giant leap from local efforts in that direction. What, then, constitutes bilingual education?

According to Gary Imhoff and former governor Richard D. Lamm of Colorado[27], there are at least four different methods of teaching English to non-English-speakers.

The *first* was the traditional method—the *English only method*—in which no special aid was given to the minority language-speaking student. Derided as the "sink-or-swim" approach by bilingual education backers, this was actually the way in which people learned their native languages, and was especially successful with children. (This reinforces the BLANK SLATE analogy).

A variant of this method was the *immersion* method, the *second* generally-accepted approach to teaching English to non-English-speakers. Even though it did not involve the use of the students' native languages—considering such use as a crutch—it provided special assistance to the students in the forum of reading exercises, flash cards, language films, and numerous other tools aimed at achieving the same level of fluency in reading, writing and speaking English in the student as in a native speaker of the language. Considered as one of the most effective and rapid ways of teaching a language, especially to adult learners, only the language to be taught (English, in this case) was used in classrooms.[28]

Supporters of bilingual education have not only encouraged confusion between these two methods (because of the use of only English in the teaching of the language to non-English-speakers) but have decried their use, especially as alternatives to bilingual education.[29]

A *third* method, on the other hand, aimed first at teaching the students' native language. After that language was mastered, it became the primary means through which English was learned. But only a little instruction was given in English, in the minimal amount of time deemed to be necessary for the student to learn that language. All other school subjects were taught in the native language. Even though this was regarded as *transitional* bilingual education, the exclusive reliance on the native language for subject matter instruction and the minimal teaching of English made the process of transition to English excruciatingly slow. Even though students took three to five years on an average in *transitional* programs, some proponents of bilingual education believe that such programs should last between five and seven years; for extremists among them, even all twelve years of school spent in native language instruction would not be a bad idea. In fact, as things stand today, *transitional* bilingual programs, with their reliance on native language instruction and the time associated with them, have degenerated into *maintenance* bilingual programs, a means of protecting and preserving the native language and culture of the language-minority students. *Transitional* bilingual programs, with the teaching of English as their primary goal, are now passé.[30]

English as a Second Language (ESL) was the *fourth* approach wherein language minority children received all subject matter instruction in English, supplemented only by an additional English language class. It was an attempt to teach English in an intensive way, with bilingual assistance provided by a bilingual teacher when the student could not understand. The native language may be one of the many tools used to teach English. This approach aimed at early predominance of English, for the purpose of moving the language minority child from ESL classes to mainstream all-English classes as soon as possible.[31] Even though this was a type of bilingual program, proponents of bilingual education do not always regard it so because of its emphasis on subject matter teaching in English. In fact, they see it as an alternative to bilingual education, betraying their belief that bilingual education meant only native language instruction.

Even though the Act of 1968 did not require the use of the students' native language in the classroom, encouraging "innovative methods" designed to teach English to LESA students instead, bilingual education today is nothing more than native language instruction, with federal law reserving three-fourths of all federal bilingual education funds for such instruction. In these programs, a student might receive as little as 45 minutes of instruction in English daily, prolonging his stay in the bilingual (actually, native language) classroom for several years before joining mainstream classes.

In Los Angeles, the city with the highest concentration of language-minority children, a common method of teaching English to non-English-speaking LEP students was to send such children out for three hours of recess on the playground each day so that they picked up enough English from their English-speaking playmates. The Los Angeles United School District regarded this method of "teaching" English as adequate, giving it the name "mixing."[32] Innovative as this may seem, it is an admission by the school district that it no longer considered the teaching of English solely a matter of classroom instruction.

As an educational technique, bilingual education may mean either the occasional use of a non-English-speaking students' native language in the classroom, or *transitional* bilingual programs designed to introduce LEP students to English slowly and gradually while teaching at least some subject matter courses in the students' native language, or *maintenance* programs primarily designed to maintain the language and culture of the students' old country.[33] Schools providing bilingual education in the United States are expected to preserve and even promote the divergent cultural and language backgrounds of their students; it is obvious they would opt for *maintenance* programs in which language-minority students take their basic subjects in their native language and are taught English as a foreign language.

For four decades bilingual education through native language instruction has remained the preferred—and the only federally-funded—method of teaching English to LEP students, to the exclusion of all others. This, despite the fact that neither the Act of 1968 nor the Supreme Court's ruling in 1974 in *Lau v. Nichols* explicitly required native language instruction. In fact, a survey sponsored by the U.S. Department of Education to look into the effectiveness of bilingual programs admitted in September, 1981 that there was no justification in assuming that it was necessary to teach subject-matter courses in the language-minority child's native tongue to ensure his satisfactory progress in school.[34] It suggested, alternatively, that *immersion* programs, which involved structured curriculums in English for both language and non-language subject areas, be given more attention, and if non-language subjects were taught in English to language-minority children, the curriculum ought to be structured differently from the way the curriculum was structured for English monolingual students.

Iris Rotberg, representing the National Institute of Education, in a similar survey in 1982, pointed out that there was no evidence to suggest that the bilingual-bicultural approach advocated by the *Lau Remedies* and Title VII was better on the average than other models.[35] Even though the Supreme Court's *Lau* ruling (1974) did not mandate native language instruction, its insistence that the same facilities, textbooks, teachers, and curricula did not constitute equal education implied that English as a Second Language (ESL) and *immersion* methods were inappropriate and ineffective ways of teaching English to limited-English-speaking ability (LESA) students. Accordingly, the 1975 guidelines (better known as the *Lau Remedies*) issued by the Office for Civil Rights of the U.S. Department of Health, Education, and Welfare to help school districts comply with the Supreme Court's *Lau* decision called for native language instruction in most cases with the support of federal funds. It actually changed the definition of bilingual education from one that provided instruction in English and in the native language of the student to one that provided native language instruction only. The 1975 *Lau* Remedies' redefinition of bilingual education converted it into *native language monolingual education*, robbing it of whatever English language component it might have had and putting an end to its *transitional* character for all times to come. The search for equal educational opportunity ended in the promotion of native languages and cultures!

Even former Rep. James Scheuer (D-NY) admitted that the Bilingual Education Act's "original purposes were perverted and politicized" and that instead of helping students learn English, "the English has been sort of thinned out and stretched out and in many cases banished into the mists and all of the courses tended to be taught in Spanish. That was not the original intent of the program."[36] Rep. Scheuer was an original sponsor of the 1968 Bilingual Education Act.

Why, then, has the federal government continued in its support for bilingual education? According to Governor Richard D. Lamm and Gary Imhoff, bilingual education exists for political, not educational, reasons like giving jobs and local power to members of the non-English-speaking community who work in the bilingual schools, reinforcing children's identification with members of their own ethnic groups, and preserving the distinguishing characteristics of those ethnic groups, which in turn served as a power base to those who identified themselves as leaders of those groups.[37]

Not only did the Hispanic community monopolize political lobbying for bilingual education—through groups like the League of United Latin American Citizens (LULAC), Mexican-American Legal Defense and Educational Fund (MALDEF), and the National Council of La Raza—an overwhelming majority of Hispanics also started supporting bilingual programs. A survey, commissioned by the Spanish language television station *Univision* and covering 755 eligible Hispanic voters in San

Francisco, Los Angeles, Miami, New York, Chicago, Houston, Dallas, and San Antonio between April 5 and 18, 1998, found that 83 per cent of those polled either strongly or somewhat supported bilingual education.[38]

Imhoff, in fact, views bilingual education as an element of a political movement, providing a power base for mostly Hispanic local and national ethnic organizations regardless of its efficacy or desirability for Hispanic students.[39] The politics of bilingualism, Imhoff accurately points out, is rooted in a particular social theory, namely, that of *cultural pluralism*, first articulated by Horace Kallen in the 1920s in his seminal work, *Culture and Democracy in the United States* (1924).[40] Sociolinguist Joshua A. Fishman—author of *Language Loyalty in the United States* (1966) and numerous other works on pluralism and languages—till date remains the high-priest of the social theory of bilingual education.

The problem arose, says Imhoff, when Hispanics began to be treated not as immigrants but as a minority ethnic community. The primary effort and the primary credit for an immigrant's success in American society belonged to him or her. The immigrant learned the language of the new society, along with its customs and folkways, and the skills that were useful to make a decent living in the new land. His or her success in achieving the American Dream depended on hard work, sometimes even harder than that of native-born Americans. If treated as a minority, however, this type of effort was not necessary on the part of the immigrant.

Going by the cultural pluralist model, the problems that arose between a minority and his/her society were presumed to be caused by that society. The responsibility for solving those problems, therefore, lay with the society. Applying this to the American situation, if Hispanics in America were a minority community and not an immigrant group, then the responsibility of learning a new language lay with American society and not Hispanics. Not only that, society's responsibility to the immigrant was to provide opportunity whereas society's responsibility to the minority was to provide entitlements. Bilingual education was one of the foremost entitlement programs that could be afforded to Hispanics.[41]

Worse, as political support to bilingual education was aimed at creating a power base for its supporters, it was not concerned with the success of bilingual programs, but with their indefinite continuance.[42] This, despite the fact that Hispanic organizations very well know that bilingual education was unpopular with the American people, especially when Americans understood its underlying theory of cultural maintenance. They could not have cared less, as the bilingual education movement is just an arm of a much wider power struggle wherein Hispanic leaders try to preserve their power by maintaining the separate identity of their ethnic group.[43]

But two observations of Imhoff stick out as remarkably unique and accurate as assessments of bilingual education. First, he views bilingual education as an attempt at ethnic segregation of American society, on the same lines as the racial segregation of the 1950s and 60s; only that the segregationists of today call themselves progressives or leftists rather than conservatives.[44] The other is the misleading nature of the term *transitional* bilingual education. The term, Imhoff says, was invented in the late 1960s to make bilingual education politically acceptable; no difference in educational theory actually distinguished *transitional* from *maintenance* bilingual education, but the term implied that the purpose of these *transitional* courses was to enable students to move from their native languages into English.[45] It would be pertinent to mention here that Senator Yarborough had confidently declared that the purpose of S.428—which became the Bilingual Education Act of 1968—was "not to stamp out the mother tongue". No doubt, then, schools providing bilingual education have succeeded in preserving and promoting the divergent cultures and languages of their students, at the cost of preparing them for life and citizenship in America.

Noel Epstein, an education writer for *Washington Post*, not only questioned the rationale for preferring bilingual education over other instructional approaches but also relentlessly criticized minority-language *maintenance* programs. The government was yet to demonstrate whether *transitional* bilingual education made much difference to the students' achievements, to their acquisition of English, or to their attitude toward school, says Epstein. Despite that, Congress had rapidly and regularly increased its commitment to bilingual education and even to "bicultural instruction", where language-minority students were taught about their own ethnic groups.[46]

Epstein questions the criteria for eligibility of students for bilingual education programs. According to him, students who were otherwise proficient in English (even though they may also speak another language) had been admitted to bilingual programs based on their surnames, Census Bureau data, and other grounds which do not necessarily measure a pupil's proficiency in speaking, understanding, reading, and writing English.

This, coupled with the absence of generally accepted and validated tests to measure language proficiency of students, has ended up in the admission of many English proficient language-minority students to bilingual programs, leaving out the most needy in their midst from the purview of such programs.[47]

Epstein attacks advocates of bilingual-bicultural education for wanting to provide such instruction to students who were already proficient in English, for opposing the use of the native language only temporarily as a bridge to English instruction, and for seeking to give equal importance to the mother tongue and culture through language and cultural *maintenance* programs. Beneath the arguments and justifications in favor of *maintenance* programs, says Epstein, was the idea that it was for the federal government to finance and promote student loyalties to their ethnic languages and histories while at the same time going through the process of learning the common English language and the common national history. Epstein calls this phenomenon *Affirmative Ethnicity*.[48]

If language and cultural *maintenance* programs, says Epstein rightly, were the goals of bilingual-bicultural education, then it would become the responsibility of the federal government to maintain other languages and cultures regardless of a student's degree of fluency in English. The ostensible purpose of bilingual education—to help LEP children achieve English proficiency and learn subject matters in English—would be defeated. That is exactly what has happened, even if one forgets Epstein.

But Epstein makes a more fundamental point: was it a federal responsibility to finance and promote student attachments to their ethnic languages and cultures, a task long performed by families, religious groups, ethnic organizations, private schools, and ethnic publications? Certainly not, when one considers the divisive nature of *maintenance* programs; Epstein, like Imhoff, cites evidence about maintenance efforts being highly segregated. In the same vein, Samuel P. Huntington calls bilingual education "educational apartheid."[49] It really is.

B. PERMANENTLY ALIEN RESIDENTS: THE BANEFUL EFFECTS OF BILINGUAL EDUCATION

After six years in a *transitional* bilingual education (TBE) program, a Hispanic student in California wrote

> I my parens per mi in dis shool en I so I feol essayrin too old in the shool my border o reri can gier das mony putni gire and I sisairin aliro sceer.[50]

Neither English nor Spanish. Neither here nor there. But this is exactly what happens when the educational bureaucracy in the Untied States, inspired by the principle of "cultural maintenance", wants children with Hispanic surnames to be forced into Spanish-speaking bilingual classes where they are taught Spanish language and culture and English only as a second language, regardless of the fact that such children understood and spoke English well and did not speak or read Spanish when they entered school.

Hispanic parents have also complained bitterly for long that throughout the day in school their children were exposed to Spanish and only for a few minutes to English. In a Los Angeles elementary school parents went on strike to get their children taught in English. One hundred and fifty Hispanic families in Brooklyn's Bushwick district sued New York State to get their children out of bilingual classes.[51] When a child with a Hispanic surname was admitted to a bilingual program even though he spoke no Spanish, by the time he was in the seventh grade he could read neither English nor Spanish.

Bilingual education—*transitional* bilingual education—had a simple and limited mission: to teach children of Mexican descent in Spanish while they learned English. That was the position of the federal government in 1968, and especially after the amendments of 1974. The method was simple too: to have students take subject matter courses in their native language while learning English as a second language. The idea was that these children's lack of proficiency in English should not hamper their progress in learning. But *transitional* bilingual education had fallen victim to *facilitation theorists* who claimed that children could not learn a second language until they were fully proficient in their first. This process was supposed to take six or seven years during which students were taught only in their native language. English was not be taught at all during these years, but worked into the curriculum slowly once the threshold was crossed. In other words, children were to learn English by being taught in Spanish! Since the basic postulate of the facilitation theorists was that children would be cognitively deprived if they were not taught in their native tongue, students (most of them Hispanics) were not allowed either to learn in English or to learn English in their years in bilingual school.

Both the early proponents of bilingual education (who championed *transitional* bilingual programs) and the later *facilitation theorists* (who introduced native language instruction) can be seriously disputed with regard to their basic premises. If lack of proficiency in English hampered the process of learning of limited English proficient (LEP) students—as the early bilingual advocates had claimed—then the only way of overcoming that drawback would be to teach such students in English in either traditional all-English classes, structured "immersion" programs in English, or in English as a Second Language (ESL) programs. In this way, LEP students would successfully make the crossover to English because such instruction would allow them to learn in English and learn English (as a language) at the same time. In fact, the longer students stayed in segregated bilingual programs, the less successful they were in school. After four decades of bilingual education, the dropout rate for Latinos was the highest in the country: among Hispanic immigrant children in the age group 16 to 19, 34% were dropouts in 2000, whereas among US-born Latinos of the same age group, 14% were dropouts in that year, among all Hispanics 16-19, regardless of where they were born, 21% had dropped out in 2000, down from 21.6% in 1990.[52]

Worse, only about 5% of children enrolled in bilingual classes ever made it to English-speaking classes each year.[53] Needless to say, most of them are Hispanics. In fact, Hispanics constitute about 75% of all students enrolled in LEP programs.[54] Hispanic students, despite bilingual education, consistently perform below the national average, as shown by the National Assessment of Educational Progress (NAEP). Disparities begin as early as kindergarten and remain through age 17. Hispanic students lag behind their non-Hispanic peers in reading, mathematics and science proficiency throughout their years in school.[55] And most of them leave school unable to

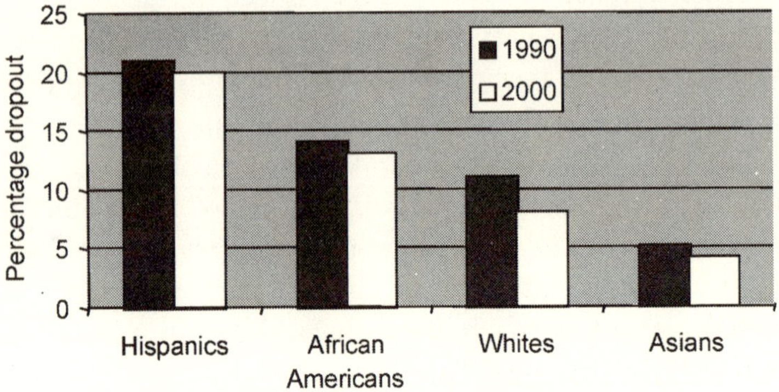

[DATA: *CNN.com/EDUCATION*]

Fig. 7. Dropout Rates Among Children of Different Ethnic Communities in the United States, 1990 & 2000

read or write English, the language of the United States.

No doubt, then, that large numbers of Hispanic parents want their children to be taught in English and not in Spanish and do not want the federal government to continue maintaining Spanish language and culture with federal funds. As Earnesto Ortiz, a foreman on a South Texas ranch put it: "My children learn Spanish in school so they can become busboys and waiters. I teach them English at home so they can become doctors and lawyers."[56] Yolanda Granados' 5-year-old son Luis, who could read simple English before he entered kindergarten in Sun Valley (California), was forced into bilingual class by the school district—without consulting his mother—for the simple reason that he had a Spanish surname and Spanish was sometimes spoken in their home. Yolanda was informed not long after the school year started that her son could not keep up. "I sent Luis to school to learn English," she said.[57] Evidently, her purpose had not been served. Such Hispanic parents look at English as the language of opportunity in the United States, refusing to be drawn into a confrontation between the language of the country and their native language for practical, if not for any other, reasons. Not that they do not converse in Spanish at home, but they would not like their children to lose out on educational and employment opportunities because of the fact that their native tongue was not English. For them, the transition to English was a matter of deliberate practical choice, and they saw no dichotomy between the occasional use of Spanish at home and the more general use of English outside by their children. According to the *National Clearinghouse for Bilingual Education*, California accounted for 40% of the 3,452,073 LEP students reported during the '96-'97 school year.[58] The 1997 Language Census of the California Department of Education put the number of LEP students in California at an alarming 1,381,393.[59] Along with it, Texas (15%), Florida (8.4%), New York (7.2%), and Illinois (3.4%) accounted for almost 75% of LEP students in the United States.

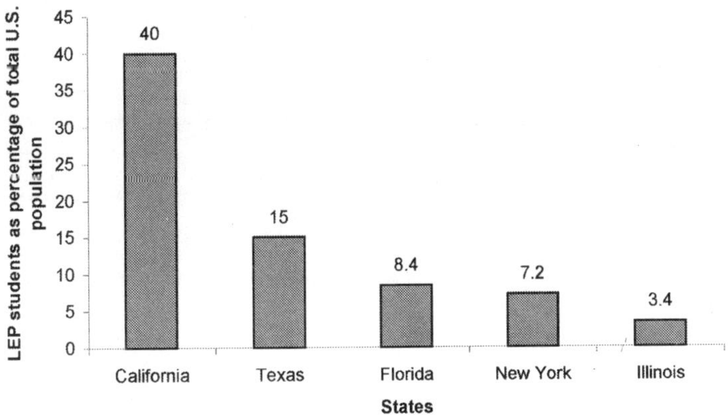

[DATA: *FAIR*, 4/03]

Fig. 8. States With The Highest Limited English Proficient (LEP) Students In The U.S. 1997

According to the U.S. Census Bureau Report (2000),

17.6% of the American population spoke a language other than English at home, up from 13.8% in the 1990 census. Among them, those who spoke Spanish at home rose from 54.5% in 1990 to 59.6% in 2000.[60]

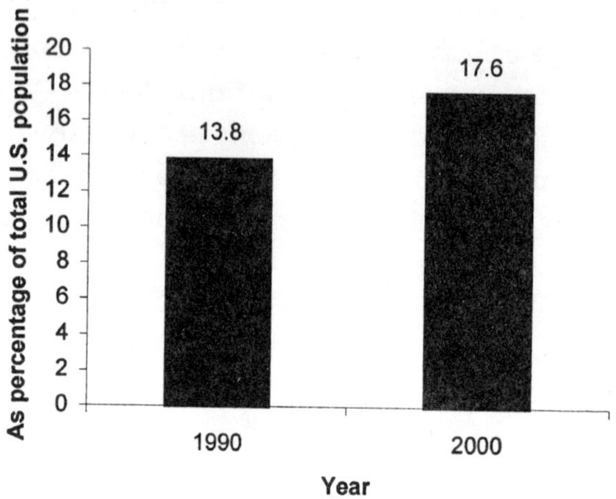

[DATA: *FAIR*, 4/03]

Fig. 9. Americans Speaking Non-English Languages At Home 1990 & 2000

To understand how well immigrants in the United States spoke English, says Gillian Stevens, it is necessary to take into account the native lands of immigrants. Potential immigrants born and raised in countries in which English was a dominant or official language had a large advantage over potential immigrants born and raised in non-English-language countries. If English was the dominant language of an immigrant's country, which made the immigrant a native speaker of English, his linguistic assimilation in the United States would not be much of an issue. Countries like the United Kingdom, Australia, Canada, and New Zealand fell into this category. Even immigrants from countries like India, where English was not a dominant language but an official language used in important social institutions such as the government and the educational system, arrived in the United States with prior knowledge of English and hence would not find living and working in their new country a difficult proposition. On the other hand, immigrants from the remainder of the world's countries, where they were much less likely to learn English as a first or second language or to use English in major social institutions, were less apt to be proficient in English on their arrival in the United States.[61] These include immigrants from Vietnam, Korea, and China. And these also include Hispanics. Spanish-speakers in the United States are drawn from Argentina, Bolivia, Chile, Colombia, Costa Rica, Cuba, the Dominican Republic, Ecuador, El Salvador, Guatemala, Honduras, Mexico, Nicaragua, Panama, Paraguay, Peru, Puerto Rico, Spain, Uruguay, and Venezuela.[62] Though frequently referred to as *Latino,* a term used to denote US residents of Latin American origin, *Hispanic* is a more preferred designation for this very diverse and multi-racial population of which Mexican-Americans (earlier known as *Chicanos*), Cuban-Americans, and Puerto Ricans are the largest groups according to national origin.

No doubt, then, that Hispanics would find linguistic assimilation and adaptation in the United States difficult; English is neither a dominant nor an official language in any of their countries of origin. The task of linguistic assimilation, however, has been made impossible by bilingual education through native language instruction. If mastery of both the native language and English, and not just English, was the goal of the facilitation theorists and their *maintenance* approach to bilingual education, that goal is yet to be achieved; Hispanic students in primary and secondary schools (K-12) in the United States master neither language after years in so-called *bilingual* classes.

Even if they become proficient in Spanish, that is of little use in the United States. Despite the recent tendency in government, business, and politics to publish Spanish translations of their literatures, American society remains overwhelmingly English speaking. One thing is certain: Hispanics seem condemned to lifelong limited English proficiency and, by extension, to continued marginal and subordinate positions in American economy and society.

In 2001, 21.4% of Hispanics were below poverty level, a slight increase from 21.2% in 2000. A gradual decline in the number of Hispanics below poverty level here was also accompanied by a rise in the level of English proficiency in that community. Whereas 39.3% of Hispanic students in K-12 reported to be speaking English less than "Very Well" in 1990, only about 33% of such students fell in that category in 2000. The Hispanic population in the United States also rose from 9% in 1990 to 12.5% in 2000. But the percentage of Hispanics speaking Spanish at home rose from 7.5% in 1990 to 12% in 2000, as part of the total US population. Interestingly, more native-born Hispanics spoke Spanish at home than the foreign born, 52.5% to 47.4% in 2000.[63]

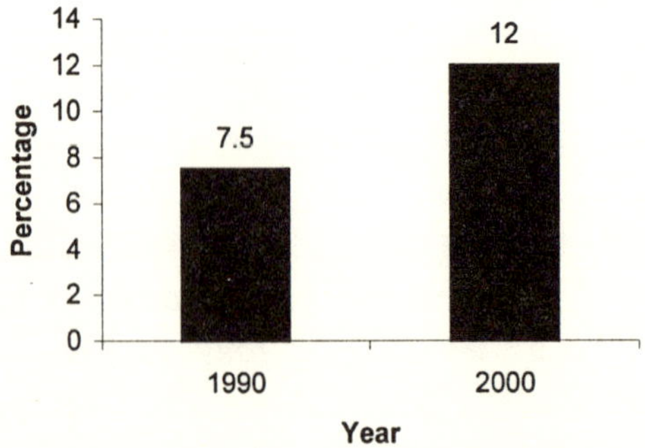

[DATA: *Current Population Surveys*, 1990 and 2000]

Fig. 10. Hispanics Speaking Spanish At Home 1990 & 2000

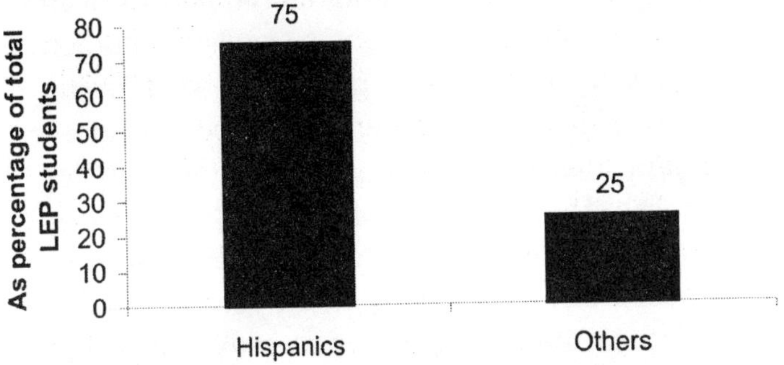

[DATA: *www.ed.gov/offices/OIIA/Hispanic*]

Fig. 11. Hispanics and Others in LEP Programs (Maintenance and ESL Programs) 2000

A decline in the percentage of LEP Hispanics in grades K-12 from 1994 through 2000 was accompanied by a gradual fall in the percentage of Hispanics below poverty level during the same period. This research revealed a perfect positive correlation between the degree of English proficiency and the level of prosperity among Hispanics. This falsifies Joshua A. Fishman's contention, made in his 1988 paper "'English Only': Its Ghosts, Myths and Dangers,"[64] that there was no relation whatsoever between acquisition of English proficiency by Hispanics and their social mobility.

Despite this, the Democratic Party—the 'party of immigrants'—continues to affirm its support for bilingual education in unambiguous terms, declaring that this "important education program" increased educational opportunities for 2.8 million LEP students.[65] The rationale for backing bilingual education is also stated clearly and with rare conviction by a party known for its equivocation:

> U.S. elementary and secondary schools have relied on bilingual education to teach limited English proficient students for over 200 years.

> Bilingual education requires limited-English proficient students to spend a significant portion of their school day learning English while allowing them to study core academic subjects in English and/or their native language until they master English. These students often fall far behind their English speaking classmates in English-only classes because they spend most of their day trying to learn English when they should be learning new academic concepts.[66]

The party not only accepted that it had increased federal funding for bilingual education between 1995 and 2000 but promised to keep the show going despite having lost control of Congress in the midterm elections of November, 1994.

It is evident that bilingual education is the cornerstone of the Democratic Party's education plank. What is also evident is that the party's claims regarding bilingual education are misleading. Americans with non-English native language backgrounds have for generations learnt English through the traditional *all-English* and *structured immersion* approaches, not through bilingual education. Though German, French, Dutch, Spanish and Navajo bilingual classes existed, they were exceptions. Federally funded bilingual programs started only in 1968.

That students in bilingual programs do not spend "a significant portion of their school day learning English" has already been written about. In fact, less than an hour is devoted to English learning in bilingual classes almost everywhere in the United States, in schools receiving Title VII grants. In bilingual programs, in which native language instruction is the norm, subject matter courses are taught in the student's native language, and language minority students have no choice in studying them in English. True, such students often fell far behind their English- speaking classmates, not because "they spend most of their day trying to learn English" but because they do not learn any English at all. The contradiction in the Democratic Party's position on bilingual education is too glaring to be missed: on the one hand, the party claims that bilingual education required limited English proficient students to spend "a significant portion" of their school day learning English and, on the other, it complains that LEP students fell behind their English- speaking classmates in English only classes because they spent most of their day trying to learn English. If the reason behind the LEP students' poor performance in school was the great amount of time they spent in learning English—time they should have devoted to learning "new academic concepts"—then why should bilingual programs require their students to spend "a significant portion" of their day learning English? No doubt, the party wants students in bilingual classes to learn "new academic concepts" in their native languages, a stand rooted in the belief of *facilitation theorists* and other bilingual advocates that a student's process of learning should not be hampered by his imperfect knowledge of English.

Not surprising, then, that speeches in the 1996 Democratic National Convention were delivered in Spanish as well as English. Latino activists, who reject both assimilation and the assimilative capacity of the English language in the United States and insist on bilingualism and cultural maintenance, want recognition of some sort accorded to Spanish in the U.S. "Ingles y mas" (English and more) is their slogan. Such demands, in fact, draw their ideological sustenance from what is known as

English Plus, initially conceived as a reaction to Secretary William J. Bennett's September 26, 1985 New York City speech on bilingual education.[67]

A Miami-based till-then little known organization, the Spanish American League Against Discrimination (SALAD), in a carefully-worded response to the Secretary's speech, outlined the English *Plus* approach to language conflicts in the United States:

> English is a key to equal educational opportunity, necessary but not sufficient. English by itself is not enough. Not English only, English *Plus*!... English plus competence in the home language... English *Plus* for everyone.[68]

During the entire period of the Reagan Administration, SALAD and the League of United Latin American Citizens (LULAC) continued to use the term English *Plus* to symbolize support for bilingual education which, they propagated, was under attack from both the President and his Secretary for Education William J. Bennett.

In October 1987, toward the end of President Reagan's second term, was launched the English Plus Information Clearinghouse (EPIC) as a coalition of thirty organizations—among which were the American Civil Liberties Union (ACLU), the Mexican American Legal Defense and Educational Fund (MALDEF), National Association for Bilingual Education (NABE), the National Council of La Raza, and the Teachers of English to Speakers of Other Languages (TESOL), all renowned Official English-baiters and strong advocates of bilingual education—to promote English *Plus* as a philosophy of inclusion and openness toward linguistic minority groups.

Established under the auspices of the National Immigration, Refugee, and Citizenship Forum and the Joint National Committee for Languages, EPIC advocated, among other things, the preservation of non-English languages and cultures:

> The English Plus concept holds that the national interest can best be served when all members of our society have full access to effective opportunities to acquire strong English language proficiency plus mastery of a second or multiple languages.... There is a need to encourage the retention and development of a person's first language, to build upon the multiple language skills of all members of our society, and to strengthen our commitment to cultural and democratic pluralism.[69]

Such a prescription is fraught with dangers not only because it is difficult to determine the "first language" of the vast majority of English speakers in the US, but also because it would turn the clock back on assimilation, apart from discouraging limited English proficient minority language speakers from assimilating into American society. EPIC is known not only for its commitment to bilingual education and bilingual ballots, but also for its support for bilingual assistance in the legal system, social services, and health care.[70]

What is more, on January 3, 2001 in the US House of Representatives of the 107th Congress (1st Session) was moved a concurrent resolution—entitled the "English Plus Resolution" (H. Con. Res. 9)—by Representative Jose E. Serrano (D-NY) which was then referred to the House Committee on Education and the Workforce. Claiming that the United States "was founded on a commitment to democratic principles, and not on racial, ethnic or religious homogeneity, and has drawn strength from a diversity of languages and cultures,"[71] the resolution stressed the need for the conservation and development of non-English native languages in the United States.[72] It envisaged no threat to the status of English in the country—spoken as it was by 94% of US residents (1990 census)—and accordingly, did not see any need "to designate any official United States language or to adopt similar restrictionist legislation".[73] But then, it recognized the need to "continue to provide services in languages other than English as needed to facilitate access to essential functions of government, promote public health and safety, ensure due process, promote equal educational opportunity and protect fundamental rights".[74] Rep. Serrano again introduced an "English Plus Resolution" (H. Con. Res. 3) in the 111th Congress on January 6, 2009.[75] Clearly, English *Plus* is the political program of bilingual education advocates.

Such ideological support to cultural maintenance has led extremists among Latino activists not only to push for civil rights for illegal immigrants and protection of Spanish language and culture in the United Sates but also to demand the return (*reconquista*) of the southwest US provinces—lost by Mexico to the United States in the war of 1848—with the avowed objective of establishing *Aztlan*, a pan-Mexican homeland. A radical group formed solely for the purpose of achieving *Aztlan*, the *Movimiento Estudiante Chicano de Aztlan* (*MECHA*), launched a political party, *La Raza Unida*, in 1970. *La Raza* tried converting Crystal City (Texas) into a Chicano city after wresting control over it in local elections. English-speaking

Americans united with Latinos in singing *Viva Mexico!* at a meeting of the National Council of *La Raza*.[76] The Mexican flag adorns the office of the mayor in El Cenizo (Texas). The Democratic Party had repeatedly branded Republicans as anti-Latino for sponsoring Official English measures and opposing bilingual education at various levels. The radical Mexican-American separatist group, *MECHA*, accused the Republican Party of being made up of racist/fascist European settlers.[77] In the end, despite the best of intentions, ideological and political support to cultural pluralism has led not only to social conflicts but also to secessionist tendencies among Latinos in the United States. Bilingual advocates have failed to recognize that repeated reminders of 'rich' cultural diversity actually undermined assimilation; cultural homogeneity was the basis of social and political unity.

The Unz initiative (California)

In June 1998, California voters approved Proposition 227—the *English for Children* initiative, introduced by Silicon Valley software entrepreneur Ron Unz and sponsored by his organization One Nation/One California—by a vote of 61% to 39%[78] (including a large vote from language minority voters) to end bilingual education in its present form, that is, through native language instruction. Despite attempts at politicizing the language debate, a *Los Angeles Times* poll showed that Latino voters favored the initiative 84% to 16%.[79] In fact, Unz collected 433,000 signatures to put the issue on the ballot. The successful Unz initiative eliminated native language instruction in most cases, and replaced it with a year of intensive English-language instruction and English language classes. Interestingly, then US Secretary of Education Richard W. Riley, who as governor of South

Carolina in 1987 had signed an Official English bill with a strong bilingual education component, denounced Proposition 227 as a "disaster", saying that though the ballot measure may satisfy people's sense of frustration, ultimately it was "counterproductive" to the goal of ensuring that children learnt English while making progress in other subjects as well. Riley, a great supporter of bilingual education through native language instruction, did not specify how that progress would be made.

Keeping in mind the high dropout rate among Latino students, the failure of Latino children in LEP programs to learn to read or write English and the poor academic performance that accompanied such failure, the opposition of language minority parents to bilingual education because of these reasons, and the fact that bilingual education did not assist assimilation in any way, Unz and other like-minded backers of the initiative proposed to abolish bilingual education after all; the *English for Children* ballot initiative called for stopping the teaching of non-English-speaking children in their native language unless their parents requested it. Instead, a year of "sheltered English immersion" was proposed for such children before being moved into mainstream English-only classes. Unz also mandated $50 million a year for ten years for adult literacy programs. There was neither any proposal in the initiative to throw all LEP children into regular classes from the beginning, nor one to cut special funding for children learning English.

Despite this, the National Association for Bilingual Education (NABE), the California Teachers' Association (CTA), the National Association for Latino Elected Officials (NALEO), the Mexican American Legal Defense and Education Fund (MALDEF), and the National Association for the Advancement of Colored People (NAACP) put up strong opposition to the *English for Children* ballot initiative, claiming that one year of "sheltered English immersion" would not be enough for LEP students. In fact, a coalition of bilingual advocates led by MALDEF and NAACP filed a class-action lawsuit in a California court on June 4, 1998, after the initiative passed the ballot. The lawsuit was an attempt to invalidate the new *English for Children* law on the ground that it violated the Civil Rights Act of 1964, the Educational Opportunity Act of 1974, and the Equal Protection clause of the US Constitution. The lawsuit further argued that the Unz measure subjected students to an "educational experiment, denied them access to critical aspects of school curriculum and severely limited their chances at academic success."[80] In fact, the *El Futuro Newsletter* of summer 1997 attacked Proposition 227 (the Unz initiative) in a language that reiterated the basic tenets of the *facilitation theory*:

> Legislation such as Proposition 227... does not represent viable alternatives to the educational systems they are designed to dismantle. Instead, it uses a one-size fits-all philosophy that may prove devastating for all children whose first language is not English ... Educators contend that ....mastery of English should not take place at the expense of advanced academic and thinking skills, or the loss of the child's first language.... If young people are not familiar with the language of instruction, it will be nearly impossible to learn educational content, thereby jeopardizing their advancement and future graduation.[81]

Clearly, Stephen D. Krashen's "comprehensible

input"[82] was playing on the minds of the opponents of Proposition 227. They were so hell-bent on not allowing Proposition 227 to become law that they challenged it in the courts a day after its passage on June 3, 1998. The federal courts, however, upheld the initiative. Since passing Proposition 227, LEP students in California—home to 41% of all students with a Primary Home Language Other Than English (PHLOTE) and where 40% of students in K-12 were limited English proficient (the highest in the country)—have shown remarkably improved scores in reading, writing and math. Classrooms in Los Angeles—with 557,640 LEP students or over 40% of California's LEP population[83], the highest number of such students of any district in the entire country—became overwhelmingly English-language. In Oceanside (CA), test-scores of language minority children increased 200% after Proposition 227 was introduced.[84]

The method mandated by Proposition 227—*sheltered English immersion*—was the indispensable method of English as a Second Language (ESL) programs and has been found to be extremely effective in teaching both English and other academic subjects. Rosalie Pedalino Porter, former director of bilingual education in Newton (MA) and then with the Research in English Acquisition and Development (READ) Institute, concluded after a recent ten-year study of ESL programs and their impact on the academic performance of LEP students that "special, English-intensive, content-based instruction from the first day of school, and the early development of literacy in English for (language-minority) students" produced superior results.[85] As a onetime director of bilingual education, she felt she was deliberately holding back the learning of English.[86] Interestingly, Mexican-American and Cuban-American parents, responding to a survey conducted by the US Department of Education, overwhelmingly declared their opposition to teaching children in their native language if it meant less time devoted to English.[87]

Evidently, bilingual education with the initial limited objective to teach Spanish-speakers English within one or two years has been perverted into a program to Hispanicize, and not Americanize, Spanish-speakers. As Ronald J. Schmidt wrote, the conflict over language policy was nothing but a conflict about the relationships between language, ethnic identity, and American nationalism.[88]

Schmidt identified three central "instrumental" advantages of a pluralistic policy for language minority groups: *first*, a pluralistic language policy would lessen some of the costs heretofore paid by non-English speakers, shifting some of the burden to the state (for example, multilingual ballots and election materials reduced costs of political participation for language minority members); *second*, many language minority members and language experts believe that a bilingual education policy which added to and built upon the students native language would be more effective in ensuring academic excellence even in English than did programs seeking to substitute the native language with English; and *third*, to the extent that bilingual skills became valued in the political economy as a result of a pluralistic language policy, the policy will directly benefit those members of language minority communities who have already invested the time and effort to become bilingual.[89] One thing is certain from Schmidt's analysis: a pluralistic language policy—of which bilingual education is the cornerstone—benefited members of language minority communities only. They benefit someone else as well, as assimilationists pointed out and

Schmidt agreed: self-appointed ethnic leaders for whom a pluralistic policy like bilingual education was a self-serving political strategy.

Schmidt also lauded assmilationists like Gary Imhoff in questioning the legitimacy of the pluralist argument by defining the beneficiaries of pluralist policies as "immigrants" and not as members of minority groups.[90] But for Schmidt, the most important and central issue dividing assimilationists and pluralists was the nature of the American identity: "costs" and "benefits" regarding language policy could only be understood when viewed in the context of whether the United States was a monocultural (as assimilationists regard it as) or a multicultural (as pluralists would have everyone believe it was) country.[91]

For Alejandro Portes and Ruben G. Rumbaut, it was necessary to take into account the social context into which immigrants settled; in their view, the basic difference was between immigrants who clustered in ethnic communities and those who became dispersed throughout the country. According to them, if a language group found itself in a minority in a city, there was always a pressure on it to become bilingual.[92] If they lived in ethnic enclaves, they would tend to be mother-tongue monolingual or at most limited bilingual.

Elaborating on their thesis, Portes and Rumbaut pointed out that the pressure on immigrants to learn English was different from the pressure on them to learn English only. The pressure to learn English only—which Portes and Rumbaut call *subtractive* acculturation—operated when the immigrant population was dispersed and not concentrated in ethnic enclaves. The outcome of such dispersed immigrant settlements was either limited or fluent bilinguals in the first generation and English monolinguals invariably in the second generation. This was true for workers, professionals and entrepreneurs, the three classes to which immigrants generally belonged. The pressure to learn English—which Portes and Rumbaut have named *additive* acculturation—was not as great as the pressure to learn English only and operated when immigrants lived in homogenous ethnic neighborhoods or ethnic enclaves. In such elements, the first generation of immigrants—whether workers, professionals, or entrepreneurs—were always invariably mother-tongue monolinguals and those belonging to the second generation were either limited or fluent bilinguals, but never English monolinguals.[93] Clearly, mother-tongue retention happened when immigrants lived in ethnic enclaves only. Nearly 50% Hispanics attend urban high-poverty schools,[94] and continue to live in ethnic enclaves. This was a situation that Senator Ralph Yarborough, while introducing the Bilingual Education Act (1968), wanted to avoid.

Horace Mann, a prominent public figure of 19th century Massachusetts and an observer of the American system of education, argued that public schools in the United States should take the lead in assimilating immigrant populations into American economic life.[95] Clearly, because of bilingual education, public schools have failed to fulfill that obligation.

REFERENCES

1 Quoted in James Crawford, *Hold Your Tongue: Bilingualism and the Politics of "English Only"* (New York, NY, 1992), p. 84

2 Secretary William J. Bennett, "The Bilingual Education Act: A Failed Path" in James Crawford, *Language Loyalties: A Source Book on the Official English Controversy* (Chicago, IL, 1992), p. 358

3 ibid.

4 ibid. pp. 358-9

5 ibid., pp. 362-3

6 ibid.

7 "Bilingual Education", *CQ Researcher* 3, August 13, 1993, pp. 704-12

8 Quoted in ibid.

9 ibid.

10 ibid.

11 ibid.

12 James J. Lyons, "The Past and Future Directions of Federal Bilingual-Education Policy", *The Annals of the American Academy of Political and Social Science*, Vol. 508, March 1990, pp. 67-68.

13 José A. Cardenas, "The Role of Native Language Instruction in Bilingual Education", *I.D.R.A. Newsletter*, January 1984, pp. 1-6

14 See also Chapter 6 (A) of this book.

15 Cardenas, op cit.

16 ibid.

17 Gary Imhoff, "The Positions of U.S. English on Bilingual Education" in *The Annals*, op cit., p.51

18 Quoted by Imhoff, ibid., p. 51

19 Stephen D. Krashen, "Bilingual Education, Acquiring English, and the Case of Richard Rodriguez", *California Association for Bilingual Education Newsletter*, May-June 1982

20 ibid.

21 Jim Cummins, "The Role of Primary Language Development in Promoting Educational Success for Language Minority Students," *Schooling and Language*

Minority Students, p. 33. Quoted in Krashen, ibid.

22 U.S. Senate, Committee on Labor and Public Welfare, Special Sub-Committee on Bilingual Education, *Hearings on S. 428*. 90th Congress, 1st Session, (May 18, 1967), pp. 50-4

23 ibid.

24 ibid.

25 Lyons in *The Annals*, op cit., p. 78

26 See next sub-chapter.

27 Lamm was the longest serving Colorado governor, holding office between 1975 and 1987

28 Gov. Richard D. Lamm and Gary Imhoff, *The Immigration Time Bomb: The Fragmenting of America* (New York, NY, 1985), pp. 102-3

29 Cardenas, op cit.

30 Lamm and Imhoff, op cit., p. 104

31 ibid, p. 103. Also Bill Piatt, *¿ Only English? Law and Language Policy in the United States* (Albuquerque, NM, 1990), pp. 47-8

32 Terri Hardy, "LAUSD Plays at Teaching", *Los Angeles Daily News*, December 21, 1997, A 1.

33 Imhoff, op cit., p. 50

34 Keith A. Baker and Adriana A. de Kanter, "Effectiveness of Bilingual Education: A Review of the Literature" (U.S. Department of Education, Office of Planning, Budget and Evaluation, Washington D.C., September 1981), Quoted in Lamm and Imhoff, op cit., p. 108-9

35 Iris Rotberg, "Some Legal and Research Considerations in Establishing Federal Policy in Bilingual Education", *Harvard Educational Review,* 52, no. 2 (May 1982), p. 157

36 Quoted in Bennett, op cit., in Crawford (ed.), *Language Loyalties*, p. 361

37 Lamm and Imhoff, op cit., p. 109

38 Bennett Roth, "Survey Says Most Hispanics Support Bilingual Education", *Houston Chronicle*, April 23, p. 108

39 Imhoff, op cit., pp. 57-8

40 Preceded by an article "Democracy *Versus* the Melting Pot", *The Nation*, February 18 and 25, 1915.

41 Imhoff, op cit., p. 57

42 ibid.

43 ibid, p. 60

44 ibid.

45 ibid.

46 Noel Epstein, *Language, Ethnicity, and the Schools: Policy Alternatives for Bilingual-Bicultural Education* (Washington, DC., 1977)

47 ibid.

48 ibid.

49 Samuel P. Huntington, *Who are We? America's Great Debate* (London, 2004), p.169.

50 Quoted in Peter Duignan, "Bilingual Education Advocates", (Hoover Essay/Hoover Institution), *www.hoover.stanford.edu*

51 ibid.

52 "Immigrant Hispanic Teens More Likely to Drop Out", *CNN.com / EDUCATION*, June 13, 2003

53 Duignan, op. cit.

54 "White House Initiative on Educational Excellence for Hispanic Americans", *www.ed.gov / offices / OIIA / Hispanic*

55 ibid.

56 *Congressional Record*, December 5, 1995, p. H. 13932

57 Cited by Linda Chavez, "One Nation, One Common Language", *Reader's Digest*, August, 1995.

58 "Immigration Affects the Whole Country", *FAIR*, 4/03, *www.fairus.org*

59 "General Information on Limited English Proficient (LEP) students in California Public Schools", *Kenji@lindy. stanford.edu,* April 2, 1998

60 *FAIR*, 4/03, *www.fairus.org*

61 Gillian Stevens, "Immigration, Emigration, Language Acquisition, and the English Language Proficiency of Immigrants in the United States" in Barry Edmonston and Jeffrey S. Passel (eds.), *Immigration and Ethnicity: The Integration of America's Newest Arrivals* (Washington, DC, 1994), p.163-65

62 *Current Population Surveys*, November 1979 and November 1989 cited in Stevens, ibid., p.166

63 *Current Population Surveys*, March 1991 to March 2002, U.S. Census Bureau.

64 Joshua A. Fishman, "'English Only': Its Ghosts, Myths, and Dangers", *International Journal of the Sociology of Language 74* (New York, NY, 1988), pp. 125-40

65 "DNC Position Paper – Bilingual Education", Democratic National Committee, *www.democrats.org,* September 19, 2000

66 ibid.

67 See subchapter (A) of this chapter for Secretary Bennet's speech.

68 "Not English Only, English Plus! Bilingual Education Issue Analysis", Oct. 15, 1985, *SALAD Press Release*, December 4, 1985

69 "Statement of Purpose", English Plus Information Clearinghouse (EPIC)

70 ibid.

71 "English Plus Resolution" (H. Con. Res. 9), 107th Congress, 1st session, January 3, 2001, *www.house.gov*

72 ibid.

73 ibid.

74 ibid.

75 "H. Con. Res. 3: Entitled the "English Plus Resolution", *http://www.govtrack.us/congress/bill.xpd?bill=hc111-3*

76 Duignan, op. cit.

77 ibid.

78 *El Futuro Newsletter*, Summer 1997.

79 Cited in Duignan, op. cit.

80 *El Futuro*, op. cit.

81 ibid.

82 See preceding subchapter

83 *1997 Language Census,* California Department of Education

84 "Language in America: Bilingual Education", English Language Political Action Committee, *www.elpac.org*, May 20, 2003

85 Rosalie Pedalino Porter, "Introduction", *READ Perspectives*, no.1, Vol. V, Spring 1998, p. 2

86 Porter, *Forked Tongue: The Politics of Bilingual Education*, Quoted in Chavez, op. cit.

87 Cited in Chavez, ibid.

88 Ronald J. Schmidt, "Language Policy Conflict in the United States", in Crawford Young (ed.), *The Rising Tide of Cultural Pluralism: The Nation-State at Bay*? (Madison, WI, 1993), p.81

89 ibid, p. 83

90 ibid., p. 84. For a fuller discussion of Imhoff's thesis, see preceding subchapter.

91 ibid.

92 Alejandro Portes and Ruben G. Rumbaut, *Immigrant America: A Portrait*, 2nd edition, (Berkeley, CA, 1976), p. 226

93 ibid., pp. 220-1, 228

94 "White House Initiative on Educational Excellence for Hispanic Americans", *www.ed.gov/offices/OIIA/Hispanic*, op. cit.

95 John B. Orr, "The American System of Education" in Luther S. Luedtke (ed.), *Making America: The Society and Culture of the United States* (Washington, D.C., 1988), p. 289

4

The Surge for the Language of America

"English unites us as Americans – immigrants and native-born alike. Communicating with each other in a single, common tongue encourages trust, while reducing racial hostility and bigotry".

- Late Senator S.I. Hayakawa (R-CA)

(A) PRESERVING AMERICA'S COMMON BOND: THE OFFICIAL ENGLISH MOVEMENT

1978. Miami, Florida. One Emmy Shafer fails to find a clerk in the Dade County Municipal Offices who could speak English to her, so widespread had Spanish become in Miami. Gravely concerned at the state of affairs in the area, she launched an English Only movement.[1]

November 4, 1980, Election Day. Dade County (FL) voters approve an "anti-bilingual ordinance" prohibiting the expenditure of public funds on the use of languages other than English. Spanish marriage ceremonies are stopped, Spanish public transportation signs are removed, and fire safety information pamphlets in Spanish are prohibited.[2] Passed by a citizen initiative (by a vote of 59% to 41%) this Official English measure repealed a 1973 resolution declaring the county to be "bilingual and bicultural", terminated a host of county services in Spanish in addition to those cited above, and prohibited the promotion of any culture other than that of the United States.[3]

The Dade County Anti-bilingual ordinance was passed on the same day a certain Ronald Wilson Reagan, former Governor of California, was elected President of the United States defeating incumbent President James Earl "Jimmy" Carter. Though Reagan, the undisputed leader of the conservative Right Wing of the Republication Party, got 40% of the Hispanic vote in 1980 (and another 47% in 1984), he was not particularly sympathetic to bilingualism. Shortly after taking office as America's fortieth president, Reagan said:

> ...it is absolutely wrong and against American concepts to have a bilingual educational program that is now openly, admittedly dedicated to preserving their (immigrants) native language and never getting them adequate in English so they can go out into the job market and participate.[4]

But the Dade County Anti-bilingual ordinance unleashed militancy among Hispanic activists. Among them was Maurice Ferré, Mayor of Miami. In a statement to *Esquire* in May 1993, Ferré said, "...citizenship is what makes us all American. Language is not necessary to the system. Nowhere does the constitution say that English is our language."[5] Ferré's militancy began bordering on the audacious. In a later interview to the *Tampa Tribune*, he made an extremely provocative separatist announcement just falling short of sedition, "Within ten years there will not be a single word of English spoken (in Miami)—English is not Miami's official language—one day residents will have to learn Spanish or leave."[6] The controversy created by the likes of Ferré came to an end with the state of Florida declaring English as its official language in 1988. It was the culmination of an aggressive campaign launched by a Washington, D.C-based national group promoting Official English. Its name: U.S. English.

As things stand today, U.S. English is *the* national organization leading the Official English Movement and is synonymous with it. Founded in 1983 by the late Senator S.I. Hayakawa (R-CA), a Canadian immigrant of Japanese descent and a semanticist by training and profession who introduced the first English Language Amendment to the U.S. Congress in 1981 (S.J. Res 72), and Dr. John Tanton, a Michigan ophthalmologist, U.S. English was the acknowledged force behind the campaigns for Official English laws in all American states since its inception. Claiming a membership of 650,000 individuals as of 1999, it declares that its purpose was to make English the official language of the U.S. government, and to promote opportunities for all in America to learn English.[7] Defined as a "national public interest organization,"[8] it welcomes to membership not only those "who agree that English is and must remain the only official language of the people of the United States",[9] but also those "who are concerned about the prospect of entrenched language segregation and the possibility of losing our strongest national bond."[10] Apart from Hayakawa as Honorary Chairman, Tanton as

Chairman and Linda Chavez as President, U.S. English had such luminaries like Saul Bellow, Bruno Bethlehem, Dr. Denton Cooley, Walter Cronkite, Norman Podhoretz and Arnold Schwarzenegger on its first Board of Advisors. The group is presently headed by Mauro E. Mujica as Chairman of the Board of Directors and CEO. Holding office from January, 1993, Mujica, a Spanish-speaking architect who migrated to the United States from his native Chile in 1965, is expected to have a "firsthand understanding of the obstacles facing non-English speakers upon their arrival" in the United States.[11] Media reports about U.S. English's philosophy and activities have been far from flattering, as have been scholarly works concerning it:

> U.S. English has promoted the idea that the influx of Latin immigrants in recent years has threatened the primacy of English. The group contends that the country risks becoming divided linguistically and culturally, like Canada. In addition to advocating a constitutional amendment to make English official, the group seeks to restrict bilingual-education programs, eliminate non-English voting ballots and tighten language-proficiency standards for prospective citizens.[12]

Hypocrisy has also been insinuated in scholarly descriptions of U.S. English:

> Rather than promote English proficiency, 99 percent of the organization's efforts go toward restricting the use of other languages. Certainly, there is nothing in Official English legislation to help anyone learn English. On the other hand,

> there is much to penalize those who have yet to do so... English Only is a label that has stuck, despite the protests of U.S. English, because it accurately sums up the group's logic: That people will speak English only if forced to do so... If U.S. English sincerely wanted to foster ethnic harmony, it would stop chastising immigrants, open its multi-million-dollar campaign chest, and join with advocates for Asians and Hispanics to remedy the scarcity of seats in adult English classes. Instead, it exploits strong feelings about language to build a new nativist movement.[13]

If liberal scholarly opinion had been unsparing in its criticism of U.S. English, branding it xenophobic, nativist and anti-minority (read anti-Hispanic), an organized smear campaign portrayed Chairman Tanton as racist and even said that U.S. English was linked to Nazi sympathizers.[14]

James Crawford, in fact, is dedicated to the building of adverse public opinion toward the Official English movement. Through countless pamphlets, articles (in journals, newspapers, magazines and websites), and books, he had spear-headed a campaign questioning the credibility of the movement, its rationale and ideology, and even resorted to character assassination of its leaders, especially Dr. Tanton. "What is the real concern here?" questions Crawford, "The proliferation of other tongues, or the people who speak them? Is the English Only campaign a new strain of nativism, as opponents have charged, a Know-Nothing movement for the 1980s?"[15]

The insinuation here is to Dr. Tanton—also founder of the Federation of American Immigration Reform

(FAIR)—and his strong views on immigration. Believing that the influx of non-English-speaking immigrants (both legal and illegal) had overwhelmed the assimilative capacity of the United States, Dr. Tanton had repeatedly pleaded for strict immigration laws and urged English-speaking Americans not to take this onslaught lying down. Rightly identifying bilingualism as an outcome of U.S. immigration policy, he sought the remedy in Official English legislation which would, among other things, put an end to bilingual ballots, increase funds for transitional bilingual education, and start written English-proficiency test for candidates for naturalization. Dr. Tanton led the Official English movement till a controversy generated by the likes of Crawford regarding a private memo authored by him forced his resignation from the chairmanship of U.S. English during the fall of 1988. The hue and cry over the aforesaid memo, in which Dr. Tanton voiced his concern over the high fertility rates among Hispanics and the consequences it might lead to, branded U.S. English anti-immigrant, even racist. In fact, the personal vilification campaign against Dr.Tanton was so strong that Linda Chavez, president of U.S. English, quit the organization in protest, convinced of Dr. Tanton's racist inclinations.

Crawford's insinuations did not end with Dr. Tanton. He even charged U.S. English of being a secretive organization trying to marginalize, and ultimately eliminate, immigrants (read Hispanics): "To be sure, the unsavory allies and hidden agendas of U.S. English are unknown to most of its supporters... the English language has acquired a broad following—which makes it defenders all the more dangerous."[16]

The "unsavory allies" Crawford alluded to refer to a network of organizations strongly opposed to liberal immigration policy like FAIR, the Centre for Immigration Studies, Americans for Border Control, and the Pioneer Fund. That the Official English movement was popular and, to a very big extent, successful is evident from the "broad following" Crawford wrote about and, evidently, accepted. But what is unacceptable is the fact that he accused U.S. English of keeping its unsuspecting followers in the dark about its real aims and objectives. For Crawford, the Official English movement and its demand for an English Language Amendment (ELA) to the US Constitution was a cover for White English-speaking nativism and racism. Furthermore, wrote Crawford, U.S. English's insistence on immigrants learning English was aimed at misleading its supporters.[17] Failing to slot the Official English movement as liberal or conservative, Crawford confused the issue further, "Such overt appeals to prejudice are usually confined to the Far Right. But not in this case. While that label may fit a few zealots, it fails to describe the movement as a whole. English Only is a political hybrid that defies easy classification."[18] That was a serious failure indeed.

Though other scholars do not display the missionary zeal of Crawford, they nevertheless have regarded the Official English movement unnecessary:

> Those Americans who fear that unless English is made the official language of the United States by means of federal and state constitutional amendments they are about to be swamped by new waves of non-English-speakers should realize that even without restrictive legislation, minority languages in the US have always been marginal... Even in the absence of restrictive language legislation, American society enforces

> its own irresistible pressure to keep the United States an English-Speaking nation... English may not be official, but it is definitely here to stay... The issue of minority languages will not soon go away, and a constitutional amendment cannot force people to adopt English if they are unwilling or unable to do so. Nor will English cease to function as the nation's official language even if it does not have a constitutional amendment to establish it...[19]

Yet others have tended to regard Official English an issue sans substance, though aimed at depriving non-English-speaking immigrants of their rights and privileges through Official English legislation.

> Making English the official language of the United States is a false policy issue. The principal argument of its proponents, namely, that the use of languages other than English fragments American society and debilitates the nation, is spurious at best. Moreover, there is little basis to their claim that the use of English is declining and that its status is threatened. Rather than promoting the mastery and use of English, the advocates of English-only policy seek instead to impose an official language of state on the American population. Rather than encouraging civic assimilation and participation, they would limit the benefits of citizenship to English speakers... The English only movement taps into and is informed by deeply rooted fears: fear of persons who are different from the majority population and fear of change... The movement to give English official status is a manifestation of

> linguistic protectionism and is inseparable from the dark and exclusionary underside of demographic protectionism. Not surprisingly, it manifests xenophobic and nativist tendencies.... There is no historical basis for the thesis that English, or language itself, holds this society together. On the contrary, the attempts to impose English on the American population have served historically to divide the nation. Language policy has been an instrument of control, used to exclude certain groups from participating fully in America's institutions as well as to deny them the rights and benefits that accrue to members of this nation.[20]

Joseph Leibowicz, a New Haven (CT) lawyer-turned-activist, condemned the Official English movement in the severest of terms. He began by ridiculing Gerda Bikales, former executive director of U.S. English, for insisting that the English language was the bond between all Americans, and went on to say:

> Unfortunately, the assumptions, arguments, conclusions, and in some cases, the motives of the ELA's supporters are highly suspect... Even accepting the idea that language and nationhood are linked, it does not follow that language is not just *a* but *the* most important bonding force of a people. Language is only one of a multiplicity of factors that can bind or rend a people... Supporters of the ELA seem to be making precisely the mistake of equating the obviousness of language usage with its importance to national unity.[21]

Leibowicz branded Official English proponents as nativists—and used nativism as a dirty word, like other cultural pluralists—and warned that they, like their Americanization movement predecessors, constituted the real threat to American institutions rather than the immigrants they were scared of. Doubting the credentials and casting aspersions on the motives of the Official English movement, Leibowicz wrote:

> Attempts to use language for "patriotic ends" must be subjected to the strictest sort of scrutiny, and that elements of jingoism, racism and xenophobia hiding behind expressed concern for linguistic unity must be identified and rooted out of the debate before proposals to impose English on our official and unofficial life are given any serious consideration.[22]

Calling Official English supporters "Anglo-conformists", using a phrase made popular by Milton M. Gordon, Leibowicz ended his essay with a customary note of sympathy and concern for the plight of Hispanics in case an English Language Amendment (ELA) was passed by Congress:

> Imposing English among Spanish speakers through a constitutional amendment would likely exclude many from political participation, sacrifice equal justice in the courtroom, narrowly restrict educational alternatives on the basis of political criteria, and mark linguistic minorities as "un American" in the eyes of the rest of society. Based on undocumented fears of separation and cultural fragmentation, passage of the ELA would insult and alienate a significant portion of our society in the name of national unity.[23]

Such scholarly diatribes against the Official English movement were complemented by equally hostile reactions from politicians. If Mayor Maurice Ferré of Miami was uncouth, Representative (and later Senator) Stephen Solarz (D-NY) was sophisticated and level-headed. He was vehemently opposed to the idea of an English Language Amendment to the Constitution, nevertheless. In his testimony to the U.S. House Committee on the Judiciary, Subcommittee on Civil and Constitutional Rights in May, 1988, Representative Solarz spoke on predictable lines:

> We are not in danger of becoming another Quebec, or the national equivalent of the Tower of Babel… There is nobody more cognizant of the disability of non-English proficiency than the individual who is struggling to make it in this country without being able to speak English. I see no reason, therefore, to enact legislation that would only punish a huge segment of a society for a disability that they themselves are earnestly trying to correct.[24]

If that was a direct attack on the basic assumption of the demand for an English Language Amendment to the Constitution, Rep. Solarz had his reasons:

> I believe that the proposals (for Official English)… are unnecessary and unwise. They are unnecessary because it is clear that English is unquestionably our primary language, and I see no evidence that its position, as such, is in danger. They are unwise for two reasons. First, there is the potential that an English Language Amendment could pose significant threats to the civil and constitutional rights of citizens with little

> or no English proficiency. Second, the proposals represent a concession to nativist instincts and are incompatible with the cultural diversity and ethnic pluralism that constitute fundamental strengths of our nation.[25]

True, Rep. Solarz was a confirmed and committed multiculturalist, in line with his party's ideology:

> The time-worn cliché dictates that America is a "melting pot." This is no longer an apt description. We are instead a tapestry of many races, creeds, religions, and ethnic backgrounds – each independent, but all interwoven with one another. Like no other country in the world, this diversity creates not a clash of cultures, but a nation in which each culture leaves its own imprint and enriches us all.[26]

He rejected the contention of Official English proponents that the use of other languages in any official capacity diluted American unity and prevented ethnic groups from participating in the mainstream of America's economic and political pursuits. He, admittedly, believed in just the opposite:

> The possible consequences of the proposed constitutional amendments are disturbing and, in my view, are not worth risking. There is too real a danger that court rulings and legislations in the wake of such an amendment could undermine the civil right of millions of Americans. But even if an English Language Amendment were purely symbolic, I would oppose it. Such an amendment would have the perverse effect of making huge segments of our society feel unwanted and *not*

> *wanted*, strangers and not citizens. In my view, this amendment would have the very opposite effect than that intended by its authors, by *serving to hinder the assimilation of non-English-speaking Americans into the mainstream of our society.*[27] (Emphasis mine)

Such forceful opposition to Official English, on the ground that it would actually hinder the assimilation of language minorities into the American mainstream, remains unprecedented. Rep. Solarz, accordingly, refused to support an English Language Amendment to the U.S. Constitution, not only because it would alienate non-English-speaking Americans, but also because such an amendment, in his view, would defeat the purpose behind the Constitution itself:

> I believe that... the English language Amendment—however well-intentioned—is not in the best interests of our nation.... They (non-English-speaking constituents in his electoral district) are as patriotic as any ethnic group in our nation and are actively involved in our political process. To prevent these individuals—and any other immigrant group—from being able to use their native language as part of any governmental activity would make it harder, not easier, for them to enter the American mainstream. The Congress would commit a grave error if it amended the Constitution in a way that would circumvent the very purposes for which that document was written.[28]

In Rep. Solarz's view, any attempt to prevent language minorities from using their languages officially would make the task of their assimilation difficult. He misses the point that the Founding Fathers never desired to assimilate individuals seeking to use non-English native tongues for official purposes.[29]

The target of this multiculturalist assault, U.S. English, which describes itself as "a national, non-profit, non-partisan organization" founded to defend the public interest in the growing debate on bilingualism and biculturalism, lists its current concerns as "bilingual education reform and multi-lingualism in government".[30] It declares, in no uncertain terms, that it "is committed to promoting the use of English in the political, economic and intellectual life of the nation."[31] Moreover, that "it operates squarely within the American political mainstream, and rejects all manifestations of cultural or linguistic chauvinism'.[32] By making such a declaration, U.S. English attempted not only to debunk impressions that it was nativist, but at the same time condemned minority separatism—especially of the Maurice Ferré variety—as unacceptable under any circumstances.

U.S. English set the tone by eulogizing English as Americans' common bond:

> Throughout its history, the United States has been enriched by the cultural contributions of immigrants from many traditions, but blessed with one common language that has united a diverse nation and fostered harmony, among its people... English prevailed, and it has served us well. Its eloquence shines in our Declaration of Independence and in our Constitution. It is the living carrier of our democratic ideals... The United States has been spared the bitter conflicts

> that plague so many countries whose citizens do not share a common tongue. Historic forces made English the language of all Americans, though nothing in our laws designated it the official language of the nation.[33]

That was an honest admission indeed, especially seen in the context of Mayor Ferre's aggressive assertion that English was not the language of America. But the emphasis here is difficult to miss: a single common language that united Americans. As the late Senator Hayakawa wrote, "English unites us as Americans – immigrants and native-born alike. Communicating with each other in a single, common tongue encourages trust, while reducing racial hostility and bigotry."[34]

Hayakawa banked on personal experience to reinforce his idea:

> As an immigrant to this nation, I am keenly aware of the things that bind us as Americans and unite us as a single people. Foremost among these unifying forces is the common language we share. While it is certainly true that our love of freedom and devotion to democratic principles help to unite and give us a common purpose, it is English, our common language, that enables us to discuss our views and allows us to maintain a well-informed electorate, the cornerstone of democratic government.[35]

The message here is loud and clear: English has made democracy meaningful in America; English was the language of freedom.

Hayakawa did see the wisdom behind a common

language forging a nation and fostering national unity:

> Because we are a nation of immigrants, we do not share the characteristics of race, religion, ethnicity, or native language which form the common bonds of society in other countries. However, by agreeing to learn and use a single, universally spoken language, we have been able to forge a unified people from an incredibly diverse population.[36]

Representative Norman Shumway (R-CA) echoed Hayakawa's sentiments when he spoke about the unifying potential of the English language in the United States in his testimony to the House Judiciary Committee in May, 1988:

> English has been the common language of the United States as a result of historical custom, not legal designation. That common language has been the "glue" which has held us together, forging strength and unity from our rich cultural diversity. From our earliest days, despite our melting pot inheritance, English has been the language in which we expressed the goals, objectives, ideas, principles, and duties of our form of government. It is the language in which the Declaration of Independence and the Constitution are written. It is the language in which the welcome at the base of the Statue of Liberty is engraved. And in my view, it is the primary language in which our government should continue to function.[37]

Shumway also warned about how, in the absence of an official language, America was fast degenerating into a bilingual society, much in the same way as Canada.[38]

Rep. Shumway, very much in line with U.S. English's assertion that "the rights of individuals and groups to use other languages must be respected in a pluralistic society,"[39] also attempted to rectify the commonly held notion that the movement for Official English was actually an 'English Only' movement, adding that "those who emigrate from their native lands should be free to maintain the language which reflects their cultural and ethnic heritage."[40] He also rubbished opponents' allegations that designating English as America's official language would deny emergency services, basic civil rights and human dignity to language minorities.

Rep. Shumway also held bilingualism—both bilingual ballots and bilingual education—responsible for alienating linguistic minority groups from the rest of American society. He accused the federal government of trying not only to encourage dependency on non-English languages through the use of multilingual ballots and voter assistance in 375 jurisdictions in 21 states but also attempting to foster "continued reliance" on language minority students' native tongues through bilingual education.[41]

Finally, Rep. Shumway made an impassioned plea to grant English official language status, explaining why it was necessary:

> We need it (the English Language Amendment) to provide English with legal protection as our national language, thereby continuing our heritage as a unilingual nation... We need it to prevent the divisiveness that is bound to result from a plurality of official languages. We need it

> to ensure that our government continues to function primarily in English... The key to being successful as a newcomer to America is to learn the language. Fluency in English is in turn the door to opportunity. By discouraging newcomers from mastering English and being assimilated into our society, we are denying them opportunity... I don't believe in "English Only". I *do* believe in English *primarily* and certainly I believe it is incumbent upon the government, which is today debating in that language to take steps to protect that primacy. I cherish our cultural diversity, but I also cherish our common bond of language.[42]

Clearly, the "unilingual nation" that Rep. Shumway spoke about meant unilingual for public and official, and not private, purposes; a publicly unilingual (or monolingual) state was sought to be created on a privately multilingual people.

According to U.S. English, the position of the English language in America was being systematically undermined, leading to "institutionalized language segregation and a gradual loss of national unity."[43] The reasons for the erosion of English and the rise of other languages in public life were not far to seek, and U.S. English had listed them meticulously:

> Some spokesmen for ethnic groups reject the "melting pot" ideal; they label assimilation a betrayal of their native cultures and demand government funding to maintain separate ethic institutions...

> Unproven theories have led to extensive government-funded bilingual education programs, ranging from pre-school through college...
>
> New civil rights assertion have yielded bilingual and multilingual ballots, voting instructions, election site counselors and government-funded voter registration campaigns aimed solely at speakers of foreign languages...
>
> Record immigration, concentrated in fewer language groups, is reinforcing language segregation and retarding language assimilation...
>
> The availability of foreign language electronic media... is a new disincentive to the learning of English.[44]

Out of the five reasons cited above, four relate to public policy, one pertains to politics. They were reasons enough to launch an Official English movement and, through it, seek an English Language Amendment to the Constitution. The late Senator Hayakawa squarely held multiculturalism—and the Hispanic leadership that believed in it and was in turn sustained by it—responsible for the linguistic and ethnic segregation visible in America:

> We are a nation of immigrant enclaves... In the past few years, strong resistance to the melting pot idea has arisen – especially among those who claim to speak for our Hispanic-American citizens. Instead of a melting pot, they say, the national ideal should be a salad bowl in which different elements do not melt but mingle, retaining their

> distinctive character. A key element in the "salad bowl agenda" is the use of so-called bilingual education to encourage the maintenance of, and primary allegiance to, the Spanish language among those of Hispanic heritage... Bilingualism can mean..."binationalism" – a course our country must escape.[45]

Hayakawa further lamented that Hispanic political leaders and lobbying organizations were very much behind a move "to split the U.S. into a bilingual and bi-cultural society".[46] Convinced that Americans must share a common language—and that language must be English—he reminded his countrymen that since "countless millions" of immigrants in earlier generations had successfully made the transition from their native tongues to English and became assimilated into the American mainstream, there was no reason to believe that today's immigrants could not do the same.[47]

But public use of non-English languages, especially Spanish, runs the risk of the United States being made officially bilingual. Already, there were those who pointed out why it was important for the United States to be bilingual and that bilingualism was very much in the American tradition. [48]

As Samuel P. Huntington point out, English has been central to American identity throughout the nation's history:

> Three hundred years of history had selected English as the language for Americans.... Only a few questioned the importance of English in American culture and the desirability of Americans being proficient in English.[49]

He regrets that English was being downgraded and its position systematically undermined (in the late twentieth century) and minority languages were being promoted by governments and other institutions in order to encourage sub-national identities.[50] Most importantly, he identifies Spanish as *the* minority language threatening the position of English in American society:

> In terms of both symbol and substance, the battles over English were a major front in the broader war over American identity.... The real issue, however, is not multilingualism but bilingualism... (T)o what extent should the U.S. government promote the knowledge and use of languages other than English and restrict the ability of governments, private businesses, and other institutions to require the use of English? In most instances, the other language is Spanish.... Should the United States become a bilingual society, with Spanish on an equal footing with English?[51]

The fear of America turning into a bilingual society was also voiced by Senator Hayakawa, cautioning against the ethnic and linguistic segregation visible even two decades back.[52]

Conservative ideologue Patrick J. Buchanan also wrote in the same vein, underscoring the need to make English the official language of the United States:

> If we are to remain one nation and one people, an end to bilingual education is essential, for two languages means two cultures and eventually two countries. The American people know this. English must become the official language of the

United States.[53]

Arthur Mann pointed to the emergence of Spanish as a rival to English due to misplaced federal policies:

> What remains to be seen is the degree to which Spanish will challenge the hegemony of English. Already a reaction has set in. Ten years after the passage of the 1968 law, it was amended to stipulate that bilingual education was being funded not as an end in itself, but as a means to teach English to foreign language-speaking children. Congress acted on a widely held belief in the country that although no federal statute ever declared English official, it is in fact the language of the United States.[54]

Mann was writing about the state of bilingual education in the United States, started by the Bilingual Education Act of 1968 and administered through native language instruction. It had led to native language *maintenance* which was not the avowed purpose of the Act of 1968. More importantly, the absence of a constitutional stipulation declaring English official may be behind the subversion of bilingual education.

The chief concern of the Official English movement is the total assimilation of non-English-speaking immigrants with the rest of the American population. Language is chosen as the instrument through which to assimilate as that is what has remained common to all Americans right from the initial days of the republic. No doubt that American society is plural, but any attempt to foster differences among people—that is what Cultural Pluralism does—would divide the nation along ethnic lines. In fact, the principal objective of the Official English Movement is to put an end to hyphenism among Americans. Hyphenism denotes ethnic identities and any attempt to perpetuate them would keep an American identity from developing among immigrants, Asian or Hispanic. In the tradition of Theodore Roosevelt, the Official English movement would want complete elimination of ethnic identities, if fostering them would mean undermining the American national identity.

What is most alarming today is that the concept of assimilation itself is being called into question as never before. Some believe that assimilation is not always a positive experience for immigrants; and with the emphasis shifting to diversity and ethnicity, it has become possible for immigrants to avoid assimilating at all.[55] There is also a pressure on immigrants to keep their unique cultures alive, even as they learn English and assimilate into the society at large. The result of all this has been a refusal by the newest immigrants to learn English and assimilate into American society.

Hayakawa's U.S. English professes that its goal was to maintain the blessing of a common language (English) for the people of the United States. Pointing out that the nation's public schools have a special responsibility to help students who don't speak English to learn the language as quickly as possible, it proposes that quality teaching of English should be part of every student's curriculum, and at every academic level. It strongly recommends that *all* candidates for U.S. citizenship should be required to demonstrate the ability to understand, speak, read, and write simple English and demonstrate basic understanding of the American system of government, while accepting the rights of individuals and groups to use other languages.[56] On a cautious note, it asserts that "in a pluralistic nation as ours, it was the duty of government to foster the similarities that unite us rather than the differences that separate us."[57]

U.S. English, thus, admits that the United States was a pluralistic nation. But what was more important than the diversity was the unity that existed among all Americans, underscored by a common language. It was the responsibility of the government to strength that unity and not undermine it by encouraging differences—especially those based on language and ethnicity—that distinguished one American from another through policies such as bilingualism.

As a national organization dedicated to making English the official language of the United States, U.S. English operates through advertisements, coalition forming, congressional testimony, congressional voting analysis, demonstrations, grant making, grassroots organizing, initiative/referendum campaigns, the internet, legislative/regulatory monitoring (federal and state), lobbying (federal, state, and grassroots), media outreach, polling, research, and speakers programs.[58] Through all these methods of operation, U.S. English "actively works to reverse the spread of foreign language usage in the nation's official life."[59] Official bilingualism in its two principal manifestations—bilingual education and bilingual ballots—has allowed Spanish (a foreign language) entry into the sphere of government activity. The idea was to stop such entry and its subsequent expansion. That could only be done if a constitutional amendment was adopted to establish English as the official language of the United States, laws mandating multilingual ballots and voting materials were scrapped, government funding for bilingual education was restricted to short-term transitional programs only, and the English language was universally enforced and made a civic requirement for naturalization.[60]

Evidently, the term English *Only* movement is a misnomer, and misleading as well. Nowhere does U.S. English, or the movement that it leads, seek the complete elimination of languages other than English. The demand is to accord official status to the English language in order to achieve assimilation of recent immigrants through a single common language (English) and undercut, and finally defeat the forces of language segregation represented by multiculturalists. As such, *Official* English movement is the appropriate term. And, this movement is best construed as a fight between the inclusivist assimilationist tendencies represented by U.S. English and the exclusivist segregationist forces represented by its multicultural opponents. As Gary Imhoff, public policy expert and consultant to U.S. English, has noted:

> The irony of the situation lies in the fact that the practitioners of today's segregation think of themselves as progressives or leftists rather than as conservatives. Like past segregationists, however, they advocate the legal segregation of racial and ethnic groups… in order to preserve these groups' cultures and traditions.[61]

The activities of U.S. English all over the United States—in states that have Official English laws and in states that do not—have turned it into a formidable political force. But other organizations have also associated themselves with the Official English movement. Among them is English First, a national petition drive seeking to influence Congress to make English the official language of the United States. Based in Virginia, English First claims in its fund raising literature:

> Tragically many immigrants these days refuse to learn English! They never become productive members of American society. They remain stuck in a linguistic and economic ghetto, many living off welfare and costing working Americans millions of tax dollars every year.[62]

A bigger effort is that of ProEnglish, launched in 1994 as English Language Advocates by Gerda Bikales, former Executive Director of U.S. English. ProEnglish addresses the issue thus:

> Today America's linguistic unity, which enabled the melting-pot crucible to create one nation out of millions of immigrants from all over the world, is under attack as never before. Record numbers of non-English speaking immigrants threaten to overwhelm the assimilative process. And instead of encouraging new immigrants to acquire the English fluency needed to succeed in our society, the policy of our government is to promote "diversity" by operating in ever growing numbers of foreign languages... Learning to speak English empowers immigrants... Official English does not mean "English Only". None of the 26 states with Official English laws prohibit government agencies from using other languages when there is a compelling public interest for doing so... Having English as our official language simply means that for the government to act officially, it must communicate in English... Official English would also reinforce American's historic message

> to new immigrants – that we expect them to learn English as the first step in their assimilation – and that we are committed to ensuring that all Americans share in the economic, social and political benefit of having a common language.[63]

Echoing U.S. English, ProEnglish maintains that "in a pluralistic nation such as ours", the function of government should be to foster and support the similarities that united Americans, rather than institutionalize the differences that divide them. Like U.S. English, it reiterates that public schools had a "clear" responsibility to help students who did not know English to learn that language as quickly as possible and recommends that quality teaching of both English and America's civic culture should be part of every student's curriculum. Like U.S. English again, it demands that not only should all candidates for U.S. citizenship be required to demonstrate knowledge of English and an understanding of the American system of government, "at a level sufficient to vote in the language of our country, English", but also that naturalization ceremonies, including the Oath of Citizenship, be conducted in English. In the end, following U.S. English, ProEnglish admits the right to use other languages in the United States.[64]

ProEnglish resembles U.S. English too closely in its vision and mission statements and in its Agenda for Action.[65] Only the demand that the admission of territories as states be opposed unless they have adopted English as their official language[66] is refreshingly original. This is a clear reference to Puerto Rico—Spanish-speaking and overwhelmingly Hispanic—and the issue of granting it statehood.

Interestingly, three people on the Board of Directors of ProEnglish had served on the Board of Directors of U.S. English earlier. One is Gerda Bikales herself. The other one is Leo Sorensen. There is yet a third: a Michigan ophthalmologist named John Tanton!

The Official English movement has achieved remarkable success in being the force behind the popular initiatives that culminated in English being made the official language in many states. Linguist Geoffrey Numberg of Stanford University commented in 1989 that the U.S. English leadership was probably justified in claiming that "no one is for us but the people", because the success of the Official English movement has been largely achieved without the support of establishment political parties.[67] Coming from a leading opponent of Official English, such admission helps underline the importance of the Official English issue in the public mind and the reason for the huge public support it had received whenever it was put on the ballot. U.S. English, despite accusations of racism and nativism, shot into national prominence with its sponsorship of H.R. 123, the first English Language Amendment passed by the U.S. House of Representatives.

(B) TOWARD OFFICIAL MONOLINGUALISM: H.R. 123

The defining moment for Official English came finally on August 1, 1996, when the U.S. House of Representatives (104th Congress, 2^{d} session) passed H.R. 123, the Bill Emerson English Language Empowerment Act, declaring English as the official language of the U.S. government and requiring the federal government to conduct most of its official business in English. The Bill also sought—by repealing the—1975 amendments to the

Voting Rights Act (1965)—to eliminate the requirement that bilingual voting ballots be provided in areas populated by large numbers of voters whose native language was not English. In a House of 236 Republicans and 198 Democrats, the Bill passed 259-169 (223 Republicans and 36 Democrats for; 8 Republicans and 160 Democrats against).[68] Introduced by the late Representative Bill Emerson (R-MO) on January 4, 1995 and sponsored after his death by Rep. Randy "Duke" Cunningham (R-CA), the bill had earlier been approved by the House Economic and Educational Opportunities Committee by a party-line vote of 19-17 on July 24 after long hours of highly partisan and passionate debate.[69]

The 104th Congress was the first Republican Congress in forty years. Egged on by House Speaker Newt Gingrich (R-GA)—architect of the 1994 Republican revolution and author of the conservative *Contract With America*, the document that had inspired that revolution—House Republicans voted overwhelmingly for the Official English measure. But this was not the first time that an Official English bill was moved in the U.S. Congress. Between the years 1981 and 1990, Congress saw the introduction of sixteen English Language Amendments (ELAs), in forms ranging from one-liners establishing English as the nation's official language to English Only mandates which sought to outlaw the official use of languages other than English by federal, state and local governments (though with exceptions). Unfortunately, though, the ELAs had never been put to a congressional vote; without fail, they were killed in committee even before the voting stage. But, interestingly, all earlier ELAs were introduced in Congress by Republicans.

The first, SJ Res. 72, came up in the Senate on April

27, 1981 and was sponsored by Senator S.I. Hayakawa (R-CA). That was the 97th Congress, elected along with Ronald Reagan in November 1980. Reagan's two terms as President saw seven more ELAs being introduced in Congress. On March 2, 1983, Representative Norman Shumway (R-CA) introduced H.J. Res. 169 in the 98th Congress. Senator Steve Symms (R-ID) followed it up with S.J. Res 167 in the Senate on September 21, 1983, with Senator Walter Huddleston (D-KY) as cosponsor. Representative Shumway reintroduced his ELA in the 99th Congress on January 24, 1985 as H.J. Res. 60. Two days back, Senator Symms had introduced S.J. Res. 20 on the Senate floor. In the 100th Congress, Representative Smith (R-NE) introduced an ELA (H.J. Res. 60) on January 6, 1987, to be followed by H.J. Res. 13 in the next session with Representative William Broomfield (R-MI) as sponsor. On his part, Senator Symms brought up S.J. Res. 13 on the same day as Representative Smith's ELA in the House. After President Reagan demitted office on January 20, 1989, Representative Shumway again sponsored an ELA the same year as H.J. Res. 81.[70] That was the last ELA of any consequence before H.R. 123. But those were years when both chambers of Congress were controlled by Democrats.

The situation changed after 1994. Though the GOP had never made Official English a plank in its party platform, individual Republicans had always spoken in its favor—and against official bilingualism in particular—and had even acted with the aim of granting English official status in the United States, as in evidenced by the ELAs placed before Congress between 1981 and 1990. Sponsors of the ELAs during that period, though, had little hope of getting their bills passed by Congress. Republicans were in a hopeless and seemingly-perpetual minority in both houses and the multiculturalist Democratic Party—the 'party of immigrants'—would never allow bipartisan consensus in support of Official English, especially as it considered such legislation anti-immigrant and discriminatory toward non-English speaking individuals (read Hispanics) in the United States. The result: the bills were invariably killed in committee. The 104th Congress gave House Republicans sympathetic to Official English an unprecedented opportunity to actually get their desired legislation passed, if they wanted to, especially when one of its chief proponents was the House Speaker himself. In his book, *To Renew America,* Gingrich had made an impassioned, though practical, plea for first acknowledging and then declaring English as the language of America:

> It is difficult for... an immigrant to get anywhere in this country without learning English... The only viable alternative for the American underclass is American civilization. Without English as a common language, there is no such civilization.[71]

As the closing participant in the debate on H.R. 123, Gingrich, expectedly, spoke in favor. Warning that continuation of multilingual trends in education would lead to "decay of the core parts of our civilization."[72] Gingrich emphasized the role of English for immigrants seeking to develop an American identity:

> Our greatness in part comes from our ability to be a melting pot. While I cherish every person who comes here legally and seeks to pursue happiness... I want them to become American, and part of becoming American involves English.[73]

Clearly, as the supreme leader of House Republicans, Gingrich was making a policy statement. His speech was aimed at dispelling fear among Hispanics and other non-Anglos that the measure intended to cut their constitutional rights and privileges. At the same time he was emphatic that illegal immigrants were unwelcome; those who had entered America legally, he would want to assimilate as soon as possible, and the process of such assimilation could be best facilitated through adoption of the English language in public discourse because English was the language of American identity.

Gingrich had earlier proposed to bring to vote, if not actually pass, the ten items in the *Contract With America* within the first hundred days of the 104th Congress.[74] Indeed, House Republicans passed all but one of those ten items in their revolutionary legislative agenda within the stipulated time.[75] A measure to designate English as the official language of the United States was not one of the *Contract* items. Even then, the Republican House passed it during the 104th Congress itself, attracting charges of a hidden agenda to shut out immigrants and other non-English speakers from the American political process, particularly because of the clause to repeal the bilingual ballot requirements of the Voting Rights Act of 1965 (as amended in 1975). Democratic opponents of the bill also called it an infringement of the First Amendment.[76] Condemning the bill as punitive, Asian and Hispanic activists said the proposed "English-only" measure would actually prevent non-English speaking immigrants from joining the American mainstream.[77] But Gingrich had the last word on the bill, calling it "a modest step in the right direction of reinforcing and reasserting the greatest civilization ever to provide freedom in the human race."

Deviating from his usual practice of not voting for bills as Speaker, Gingrich voted for H.R. 123.

Gingrich's *bete noire*, President William Jefferson "Bill" Clinton, did not immediately speak out on his course of action in the event of Official English legislation being approved by Congress. But, reportedly, he considered the bill in bad taste. Reflecting the administration's view on H.R. 123, a statement released by the White House Office of Management and Budget (OMB) said, "This highly objectionable bill is unnecessary, inefficient and divisive."[78] A confirmed multiculturalist who got 61% of the Hispanic vote in 1992 (and an unprecedented 72% in 1996), Clinton was expected to veto any Official English bill coming out of Congress. But as Governor of Arkansas in 1987, he had signed into law a bill that declared English the official language of the state. As of August 1996, 23 states including Clinton's Arkansas had passed Official English laws. Though Clinton's *volte face* was meant to suit his political ambitions, his opposition to H.R. 123 forfeited him the role of opinion-maker. Trained in the Kennedy Johnson-Humphrey-McGovern-Mondale liberal multicultural tradition of the Democratic Party, the President was eyeing the Hispanic vote for his re-election bid. The unprecedented 72% of the Latino vote that he received in 1996 can, to a big extent, be attributed to his opposition to H.R. 123 and commitment to multilingual ballots (and, of course, bilingual education), which the bill sought to abolish.

But the President's committed multiculturalism could not prevent thirty-six of his party colleagues in the House from voting for the bill. Congressional Democrats from twenty-one states supported the Official English measure. Of them, fourteen states—Alabama, Arkansas,

California, Florida, Illinois, Indiana, Kentucky, Mississippi, Missouri, North Carolina, South Carolina, South Dakota, Tennessee, and Virginia—already had Official English laws. Noticeably, almost all of them are southern states. States without Official English laws which comprised this supporting group of congressional Democrats were Minnesota, New York, Ohio, Oklahoma, Pennsylvania, Texas, and Wisconsin. Compared to them, only eight congressional Republicans voted against H.R. 123, spread over six states. Of them, only one—Florida—had an Official English law. Interestingly, a majority of these Republicans were Hispanics: Ileana Ros-Lehtinen and Lincoln Diaz-Balart from Florida, Constance A. Morella from Maryland, John Ensign from Nevada and Henry Bonilla of Texas. If the number of Democrats voting for the bill was more than Republicans voting against it, that in itself explains the emotional and practical appeal of Official English.

On February 3, 1995, almost a month after H.R. 123 was introduced in the U.S. House of Representatives, Senator Richard C. Shelby (R-AL) placed before the U.S. Senate S. 356, titled as the Language of Government Act of 1995, to declare English as the official language of the government of the United States. Referred to the Senate Committee on Governmental Affairs, S.356 was identical to H.R. 123; only that, unlike H.R. 123, it did not contain any provision to abolish multilingual ballots by repealing the 1975 amendments to the 1965 Voting Rights Act. S.356 met with an unfortunate end; it never emerged from committee and eventually lapsed at the end of the 2^{d} session of the 104th Congress. The gains made by the House on the path to declaring English as the official language of government of the United States by approving H.R. 123

were squandered by the Senate. Since neither H.R. 123 nor S. 356 sought to restrict government involvement in bilingual education, no viable reason can be attributed to the killing of S.356 in committee, more so when it also remained silent on the issue of bilingual ballots.[79] Even though both the measures required that all government business be conducted in English, they allowed agencies to use other languages in certain cases to protect public health and safety, provide for national security, and protect the rights of crime victims or criminal defendants.[80]

But H.R. 123, as did S. 356, sought to tighten the noose where it was needed. Reiterating that full citizenship in the United States was incumbent on fluency in English, H.R. 123 required all naturalization ceremonies to be conducted entirely in English. The reason, admittedly, was simple: English was the language of opportunity for all immigrants to take their rightful place in society in the United States. H.R. 123 further required that governmental documents, including publications, income tax forms, and informational materials (with the exceptions cited above), be printed in English.[81] Making the emphatic declaration that English was the official language of the federal government, both H.R. 123 and S. 356 made it obligatory on representatives of the federal government to preserve and enhance the role of English as its official language. And such an obligation could only be fulfilled if immigrants were encouraged and provided greater opportunities to learn the English language.

Declaring English the official language of government meant also that the rights and privileges of speakers of English be secured. Under H.R. 123, no person could be denied services, assistance, or facilities, directly or indirectly provided by the federal government, solely because that person communicated in English. Not only that. Every person in the United States was entitled to communicate with federal representatives in English, receive information from or contribute information to the federal government in English, and be informed or be subject to official orders in English. Moreover, if any person stood injured by a violation of any of these provisions, he could initiate civil action to obtain appropriate relief.[82] H.R. 123, thus, sought not only to protect the rights of individuals to learn English and communicate in English with the federal government, but also to ensure that English-speakers were not disadvantaged or discriminated against anywhere in the United States or at any level because of their language. Though the primacy of English for all official purposes was proclaimed, the wisdom and efficacy in the use of other languages, when required, was admitted as well.[83]

U.S. English claimed direct involvement with H.R. 123.[84] The issue of Official English is explained thus:

> Declaring English the Official language means that official government business at all levels must be conducted solely in English. This includes all public documents, records, legislation and regulations, as well as hearings, official ceremonies and public meetings. Official English legislation contains common-sense exceptions permitting the use of languages other than English for such things as public health and safety services, judicial proceedings (although actual trials would be conducted in English), foreign language instruction and the promotion of tourism.[85]

The similarities with H.R. 123 are evident; in fact, it seems like a summary of the bill. Alternatively, H.R. 123 can be construed as a reflection of the policy-paper of U.S. English, posted on its website for the public. Though the Republican Party had never admitted to a formal relationship with U.S. English, the organization did claim responsibility for passing Official English legislation for the first time in the U.S. House of Representatives. There is no doubt that U.S. English's involvement with H.R. 123 ranged from helping to draft the bill to lobbying for support among congressmen. Derided by opponents as a chauvinist (even racist) organization, perhaps its biggest accolade came in the form of a statement by Raul Yzaguirre on February 27, 1989, president of the National Council of La Raza, a Hispanic forum bitterly opposed to Official English: "U.S. English is to Hispanics as the Ku Klux Klan is to Blacks."[86]

Its online policy-paper also outlined the necessity of having English as the official language of government in the United States and explained that Official English not only promoted unity among Americans and empowered immigrants, it also meant common sense government. Said the policy-paper:

> Our national motto is *E Pluribus Unum* – out of many, one. Immigrants of many nationalities built our nation, but the "melting pot" melded us into one people. This long tradition of assimilation has always included the adoption of English as the common means of communication. Unfortunately, the proliferation of multi-lingual government sends the opposite message to non-English speakers: it is not necessary to learn English because the government will

> accommodate them in other languages... multilingual government services actually encourage the growth of linguistic enclaves. This division of the United States into separate language groups contributed to racial and ethnic conflicts. Designating English as the official language will help reverse this harmful process.
>
> The designation of official English will eliminate the needless duplication of government services in multiple languages. It is not the responsibility of government to provide services in the 329 different languages spoken in the United States. It is the responsibility of each individual to...learn English. The money formerly spent on multilingual services can instead provide immigrants with the assistance they really need – classes to teach them English.
>
> English is the key to opportunity in this country. It empowers immigrants and makes us truly united as a people... Without a common language, how long would we remain the "United" States? [87]

Speaker Gingrich's defense of H.R. 123 on the floor of the House closely resembled these arguments. On its part, H.R. 123 stated in its findings:

1. The United States is comprised of individuals and groups from diverse ethnic, cultural, and linguistic backgrounds.

2. The United States has benefited and continues to benefit from this rich diversity.

3. Throughout the history of the United States, the common thread binding individuals of

differing backgrounds has been a common language.

4. In order to preserve unity in diversity and to prevent division along linguistic lines, the federal government should maintain a language common to all people.

5. English has historically been the common language and language of opportunity in the United States.

6. The purpose of this title is to help immigrants better assimilate and take full advantage of economic and occupational opportunities in the United States.

7. By learning the English language, immigrants will be empowered with the language skills and literacy necessary to become responsible citizens and productive workers in the United States.

8. The use of a single common language in conducting official business of the Federal Government will promote efficiency and fairness to all people.

9. Any monetary savings derived from the enactment of this title should be used for the teaching of the English language to non-English speaking immigrants.[88]

This resemblance between the rationale for Official English set out by U.S. English and that given in H.R. 123 is no mere coincidence: H.R. 123 does address itself to the task of realizing the objectives of Official English legislation laid down by the U.S. English policy paper.

Professor Geoffrey Numberg, teaching linguistics at Stanford University, accused proponents of Official English of sending "a message that [non-English-speakers] cannot be trusted to become American like their ancestors did and their assimilation must be imposed by statute".[89] But as S.I. Hayakawa had noted before him:

> Countless millions of immigrants successfully made the transition from their native tongues to English and became assimilated into the American mainstream. It is condescending and insulting to single out today's immigrants and suggest they cannot do the same.[90]

H.R. 123—the Bill Emerson English Language Empowerment Act of 1996—was aimed at arming the federal government with an official language (English) and empowering it (through use of that language) to preserve and foster national unity, help immigrants assimilate better and faster into American society, and provide cheaper English monolingual services to U.S. citizens. It was also meant to prevent something the Founding Fathers had failed to foresee: linguistic fragmentation of the United States. Unfortunately, though H.R. 123 was approved and adopted by voice-vote,[91] the voice of the House of Representatives did not reach the Senate. The measure fell through. That was the closest Official English, till date, had come to being enacted by the U.S. Congress.

Interestingly, a new immigration reform bill, introduced in the 111th Congress by Rep. Luis V. Gutierrez (D-IL), seeks to provide legal status to nearly 12 million illegal immigrants. If this bill became law, it would require these immigrants — mostly from Latin America who entered the United States via Mexico – to learn English before they ware granted legal status.[92]

REFERENCES

1 Margaret Carlson, "Only English Spoken Here", *Time*, December 5, 1988, p. 29

2 Jamie B. Draper and Martha Jimenez, "A Chronology of the Official English Movement", in James Crawford, ed., *Language Loyalties: A Source Book on the Official English Controversy* (Chicago, IL, 1992), p. 90

3 "Dade County "Anti-bilingual" Ordinance" in Crawford, ibid., p. 131

4 Quoted in James Crawford, *Bilingual Education: History, Politics and Practice* (Trenton, NJ, 1989), p. 114

5 Quoted by U.S. English, "In Defense of our Common Language...," in Crawford, ed., op cit., p. 147

6 Quoted by S.I. Hayakawa, "Bilingualism in America: English should be the *Only* Language", *USA Today*, July 1989, p. 32

7 *Public Interest Foundation for Public Affairs*, (Washington, DC, 1998), p. 214

8 Thomas S. Donahue, "U.S. English: Its life and Works", *International Journal of the Sociology of Language*, 56(1985), p.100

9 Guy Wright, "U.S. English" in Crawford, ed., op cit., p. 127

10 U.S. English, "In Defense of Our Common Language...", in ibid., p. 146

11 Biography of Mauro E. Mujica, Chairman of the Board / CEO, *www.us-english.org*

12 Eloise Salholz etc., "Say It is English", *Newsweek*, February 20, 1989, p. 34

13 James Crawford, "What's behind Official English?" in Crawford, ed., op cit., pp. 176-7

14 James Crawford, "U.S. English – Agendas Hidden Between the Lines", *Houston Chronicle*, 30 October, 1988, p. 44

15 Crawford, ed., op.cit., p. 171

16 ibid., p. 175

17 ibid.

18 ibid., pp. 173-4

19 Dennis Baron, "English in a Multicultural America", *Social Policy*, 21 September 1991, pp. 5-14

20 Arturo Madrid, "Official English: A False Policy Issue", *The Annals of the American Academy of Political and Social Science*, Vol. 508, March 1990 (Newbury Park, CA, 1990), pp. 62-3

21 Joseph Leibowicz, "The Proposed English Language Amendment: Sword or Shield?" *Yale Law and Policy Review 3*, No. 2, (Spring 1985), pp. 519-50

22 ibid.

23 ibid.

24 *English Language Constitutional Amendments: Hearing on H.J. Res 13, H.J. Res. 33, H.J. Res. 60, and H.J. Res. 83*, 100th Congress, 2^{d} Session, May 11, 1988, pp. 67-70

25 ibid.

26 ibid.

27 ibid.

28 ibid.

29 For a fuller discussion, see Chapter 1 (A) of this book.

30 *Public Interest Profiles*, 1998-99, op cit., p. 215

31 U.S. English, "In Defense of Our Common Language", *Fundraising Brochure*, 1984.

32 ibid.

33 ibid.

34 Hayakawa, op cit., p. 32

35 ibid.

36 ibid.

37 U.S. House Committee on the Judiciary, Subcommittee on Civil and Constitutional Rights, *English Language Constitutional Amendments: Hearing on H.J. Res. 13, H.J. Res. 33, H.J. Res.60, and H.J. Res. 83*,, 100th Congress, 2d Session, May 11, 1988, pp. 36-44

38 ibid.

39 U.S. English, *Fundraising Brochure*, 1984, op cit.

40 *English Language Constitutional Amendments, Hearing...*, May 11, 1988, op cit.

41 ibid. For a more detailed discussion on bilingualism, refer to Chapter 3 of this book.

42 ibid.

43 U.S. English, *Fundraising Brochure*, 1984, op cit.

44 ibid.

45 S.I. Hayakawa, "Why English should be our Official Language", *The Education Digest 52*, May 1987, p. 36

46 ibid., p.37

47 ibid.

48 Rolf Kjolseth, "Cultural Politics of Bilingualism", *Society*, Vol. 20, no. 4, May-June 1983, p. 47

49 Samuel P. Huntington, *Who Are We? America's Great Debate* (London, 2004), p. 158

50 ibid. pp. 159-60

51 ibid. pp. 158-9

52 Hayakawa (1987), op. cit., p. 36

53 Patrick J. Buchanan, *The Death of the West* (New York, NY, 2002), p. 236

54 Arthur Mann, "From Immigration to Acculturation" in Luther S. Luedtke, ed., *Making America: The Society and Culture of the United States* (Chapel Hill, NC, 1992), p. 79

55 William Branigin, "Immigrants Shunning Ideas of Assimilation", *The Washington Post*, May 25, 1998, p. A1

56 U.S. English, *Fundraising Brochure*, 1984, op cit.

57 ibid.

58 *Public Interest Profiles*, 1998-99, op cit., p. 215

59 U.S. English, *Fundraising Brochure*, 1984, op cit.

60 ibid.

61 Gary Imhoff, "The Position of U.S. English on Bilingual Education", *The Annals of the American Academy of Political and Social Science*, Vol. 508, March 1990 (Newbury Park, CA, 1990), p. 60

62 English First, *Fundraising Letter*

63 ProEnglish, "Making English Our Official Language", *www.proenglish.org*

64 ProEnglish, "Our Guiding Principles", ibid.

65 ProEnglish, "Agenda for Action", ibid.

66 ibid.

67 Geoffrey Numberg, "Linguists and the Official Language Movement", *Language*, 65 (September, 1989), p. 581. Quoted in Huntington, op.cit., p. 168

68 *The 52^{d} Annual CQ Almanac, 1996, 104th Congress, 2^{d} Session* (Washington, D.C.1997), p. H.126-7

69 ibid., p. 5-43; *Migration News*, September 1996, Vol. 3, No. 9

70 Nancy M. Hornberger, "Bilingual Education and English-Only: A Language-Planning Framework in English Plus: Issues in Bilingual Education", *The Annals of the American Academy of Political and Social Science,* Vol. 508, March 1990, p. 15; also James Crawford, ed., op.cit., pp. 112-13

71 Newt Gingrich, *To Renew America* (New York, NY, 1995), pp.159-62

72 Cassandra Burrell, "House Passes Official English Bill", *English Only Update EXTRA*, August 2, 1996, also "Immigration and Official English Legislation", *Migration News*, op cit.

73 John E. Yang, "House Votes for Official English Language", *The Washington Post*, August 2, 1996; also Burrell, ibid.

74 Saumyajit Ray, *The Unmaking of Big Government: Lockean Conservatism in the G.O.P.'s Contract with America*, unpublished M. Phil dissertation (submitted to Jawaharlal Nehru University, New Delhi, 1999), p. 67.

75 ibid., pp. 157-8

76 Burrell, op cit.

77 Yang op cit.

78 Quoted in Burrell, op cit. Also, Yang, ibid.

79 Text of H.R. 123 and S. 356, *www.house.gov* and *www.senate.gov*

80 ibid.

81 ibid.

82 ibid.

83 ibid.

84 *www.us-english.org*

85 ibid.

86 Quoted by Imhoff, op cit., p. 49

87 *www.us-english.org*, op cit.

88 Text of H.R. 123, *www.house.gov*. op cit.

89 Eloise Salholz etc. "Say it in English", *Newsweek*, February 20, 1989, p. 35

90 Hayakawa (1987), op.cit., p. 37.

91 Yang, op cit.

92 "New US migrant reform bill," *Hindustan Times* (Delhi), December 17, 2009, p. 16.

5

Nation versus Hyphenation

> "While I cherish every person who comes here legally and seeks to pursue happiness.... I want them to become American, and part of becoming American involves English."
>
> **- Former Speaker Newton L. Gingrich (R-GA)**

(A) A MORE PERFECT UNION: OFFICIAL ENGLISH LAWS IN THE STATES

None of the thirty states with Official English laws today had declared English as its official language of government from the time of adopting its Constitution. Save one: Louisiana. In 1812, at the time of its admission into the Union, Louisiana had been overwhelmingly French-speaking. But as a condition of its admittance into the American Union, the state adopted English as its official language in 1807 (confirmed in 1811). Despite French being its major language, Louisiana had Official

English from the beginning. The irony of the other twenty-nine states is that, in spite of their English-speaking majorities, they only thought it fit to have Official English laws years after they had joined the Union. But then, it is an irony when viewed in the context of Louisiana. When seen in the backdrop of the federal Constitution, the arrangement seems absolutely perfect: the Founding Fathers were of British ancestry, and so were the overwhelming majority of Americans in the thirteen states.

The need for an official language was not felt in 1789, so it was with the states, including those which adopted Official English later. Of those original states that woke up to the need of having Official English laws were Georgia (entered the Union January 2, 1788; 4th), Massachusetts (February 6, 1788; 6th) New Hampshire (June 21, 1788; 9th), North Carolina (November 21, 1789; 12th), South Carolina (May 23, 1788; 8th), and Virginia (June 25, 1788; 10th).[1] The rest—Connecticut, Delaware, Maryland, New Jersey, New York, Pennsylvania, and Rhode Island—never had statewide Official English legislation.

Other states which declared English as their official language were late entrants into the Union: Alabama (December 14, 1819; 22nd), Alaska (January 3, 1959; 49th), Arizona (February 14, 1912; 48th), Arkansas (June 15, 1836; 25th), California (September 9, 1850; 31st), Colorado (August 1, 1876; 38th), Florida (March 3, 1845; 27th), Hawaii (August 21, 1959, 50th), Idaho (July 3, 1890; 43rd), Illinois (December 3, 1818; 21st), Indiana (December 11, 1816; 19th), Iowa (December 28, 1846; 29th), Kansas (January 29, 1861; 34th), Kentucky (June 1, 1972; 15th), Mississippi (December 10, 1817; 20th), Missouri (August 10, 1821; 24th), Montana (November 8, 1889; 41st), Nebraska (March 1, 1867, 37th), North Dakota (November

2, 1889; 39th), South Dakota (November, 2, 1889; 40th), Tennessee (June 1, 1796; 16th), Utah (January 4, 1896; 45th), and Wyoming (July 10, 1890; 44th).[2]

Massachusetts

Among the original states that went for statewide Official English laws, Massachusetts was the earliest. In 1975, it amended its Constitution to declare English as its official language, though in very general terms: "No person shall [have the right to vote, or] be eligible for office under the Constitution of this commonwealth, who shall not be able to read the Constitution in the English language..." (Article XX).[3] This is more an assertion of the primacy of English in the state for official purposes than an explicit declaration that English was the official language of the commonwealth of Massachusetts. It does not say that government business should always and invariably be conducted in English, only that knowledge of English—in which the Constitution of the commonwealth was written—was necessary for holding public office and even for enjoying the political right to vote; and the only way to demonstrate such knowledge was the ability to read the Constitution in English. Inability to demonstrate sufficient competence in the English language, then, would result in withdrawal of voting rights by the government. Such punitive action against non-English-speakers envisaged by the Constitution reminds one of the early assimilationists.[4]

But more important than that, if voting rights were incumbent on the knowledge of English—that too judged by the ability to read the Constitution in that language—then multilingual ballots, voting materials, and voter assistance must also be forbidden by this Official English law of Massachusetts. No doubt that federal law would prevail if there was a discrepancy, but what is most interesting is that such conflicting laws had to be passed—one at the federal level and the other in the state—in the same year.

There are two other astounding aspects of this Massachusetts Official English law: it was passed in the liberal heartland of the United States, and at a time when Democrat Michael Dukakis was state governor. Dukakis, himself born of Greek parents, could not prevent English from becoming the official language of Massachusetts. Thirteen years later, he secured his party's nomination for president and ran unsuccessfully against Vice President George Bush on a liberal platform, netting a big chunk of immigrant votes! In fact Dukakis even campaigned in Spanish (he is fluent in the language) to woo Hispanic voters.[5]

In 1987, the Carolinas made laws declaring English their official language.

North Carolina

The General Statutes of North Carolina (1987) designates English as the "state language" and asserts that "English is the common language of the people of the United States and the State of North Carolina." [Section 145-12 (a)][6] It then makes the simple declaration: "English is the official language of the State of North Carolina" [Section 145-12(b)]. The law also states its purpose in clear terms: "This section is intended to preserve, protect, and strengthen the English language". [Section 145-12(a)] The function of preserving, protecting, and strengthening the English language is, according to the statute, a state responsibility. Something that John Adams wanted, and Noah Webster advocated. The rationale behind the law is stated in the law itself: that English was the common language of the people of the United States and of the state of North Carolina. There is need to state in law what is generally accepted in fact. But the fact that English was the common language of all Americans does not mean that there was no need to preserve, protect, and strengthen it. No doubt, Republican Governor James G. Martin had no problem in signing into law such a piece of legislation, consistent as it was with an assimilationist position.

South Carolina

The Annotated Code of Laws of South Carolina (1987)[7] declares that "The English language is the official language of the State of South Carolina" (Section 1-1- 696) and prohibits the use of languages other than English for all official purposes (Section 1-1-697). But the law does not prohibit the use of languages other than English for academic and educational purposes in order to make students who use a language other than English proficient in English or to make students proficient in a language other than English (Section 1-1-698).

The South Carolina Official English law, then, leaves room for bilingual education and that too through native language instruction. Apparently, the law supports *transitional* bilingual education, but also admits that the student's native language can become a means for acquiring proficiency in English; hence, native language instruction merits statutory sanction—a reiteration of the Democratic position on bilingual education.

That the law received the assent of Democratic Governor Richard W. Riley (he later served as Bill Clinton's Secretary of Education and was named by the *Christian Science Monitor* as "one of the great statesmen of education in this century") seems more than a coincidence. Riley, who was so popular that the people of South Carolina amended their Constitution to enable him to run for a second term and whom President Clinton retained as Education Secretary after his re-election in 1996, is remembered for his successful efforts for improving education at both the state and federal levels. Not only did he assent to an Official English law with a strong bilingual education component, in a major address to Hispanics as US Education Secretary in March 2000 he endorsed "two-way" bilingual education (in which students were taught half the time in their native tongue and half in another language, with the goal of making them proficient in both).[8]

New Hampshire

This belief in bilingual education through native language instruction is echoed by the Official English law of New Hampshire. The New Hampshire Revised Statutes, Annotated, Chapter 3-C (1995) states: "The official language of the state of New Hampshire shall be English. English is designated as the language of all official public documents and records, and of all public proceedings and nonpublic sessions" (3-C:1).[9] This is a positive statement, given that it does not explicitly prohibit the use of other languages, nor is punitive action envisaged against individuals with little or no knowledge of English. But then, there is an exception to the operation of this law: "The provisions of this chapter shall not apply to instruction designed to aid students with limited English in a timely transition and integration into the general education system" (3-C:2). This law ostensibly supports *transitional* bilingual education. "Instruction designed to aid students with limited English" is nothing but native language instruction in this context. This clubbing of bilingual education through native language instruction—based on the Democratic belief that native language instruction is the only vehicle for a smooth and "timely" transition of limited English proficient (LEP) students to regular all-English classes—with the general declaration of English as the official language of the state seems to be a Democratic-Republican compromise, a precedent of South Carolina followed in New Hampshire. But this time the governor who signed the Official English law was from the other party: Republican Steve Merrill, 87th governor of the state.

Georgia

The spirit of Democratic-Republican compromise seems to have pervaded the Official English law of Georgia as well. The Official Georgia Code, Section 50-3-100, Official Language (1996) designates English as the official language of the state of Georgia, adding that the official language shall be the language used for public records and public meetings, and for official Acts of the State of Georgia, including those governmental documents, records, meetings, actions, or policies which are enforceable with the full weight and authority of the State of Georgia [Section 50-3-100 (a)]. But then, the Act cannot be applied when in conflict with federal law. Also, it cannot inhibit instruction designed to aid students with limited English proficiency "in their transition and integration into the education system of the state" [Section 50-3-100 (d)].[10]

This provision accommodating bilingual education is not only couched in a language similar to that in the New Hampshire law, but also reiterates the belief that bilingual education through native language instruction is a viable means of teaching English to LEP students. Such a belief acquires constitutional sanction and significance when it comes in the form of a statutory provision, whether in South Carolina, New Hampshire, or Georgia.

As far as conflict with federal law is concerned, Article VI of the federal Constitution had already settled matters: "This constitution, and the laws of the United States which shall be made in pursuance thereof...shall be the supreme law of the land; and the judges in every state shall be bound thereby, anything in the constitution or laws of any state to the contrary notwithstanding." Viewed in the backdrop of Official English, the 1975 amendments to the Voting Rights Act of 1965 allowing multilingual ballots, voting materials and voter assistance shall be applicable to Georgia in spite of English having been declared the state's official language. In fact, they shall be applicable throughout the United States, regardless of Official English laws in the states. Only that the Georgia law—signed by Democratic Governor Zell B. Miller—makes an explicit declaration to the effect that it would not apply when in conflict with federal laws. It would also not apply if "justice" required the use of other languages, and provision of multilingual ballots to non-English speaking voters may constitute such "justice" [Section 50-3-100 (d) (2)]. It is noteworthy that Governor Miller, who had been U.S. Senator between 2001 and 2005, had backed George W. Bush over Democratic nominee John F. Kerry in the 2004 presidential election and supported several Republican candidates besides frequently criticizing the Democratic Party on a range of issues. A "cultural conservative" who had later shifted his stance from "pro-choice" to "pro-life", Governor Miller signed Georgia's Official English bill not long after his successful re-election bid in 1994.

Virginia

English is designated as the official language of the Commonwealth of Virginia by the Code of Virginia, Chapter 829 (1996), Chapter 7 (Section 7.1-42)[11]. It also forbids state agencies or local governments from providing any documents, information, literature or other written materials in any language other than English. In other words, neither the Commonwealth of Virginia nor its political sub-divisions shall have any obligation to provide multilingual assistance to its citizens.

But what is most interesting is that the Official English law of the Commonwealth of Virginia, signed by Republican Governor George F. Allen, categorically rejects *transitional* bilingual education through native language instruction, upholding the English as a Second Language (ESL) approach instead. Native language instruction is outlawed, and the ESL approach—that aims at the predominance of English from the earliest stages—is mandated.

Nebraska

Among the states that have amended their constitutions to make English their official language, other than Massachusetts, was Nebraska. In fact, Nebraska had done it more than a half century before Massachusetts. Article I, Section 27 of the Nebraska State Constitution, inserted by way of amendment in 1920, says, "The English language is hereby declared to be the official language of this State, and all official proceedings, records and publications shall be in such language, and the common school branches shall be taught in said language in public, private, denominational and parochial schools".[12] This amendment to the state Constitution was passed when even the Nebraska Supreme Court was yet to pronounce on *Meyer V. Nebraska.*[13] The amendment was also broader in scope than Chapter 249 of the Nebraska Sessions Law of 1919 that prohibited the teaching of any foreign language before the completion of the eighth grade. No doubt the prevailing anti-German sentiment and the controversy created by *Meyer V. Nebraska* spurred the amendment, but it was a bold and necessary step nevertheless; it was the first Official English measure to deal with both the official language of government and school education in one go.

Hawaii

Nineteen years after Hawaii joined the Union, its state legislature adopted a constitutional amendment according official status to both English and Hawaiian. Interestingly, though Japanese was the major second language in Hawaii, Hawaiian was selected for legal protection because it was an indigenous language perceived to be endangered.[14] Article XV, Section 4, Official Languages (1978) as inserted in the state constitution that year says, "English and Hawaiian shall be the official languages of Hawaii except that Hawaiian shall be required for public acts and transactions only as provided by law."[15] With this constitutional amendment, Hawaii became the first and till date the only officially bilingual state. The March 1989 non-binding resolution adopted by the New Mexico legislature—better known as the English *Plus* Resolution—does not accord official status to English or, for that matter, to any other language along with English; it only mentions the need to encourage proficiency in "other languages".[16] Coming back to Hawaii, Democratic Governor George R. Ariyoshi (born to Japanese immigrant parents, he became the first American of Asian descent to be elected state governor) assented to the state becoming officially bilingual, even though Hawaiian was in most cases a second language for people in the state.

California

In November 1986, California voters passed Proposition 63 with 73% of the vote making English the official language of the state. It was the first Official English measure passed by ballot initiative in any state in the country.[17] Governor George Deukmejian, surprisingly a Republican, was the most prominent opponent of Proposition 63 that intended to amend the California State Constitution to make English its official language. Deukmejian, an American of Armenian descent, called the proposal "unnecessary", because English was already the "dominant" language of California, and amending the state Constitution to make English the official language "would not result in any individual learning English any faster or better."[18] The governor also added that the proposal "would also cause fear, confusion and resentment among many minority Californians, who see the measure as an effort to legislate the cultural superiority of native English-speaking people. Without questioning the sincere motives of its sponsors, the initiative as drafted is insensitive to our state's ethnic diversity, which is one of our great strengths."[19] Deukmejian may have been alarmed by statewide protests against the ballot initiative, especially by Hispanic activist groups (Hispanics, incidentally, constitute more than a quarter of the state's population) and thought that he might lose his re-election bid if he supported Proposition 63, but the way he associated an Official English measure with "cultural superiority" of English-speakers and raised the issue of "fear" among language minorities in California of such a measure is very uncharacteristic of a Republican leader. Interestingly, despite Deukmejian's opposition, 82.1% of California voters who supported Deukmejian backed Proposition 63 in the election of 1986.[20]

The California State Constitution, amended by Proposition 63, 1986, reads; "English is the common language of the people of the United States of America and the State of California. This section is intended to preserve, protect and strengthen the English language..." [Article III, Section 6, 1 (a)] [21] California had for long been the destination of Hispanic immigrants, both legal and illegal, effecting a demographic change that sharply and irrevocably increased the number of Spanish speakers in the state. California is also home to the biggest concentration of Asians in the country: Chinese, Japanese, Koreans, Vietnamese, Filipinos, and Asian Indians. No doubt, speakers of English perceived a threat to their language, what with bilingual education, multilingual ballots, and various public services offered through an increasing number of foreign languages. Hence the need arose to "preserve, protect, and strengthen the English language". The insecurity about the future of English in California is writ large on the amendment: "The Legislature and officials of the State of California shall take all steps necessary to insure that the role of English as the common language of the state of California is preserved and enhanced. The legislature shall make no law which diminishes or ignores the role of English as the common language of the State of California" [Article III, Section 6, 1 (c)].[22] Not only is the state legislature prohibited from curbing the role of English (and threatening its predominant position in the process) it is required to uphold English as the "common language" of the state of California, not only as its official language. The law makes it incumbent on the state legislature to ensure that the status of English as the "common language" of the people of the state is perpetuated, thus entrusting it with a social responsibility along with a political one. The law does not stop at declaring that "English is the official language of California" [Article III, Section 6, 1 (b)]. To make English the language of the people was as important as making it the official language of the state. So important, that "any person who is a resident of or doing business in the State of California shall have standing to sue the State of California" if it failed to fulfill its obligation in this regard [Article III, Section 6, 1 (d)][23]. Evidently, only declaring English as the official language of a state (or of the Union, for that matter) may not suffice; its social pre-eminence may have to be upheld by law to ensure its political preponderance.

Two years later, Colorado and Florida moved constitutional amendments to declare English their official language.

Colorado

Colorado's case is most interesting. Democratic Governor Richard D. Lamm, a leading opponent of bilingual education who co-authored *The Immigration Time Bomb: The Fragmenting of America* with Gary Imhoff was ostensibly comfortable with Official English. Wrote Lamm in the book, supporting late Senator S.I. Hayakawa's proposed English Language Amendment (ELA) of 1981:

> The bill is important: it reverses the long-standing process of the federal government's promotion of bilingualism. It emphasizes the centrality of the English language to citizenship, to belonging to this polity...... If nothing else, an English-

> language amendment would certainly mandate that voting be done in English.[24]

Lamm, who was Colorado's longest-serving governor (between 1975 and 1987), however criticized Official English by comparing it with a statue in a park ("its poise was heroic, but it went nowhere") in a personal correspondence with this author. How children were taught, said Lamm, was more important.[25]

It was during the tenure of Lamm's successor, Democratic Governor Roy Romer, that Colorado amended its constitution to make English official. The amendment, which was the culmination of a 1988 ballot initiative opposed by Governor Romer but approved by 64% of Colorado voters,[26] nevertheless, was a simple one. Article II, Section 30 (1988) of the Colorado Constitution declares: "The English language is the official language of the state of Colorado".[27] Such one-liners indeed have sweeping and far-reaching consequences.

Florida

Eight years after Dade County (Florida) voters approved an "anti-bilingual ordinance" prohibiting the expenditure of public funds on the use of languages other than English, the Constitution of the State of Florida underwent an English Language Amendment in 1988. The Florida amendment, like that of the state of Colorado, was a simple one. Article II, Section 9 (a) of the Florida Constitution, as inserted by the amendment of 1988, says that "English is the official language of the state of Florida." What is interesting is that Florida became the second state to pass an Official English law by way of a ballot initiative over the opposition of a Republican governor. Robert 'Bob' Martinez, the governor, had opposed the ballot initiative that wanted to make English the official language of Florida, calling it "unnecessary". As Martinez said, "We don't select a religion for Americans. We don't select a race for Americans. And we have not selected a language for Americans".[28] He was wrong, because 84% of Florida voters approved the ballot initiative on November 8, 1988. Subsequently, Governor Martinez promised to "work with the state legislature to keep the amendment from intruding into Floridians' private lives".[29]

The Florida amendment, though, was the culmination of a longstanding Official English movement begun in the state in 1978. Dade County's "anti-bilingual ordinance" of 1980 served as a motivation and inspiration for Official English backers in the state, afraid of a total takeover by the Spanish language of all spheres of life, public and private.

Alabama

Alabama's Official English amendment is a reiteration of California's Proposition 63 in letter and spirit. What is remarkable is not only the similarly in the language of the two amendments, but the vast differences in the conditions in which they were carried out.

English-speaking Alabamans could not have felt threatened from speakers of other languages who constitute only 3.9% of the state's population. There is no sustained immigration to Alabama—legal or illegal, Hispanic or Asian—and hence no immediate provocation. Despite its Official English amendment, California is socially liberal. Alabama is conservative. It had been home to nativist movements, both Know Nothings and the Ku

Klux Klan. Along with Mississippi and Missouri—which went for Official English laws and not amendments—Alabama reflects the assimilationist response of white Anglo-Saxon middle class America to the question of Official English. The absence of non-English speakers in large numbers in the state proves that Official English has deep sentimental value apart from being a political statement. Not surprisingly, then, 89% of Alabamans voted to make English their official language.

Signed by Republican Governor Guy Hunt, Amendment 509 to the 1901 Constitution of Alabama declared English as the Official Language of State in 1990:

> English is the official language of the state of Alabama...The legislature and officials of the state of Alabama shall take all steps necessary to insure that the role of English as the common language of the state of Alabama is preserved and enhanced. The legislature shall make no law that diminishes or ignores the role of English as the common language of the state of Alabama.[30]

As in California, the assimilationist capacity of the English language is admitted, and reiterated in law. And then, like California again, a warning to state authorities against faltering on their responsibility to uphold the pre-eminence of the English language by entrusting the common man with a positive responsibility of legally pulling up the state if it failed on this count. "Any person who is a resident of or doing business in the state of Alabama shall have standing to sue the state of Alabama to enforce this amendment....[31] In May 2001, the Alabama Supreme Court upheld this Official English amendment, eleven years after it was passed.

Alaska

In 1998, Ballot Measure No. 6—An Initiative Adopting English as the Official State language of Alaska—was adopted by the Alaska legislature in the form of a constitutional amendment. The amendment says that "The English language is the official language of the State of Alaska" (Section 2). The English language was "to be used by all public agencies in all government functions and actions" and "in the preparation of all official public documents and records" (Section 3).[32]

However, the government of the State of Alaska was free to "use a language other than English when necessary" for certain purposes, including when it was required to teach another language to students proficient in English and to teach English to students of limited English proficiency [Section 5, (2)(3)].[33] As far as teaching another language to students already proficient in English is concerned, there is nothing wrong with it if it did not impede or impair that proficiency in any way. Many students were fluent bilinguals and it was not impossible for students to acquire an academic level of proficiency in two languages. But what is noticeable is that the amendment believes that other languages may be required to be used to teach English to LEP students. This is based on the belief of *facilitation theorists* that native language instruction was the only way through which English could be taught to students with limited English proficiency. A state in which 14.3% of residents spoke a language other than English, native language instruction held a special import. No doubt, bilingual education in Alaska was nothing but native language instruction. The fact that students with limited English proficiency have been mentioned in the amendment means that there were a significant number of LEP students in the state. Not only that. Bilingual education through native language instruction was relied upon as the most viable method of teaching English to LEP students. The fact that such bilingual education was not *transitional* but ended up in the *maintenance* of native languages and cultures was a different question altogether, though not something that could be overlooked by the backers of the initiative in the fist place.

Illinois

Among the states which joined the Union later, Illinois was the first to declare English as its official language through a statute way back in 1969. This Official English law repealed a 1923 legislation declaring "American" to be the state's official language. Chapter 5, Section 460/20 of the Illinois Annotated Statutes (1969) simply says: "The Official language of the State of Illinois in English".[34] One-line legislations are always vulnerable, especially to broad interpretations, and this Act of 1969 proved no exception. The 7th U.S. Circuit Court of Appeals ruled in 1973 that this simple Official English law of Illinois did not justify practical restriction on bilingual services and that Puerto Ricans residing in Illinois were entitled to voting materials in Spanish, in *PROPA v. Kusper*.[35] Interestingly, this was two years before Congress mandated bilingual and multilingual election materials and voter assistance in its 1975 amendments to the Voting Rights Act (1965). In fact, the court decision in *PROPA v. Kusper* was one among several that prompted Congress to pass the 1975 amendments. A more specific Official English law banning the provision of multilingual voting materials and voter assistance would not have allowed the court to rule in favor of such provision, if not put an end to the controversy surrounding it. With the 1975 amendments now in place, state Official English laws cannot prevent multilingual voting materials from reaching non-English-speaking voters refusing to learn the language of America. Evidently, the Illinois Official English statutes—signed by Republican Governor Richard B. Ogilvie—were not prepared for the dangers it were to countenance.

Both Indiana and Kentucky passed Official English laws in 1984.

Indiana

Section 1-2-10-1 of the Indiana Statues [State Language (1984)]—inserted by a constitutional amendment and signed by Republican Governor Robert D. Orr—states that "The English Language is adopted as the official language of the State of Indiana."[36] Except as provided by laws enacted by the General Assembly of the State of Indiana or required by federal law, the amended Article 15 of the Indiana Constitution mandated that all laws, rules, official documents, orders, transactions, proceedings, programs, meetings, publications, or actions enacted, adopted, issued, conducted, regulated, or taken by, on behalf of, or representing the state or a political subdivision of the State should be in the English language.

Kentucky

Section 2.013 of the Kentucky Revised Statutes [State Language (1984)] designates English as the official state language of Kentucky.[37] The one-line statute was authored by State Senator Louis T. Peniston (D-New Castle) as Senate Bill 145, passed the Committee on State Government with an overwhelming 35-0 margin, and adopted 84-7 in the State Senate.[38] The companion measure in the State House also passed comfortably. Democrat Martha Layne Collins became the first woman governor to sign an Official English law when she gave her assent to this Kentucky statute. Incidentally, in the same year that her state passed an Official English statute, Collins became chair of the Democratic National Convention at San Francisco (CA) that put a woman (Geraldine Ferraro) for the first time on the presidential ticket of a major party.

Mississippi

Three years later, Mississippi passed its own one-line Official English law, signed by Democratic Governor William A. "Bill' Alain, known for his conflicts with the legislative branch. Section 3-3-31 of the Mississippi Code Annotated [State Language (1987)] declares: "The English language is the official language of the state of Mississippi."

North Dakota

In the same year, North Dakota passed an Official English law, again a one-line legislation signed by Democratic Governor George Sinner. Section 54-02-13 [English As Official Language (1987)] of the North Dakota Century Code reads: "The English language is the official language of the state of North Dakota".[39] Such one-line declarations of official language have prompted many to depict the state language—English, that is—as having only symbolic status as state bird or state flower and being of no practical value.

Tennessee

In 1984, Tennessee passed a more specific Official

English law, taking both bilingual ballots and bilingual education out of the host of services provided by the state. Section 4-1-404 [English and Legal Language (1984)] of the Tennessee Code Annotated declares: "English is hereby established as the official and legal language of Tennessee. All communications and publications, *including ballots*, produced by governmental entities in Tennessee shall be in English, and instruction in public schools and colleges of Tennessee shall be conducted in English *unless the nature of the course would require otherwise*."[40] (*Italics* mine).

The requirement that ballots be produced in English only does not necessarily contradict the 1975 amendments to the Voting Rights Act (1965) requiring bilingual voting materials, but denotes that no electoral district in Tennessee has the required number of non-English-speaking residents to evoke the provisions of the amendment. More importantly, if ballots were printed in English only, voters with non-English backgrounds would be compelled to learn English and ultimately become part of the political mainstream. Only 4.9% of the state's residents spoke a language other than English and it would not be imprudent on the part of the state to assist them in making a smooth transition to the English language.

Similarly, as far as education in public schools and colleges in Tennessee is concerned, it is to be imparted in English only. Only when "the nature of course would require otherwise" are other languages to be taught or subject matter courses taught in non-English languages. The "nature of the course" may range from a course in a foreign language to bilingual education through native language instruction. No doubt the use of non-English languages cannot be construed as illegal under Tennessee's Official English law, but the statute does not explicitly rely on native language instruction as the sole viable method of bilingual education. In fact, it does not mention bilingual education at all and mandates an all-English education for students in public schools and colleges in the state. Signed by Republican Governor Lamar Alexander, the Tennessee Official English law is the only example of its kind to deal with the twin problems of bilingual ballots and bilingual education in a simple and direct manner.

Arkansas

Democratic Governor William Jefferson "Bill" Clinton of Arkansas signed the state's Official English law in 1987. Nine years later, as President of the United States, he opposed H.R. 123—the Bill Emerson English Language Empowerment Act of 1996, passed by the Republican House of Representatives in the 104th Congress—calling the measure "objectionable" and "divisive".[41] He even said that his action in assenting to Official English as governor of Arkansas was a mistake.[42] As president, Clinton may have been eyeing the Hispanic vote for his re-election bid and for improving the chances of his party in Congress, but in a state with less than 1% of the population being Hispanic, Governor Clinton had no problems with the bill at all.

Nevertheless, Section 1-4-117 (a) of the Arkansas Code Annotated declares: "The English language shall be the official language of the state of Arkansas".[43] But the Act does not end with this simple declaration: it takes care to protect bilingual education without, however, mentioning it by name. Section 1-4-117(b) reads: "This section shall not prohibit the public schools from performing their duty to provide equal educational opportunities to all children."[44] In 1974, the U.S. Supreme

Court ruled in *Lau V. Nichols* that an all-English education did not constitute equal educational opportunities for language-minority students unable to understand English, and that special assistance must be offered to such students.[45] This special assistance for the purpose of providing "equal educational opportunities" to LEP students later took the form of native language instruction, especially after the *Lau Remedies*. Viewed in this context, the Arkansas Official English law does not prevent subject matter courses from being taught to language minority students in their native languages.

Arizona

Arizona's 1988 Official English law was overturned by the state's Supreme Court ten years later. The 1988 law—which amended the state Constitution to declare English as Arizona's official language—was passed through a referendum, but the Arizona apex court struck it down on the ground that it was unconstitutional. Arizona enacted Official English legislation again in 2006, through a ballot initiative called Proposition 106. The state Constitution was amended once again to declare English as its official language vide Article 28.

This article declared that English was the official language of Arizona (Section 2) and that all official actions were to be conducted in English (Section 4). However, "official action" did not include the "teaching of or the encouragement of learning languages other than English" [Section 1.2 (a)]. Thus bilingual education through native language instruction and the teaching of foreign languages were forbidden. In fact, Arizona had passed a law in 2000 mandating the use of English immersion programs in public schools for students who did not speak English. A report submitted in January that year by the Superintendent of Public Instruction to the Arizona legislature said that English as a Second Language programs—which were modified English immersion programs—were more successful in teaching English to LEP students than bilingual education programs.[46] The 2006 Official English law scrapped bilingual education in the state altogether.

This law also required representatives of government in Arizona to "preserve, protect and enhance the role of English as the official language of the government of Arizona" (Section 3A). More specifically, "preserve, protect and enhance the role of English" included "avoiding any official actions that ignore, harm or diminish the role of English as the language of government, protecting the rights of persons in this state who use English, encouraging greater opportunities for individuals to learn the English language, and to the greatest extent possible under federal statute, providing services, programs, publications, documents and materials in English" [Section 3 (a)-(d)]. Not only was the role of English sought to be strengthened, the rights of English speakers were also upheld. Not only that. The law also asserted that "a person shall not be discriminated against or penalized in any way because the person uses or attempts to use English in public or private communication" (Section 3B). Clearly, English speakers in Arizona felt threatened by the use of non-English languages in the state. That is the reason why Proposition 106 passed by a 74% majority on Election Day in November 2006.

Both South Dakota (1995) and Wyoming (1996) rely on the use of other languages for helping LEP students achieve English proficiency as early as possible.

South Dakota

South Dakota's Official English law, signed by four-term Republican Governor William John "Bill" Janklow in 1995, shall not apply to "instruction designed to aid students with limited English proficiency in a timely transition and integration into the general education system."[47] Even if the statute envisages resorting to non-English native languages for teaching English to LEP students, it asserts that English was "the common language of the state" and the language "of any official public document or record and any official public meeting" [South Dakota Codified Laws, Section 1-27-20 (English as common language)].

Wyoming

Similarly, Wyoming's Official English law—signed in 1996 by Republican Governor James Edward "Jim" Geringer—authorizes "a state agency or political subdivision or its offices or employees" to act in a language other than English "to provide instruction designed to aid students with limited English proficiency so they can make a timely transition to use of the English language in the public schools". This statute, however, relieves the state of Wyoming from any obligation to provide services in non-English languages: "English shall be designated as the official language of Wyoming. Except as otherwise provided by law, no state agency or political subdivision of the state shall be required to provide any documents, information, literature or other written materials in any language other than English" [Wyoming State Statutes, Title 8, Chapter 6, Official Language (1996)].[48] Non-English-speaking residents should teach themselves English if they wished to avail of services provided by the state; the state would not cater to them in their non-English native languages.

Missouri

In fact the importance of language-minority residents teaching themselves English is highlighted by Missouri's Official English law of 1998—signed by Democratic Governor Mel Carnahan—which, interestingly, does not designate English as the official language, but calls it "the common language of the state." The emphasis of the law, however, is on English language education and the acquiring of fluency in English by non-native speakers of the language.

Section 2 of the Missouri Revised Statutes (1998) [English as common language of the state] devotes itself to teaching English to non-English speaking adults so that they are enabled to avail of services in the English language: "The adult basic education program administered by the department of elementary and secondary education shall include the provision of English language services to non-native speakers who need assistance in learning English" (Section 2.1). Non-English-speaking adults would also be actively encouraged to seek services in English (Section 2.2). Missouri becomes the only state to underscore the teaching of English to non-English-speaking adults through family and home-based curriculum and programs designed to enhance the English fluency of all family members and even encourage family members to teach each other the English language (Section 2.3). The reason for this emphasis on teaching English to non-native speakers of the language is simple: it would be difficult to survive in American society without assimilating into the culture and way of life of America (Section 1).[49]

Montana

Despite this emphasis on English education for non-English-speaking adults in Missouri, Montana has stuck to the importance of English education for LEP students in K-12 in its Official English law, signed by Republican Governor Marc F. Racicot in 1995. But Montana is unique: it permits the teaching of foreign languages—actually, the native languages of language-minority students—but only as a second language. The message is loud and clear: native language instruction is not to be permitted; if non-English languages are taught in school, they cannot be taught as the student's primary language.

Section 1(2) of Act 319 (1995) [English as official and primary language of state and local governments] of Montana says that a state statute, local government ordinance, or state or local government policy "may not require" a specific foreign language to be taught in a school as a student's primary language. However, it does not prohibit the teaching of other languages in school "for general educational purposes or as secondary languages" [Section 1(3)]. The Act also declares that in Montana English was the official and primary language of state and local governments, of government officers and employees acting in the course and scope of their employment, and of government documents and records [Section 1(1)].[50]

Utah

Utah Voters passed a ballot initiative 7 November, 2000—An Act Relating to State Affairs in General; Declaring English to be the Official Language for the Conduct of Government Business in Utah—which enacted Section 63-13-1.5 of the Utah Code Annotated (1953) to declare English as the official language of Utah and the "sole language of the government".[51] The Act permits the use of other languages for certain important purposes, the teaching of English to language-minority children and adults being one of them.

Utah's Official English law incorporates Missouri's emphasis on the teaching of English to non-English speaking adults—including parents whose children were already learning English in school—along with the need to make LEP students proficient in English [Section 63-13-1.5(5) (a), (c), and (d)]. Dr. Jim Cummins' concern that if parents were not fluent in English, the quality of their interaction with their children in English was likely to be poor—cited earlier in this book—has been adequately addressed by Utah's Official English law. The provision of public services in other languages is deemed unnecessary and any expenditure incurred on such provision is rightly regarded wasteful. With this ballot initiative (called Initiative A) Utah voters overwhelmingly approved a measure lawmakers had failed to pass on three previous occasions[52], making Utah the 26th state to declare English its official language.

Iowa

Despite Democratic opposition, the Republican-dominated Iowa House gave final approval to the Iowa English Language Reaffirmation Act of 2001 on February 26, 2002. Three days later, Democratic Governor Tom Vilsack, in spite of initial reservations about the bill, signed it into law (March 1, 2002).

Governor Vilsack had criticized the bill as lacking substance because it allegedly provided no funding to teach English to those for whom English was not their first language. Nevertheless, he admitted the importance of the

English language, thus accepting the need for the bill: "We all agree that everyone who lives and works here should be proficient in English because it is the language that unites us, and it is the language of opportunity."[53]

The Iowa English Language Reaffirmation Act of 2001 reaffirms that throughout the history of Iowa and of the United States, "the common thread" binding individuals of differing backgrounds together has been the English language [Section 1.18(1) (b)]. It is also the only state Official English law to reaffirm that the power of a state to establish English as its official language and to promote the English language within the state was well within the powers delegated to the states by the Constitution of the United States [Section 1.18 (1) (c)].[54]

The Act of 2001 also declares that in order to encourage every citizen of the state to become more proficient in the English language, "thereby facilitating participation in the economic, political, and cultural activities of this state and of the United States", it was necessary to make English the official language of Iowa [Section 1.18(2)]. While declaring English as "the language of government in Iowa" [Section 1.18(3)], the Act did not "disparage any language other than English or discourage any person from learning or using a language other than English" [Section 1. 18(5) (c)]. However, the law does not mention whether other languages could be resorted to while teaching English to LEP children. In fact, the Act does not mention school education at all.

Idaho

Republican Governor C. L. "Butch" Otter's assent to Senate Bill No. 1172 in 2007 made Idaho the 29th state with an Official English law. S.B. 1172, which had passed the State Senate 20-15 and the State House 46-20, amended Section 73-121 of the Idaho Code to declare English the official state language, to provide that English was the sole language of government (subject to exceptions), and to provide that specified actions shall be in English (subject to exceptions), among other things. However, languages other than English may be used when the state board of education ruled that the use of foreign languages was necessary to make non-English speaking children and adults read, write, and understand English as quickly as possible [Section 73-121 (6) (a)]. The argument that the use non-English native languages could help language minority children acquire fluency in English seems to have a wide following. The end result becomes obvious: bilingual education through native language instruction remains untouched.

Kansas

Kansas became the 30th state to get an Official English law when Democratic Governor Kathleen Sebelius (presently U.S. Secretary of Health and Human Services) signed H.B. 2140 on May 11, 2007. Under H.B. 2140, which had earlier passed the State House 114-7 and the State Senate 32-8 and declared English the official language of Kansas, state agencies would not be required to conduct business and provide documents in languages other than English, except where necessary to comply with federal law, protect public safety, and maintain constitutional rights.[55] As things stand today, bilingual education through native language instruction is a constitutional right of language minority children. As such the Kansas Official English law leaves the room wide open for bilingual education.

It is most interesting to note that nowhere has an Official English proposal been defeated at the polls. But wherever states legislatures have been reluctant or failed to act on Official English proposals, they had become the subject of statewide ballot initiatives and approved by voters with huge majorities. This has happened whenever English-speaking voters—always a majority in every state—have felt threatened by an increasing presence of non-English-speakers in their midst and found it necessary to reassert their American identity through an Official English measure. No doubt, then, that English remains an important symbol of national identity for the masses.

Again, if Republicans are widely perceived as champions of Official English, the record of language legislation in the states tells a different story. Democratic governors have willingly signed Official English bills, whereas Republican governors have opposed ballot initiatives seeking to make English the official language of their states. On the other hand, most state legislatures that have passed official language legislation have been Republican-controlled. Against this backdrop, it is necessary to explore the partisan contours of Official English.

(B) FROM IMMIGRANTS TO AMERICANS: THE GOP AND THE POLITICS OF INCLUSION

When the Louisiana Constitution was being re-written in 1864, many delegates to the convention opposed any official status or protection for the French language whatsoever. One Alfred C. Hills said that if Americans failed to learn or use English, they should return to their old countries:

> I believe the English language is the official language of this country. I believe in a homogenous people, in one language... and I believe that the publication of the laws of this state... in the French language is a nuisance and ought to be abolished in this state or any other... If there are any in the state who cannot speak, read or write the language (English), they should learn to do so before they reside in the country any longer.[56]

132 yeas later, the House Republican Policy Committee in the 104th Congress issued a statement in support of Official English, shifting the onus of making immigrants learn English to the government rather than on the immigrants themselves:

> The use of English is indispensable to immigrants and their children who wish to participate fully in American society and realize the American Dream. As we seek to promote the rich and varied traditions new Americans bring, we must simultaneously work to insure that all of us share some basis for common understanding. Securing both these important goals requires overcoming the divisive influence of linguistic separatism. English should be and remain the official language of our national government.... Unlike their predecessors, today's immigrants are met with government policies allegedly concerned with the preservation of their ethnic separateness. Chief among these misguided policies is the mandate of a multilingual government. By discouraging immigrants and their children from using the English language, this policy has

erected a linguistic barrier that keeps many immigrants from becoming full participants in a society they have chosen to join...

English, our common language, provides a shared foundation which has allowed people from every corner of the world to come together to build the American nation...

While English is our common language, government at all levels is actively undermining its unifying function. All of the benefits our Nation reaps from our linguistic harmony will be lost if ill-advised government policies continue to foment linguistic separatism...In America, where the principal language of interaction is English, its use and active promotion through government policy can pave the way for unprecedented opportunity and national prosperity. But just as a common language opens the door to communication, so too the lack of it erects a barrier not easily overcome. If the common bond of a national language is neglected and denigrated long enough... the nation itself will ultimately suffer. Such an important key to realizing the American Dream ought not to be kept from those who come to the United States. As we continue to welcome new Americans to our shores, we must ensure that misguided national policies do not undermine the important role of the common language of national understanding. English as the official language of our government encourages its use by all Americans, so as to secure brighter opportunities and better future for us all.[57]

That was June 5, 1996, nearly two months before the U.S. House of Representatives passed the Bill Emerson English Language Empowerment Act (H.R. 123), the first ever English Language Amendment (ELA) to the federal Constitution passed in Congress.[58] This statement was the only one the Republican Party has ever issued in support of Official English at the federal level. Neither does the Republican National Committee (RNC) support Official English as party policy, nor has Official English ever found a place in the presidential platforms of the GOP.

But that has not kept Republican State Committees from supporting Official English in any way. Minnesota is not one of the 30 states that have declared English as the official language of their governments, but the Minnesota Republican Party declared in its 2002 platform: "Republicans want government to be honest, efficient and responsive to individual citizens. Therefore, we advocate: Making English the official language in Minnesota."[59]

Texas does not have an Official English law either and its then governor, George W. Bush—president of the United States between 2005 and 2009—even refused to take notice when a small town on the Mexican border, El Cenizo, declared Spanish as its official language and banned the use of English in August, 1999. Even then, the Jefferson County Republican Party of Texas supported Official English in its 2002 resolutions:

> We recognize that the majority of bilingual education programs in Texas have not been successful. Thus, we urge the Texas legislature to follow the state of California's lead in terminating bilingual education. Further, we support the immediate adoption of American English as the

> official language of the government of Texas and of the government of the United States of America.[60]

In Nebraska, which had declared English as its official language through a constitutional amendment way back in 1920, the state Republican Party categorically stated in 2002 that it was high time English became the official language of the United States through an English Language Amendment to the federal Constitution.[61]

Though Wyoming got its Official English law in 1996, the state's Republican Party, in its 2002 resolutions, declared English as "the official language" in the American education system, virtually ruling out bilingual education.[62]

But 2000 was not 1996. Texas governor George W. Bush was fast emerging the frontrunner for the Republican presidential nomination. Bush hailed from a state with a huge Latino population (28%), and though he was popular among Latinos, he needed to win as any votes he could from the community if he wanted to be president. In 1998, addressing delegates to the national convention of the League of United Latin American Citizens (LULAC), Governor Bush had tried distancing himself from his party colleagues' attacks on bilingual education and support for Official English. He told LULAC delegates at the Dallas convention that his approach was not English *Only*, but English *Plus*. He, however, added that he did not favor bilingual education if it failed to achieve the objective of teaching English to Spanish-speaking children:

> If the bilingual program serves to teach our children English, then we ought to say, 'Thank you very much, and leave them in place'. And if the

> bilingual program locks someone into Spanish and does not achieve stated objectives, then we must say 'Change the program, eliminate the program'.[63]

The delegates had roared their approval of the governor's approach. They also lauded Bush when he spoke out against the use of the U.S. military to patrol the border with Mexico. Interestingly, along with its Spanish-only measure of 1999, El Cenizo also passed a Safe Haven Ordinance, forbidding city employees and officials from asking residents whether they were legal immigrants or citizens or to help agencies like the Border Patrol and the Immigration and Naturalization service find illegals; city employees who violated the ordinance were liable to be fired.[64] Governor Bush did nothing to reverse either the Spanish-only measure or the Safe Haven Ordinance.

Again, in an interview to Chris Matthews on May 31, 2000, Governor Bush reiterated his commitment to English *Plus* and opposition to English *Only*.[65] What is noticeable here is the use of the term English *Only*, and not Official English, by Governor Bush. There might be electoral compulsions behind the use of this offensive and misleading term: in order to attract as many Latino votes as possible, Bush painted a false picture of Official English, saying it was nothing but English *Only*. No doubt then that Bush got 35% of the Hispanic vote in the presidential election, up from 20% that Senator Bob Dole (R-KS) captured in 1996. Vice President Al Gore, Bush's challenger, secured 62%. But none could beat the record of President Bill Clinton who carried 72% of the Latino vote nationwide in 1996 and 61% in 1992 (much higher than Bush as a first time candidate). Clearly, Democrats were way ahead of Republicans in terms of Hispanic electoral support.

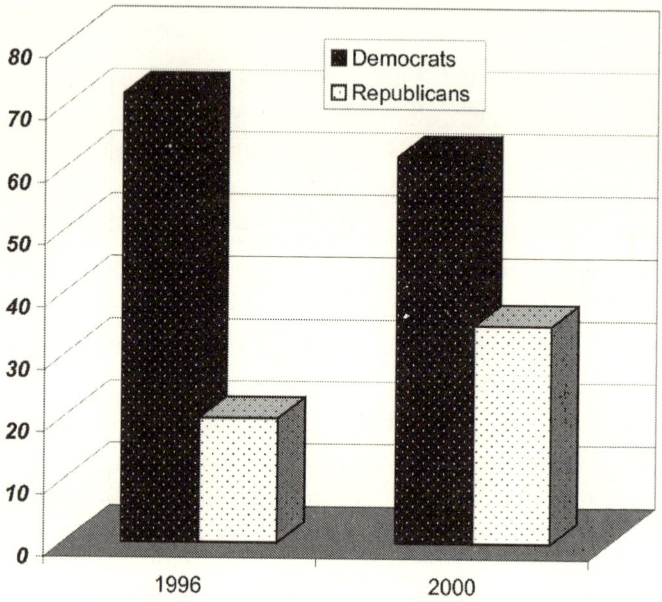

[DATA: *The Washington Post* (see text)].

Fig. 14. Latino Voter Support for Democrats and Republicans in Presidential Elections, 1996 and 2000

A national survey of Latinos conducted by *The Washington Post*, Henry J. Kaiser Family Foundation and Harvard University between June 30 and August 30, 1999 interviewed 2,417 Latino adults (818 Mexicans, 318 Puerto Ricans, 312 Cubans and 593 Central or South Americans and others). Of them, 44% identified themselves as Democrats and 16% as Republicans, whereas 40% were undecided. 58% Latinos believed Democrats always did a better job in coping with the main problems facing the nation whereas 25% trusted Republicans. Most important—and this is bad news for Republicans ideologically—67% Latinos favored bigger government whereas only 28% of Whites wanted it.[66]

Republicans would do better to try and tap the 40% floating Latino vote. Already, there are indications that Latinos believe the Democratic Party has taken them for granted, and realization has dawned that they have been treated as a voting bloc by the party. Hispanic leaders have told Democratic officials that Hispanics no longer constituted the party's political base because President Bush and Republicans have made inroads into it.[67] In fact, a New Democrat Network Poll conducted by Sergio Bendixen in June, 2003 showed that Hispanic presidential preference for Democrats have fallen to 48%, down from 62% in the 2000 elections.[68] The same poll found that 58% of Hispanics still preferred to vote Democratic in the 2004 congressional elections, 20% said they will vote Republican, another 20% were undecided. Clearly Latinos have no problem with amiable candidates like President Bush, even if he was a Republican; only that they are still apprehensive of the intentions and inclinations of the Republican Party. Large numbers of Latinos still perceive the Republican Party—and Democrats are to a great extent responsible for this perception—as immigrant-baiting, supportive of English *Only* laws and the dismantling of bilingual education, and favoring the denial of government services even to legal immigrants.[69] Then RNC Co-Chairman Pat Harrison's hard-selling of his party to Latinos as the party of upward mobility, entrepreneurial freedom and patriotism does not seem to have cut much ice among the nation's largest minority voting bloc.

But there is no doubt that Latinos are increasingly looking at the Republican Party as an option. Maria Cardona, a former Democratic National Committee (DNC) official and director of the Hispanic Project at the New Democratic Network (NDN) said in an interview:

> We can no longer be considered a base vote (for the Democrats). If they don't follow up, they risk losing additional (Hispanic) support to the Republicans. Democrats cannot take Latinos for granted, or they will suffer the consequences. Democratic support among Latinos has been trimmed.[70]

Both the Bush brothers, the former president (also when he was Texas governor) and former Governor Jeb Bush of Florida, had realized the need to have good, working relationships with the considerable Hispanic populations in their respective states and had indeed labored long and hard to foster a strong bond with Hispanic voters, dispelling in the process the old impression that minorities always supported Democrats. In their states, the Bush brothers' message of promoting small businesses and cutting taxes hit the right note with Hispanics. This achievement, though limited, is generally considered remarkable because African American and other minorities have traditionally seen no merit in Republican policies; as a result, Republican efforts to reach out to minorities were almost always doomed to failure.[71] Since African Americans are known to vote en bloc for the Democratic Party, a swing in many states of the Hispanic vote in favor of Republicans may be enough to offset the African American recalcitrance. Cuban Americans, because of the GOP's stringent anti-Castro ideology, have always identified with the party. A 2001 survey on Latinos' party alignment by the Tomás Rivera Policy Institute shows Florida to be the only state where more Hispanics identified themselves as Republicans (56%) than as

Democrats (34%).[72] Republicans may also find favor with Puerto Ricans whom the Newt Gingrich (R-GA)-led US House of Representatives gave the right to vote 'yes' or 'no' through the only legislation of its kind. And, Republicans can look forward to a new camaraderie on the part of Mexican Americans whose longstanding demand for relaxing laws on illegal immigrants was met by President Bush's latest measure in that regard.

But Republicans should never use Latinos as voting blocs; otherwise, there would be no difference between them and Democrats. The GOP should make all efforts to reach out to Latinos, disabusing them of the notion that it was a party of 'Anglos'. As a first step, it should purge itself of whatever nativist tendencies there still are within the party. Virulent anti-immigrant party leaders like former California governor Pete Wilson should be reined in. Most importantly, as one Republican activist has pointed out, the GOP should ideologically win over Latinos. There is no reason to believe that Latinos will not vote for the party if it stuck to its core beliefs like equality of opportunity, traditional values like faith and family, individual rights and responsibilities, smaller but efficient government, lower taxes, merit, economic opportunity, and strong national defense; only that Republicans should not alienate Latinos by stereotyping them and calling them un-American.[73] The objective should be to develop, and then sustain a permanent relationship with Latinos; if they are no more treated as immigrants but as an integral part of American society, they would never hesitate to embrace the "party of Americans".

The support of Cuban Americans for Republicans needs to be replicated among Puerto Ricans and Mexican Americans as well. As Cuban Americans have been won over ideologically, so too should Mexican Americans and Puerto Ricans. By its very nature, the GOP can appeal to various minorities only on the basis of its ideology and not on ethnic lines. An ethnic appeal would mean treating minorities as voting blocs, something Republicans have never done.

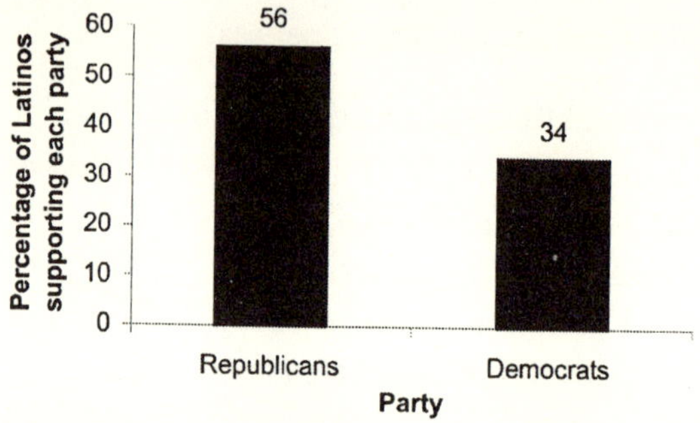

[DATA: *Tomás Rivera Policy Institute*, 2001 (see text)].

Fig. 15. Party Identification Of Latinos In Florida 2001

George W. Bush has walked the extra mile to court Latinos; however, he had got the lowest percentage of Latino votes (35%) when compared to the last two Republican presidents: his father George H.W. Bush (47%) in 1988 and the late Ronald W. Reagan (40% and 47%) in 1980 and 1984 respectively.

But what is it about Latinos that has kept them from the Republican Party, the "party of Americans"? Why has Americanization, which had succeeded among earlier generations of immigrants, failed among Latinos?

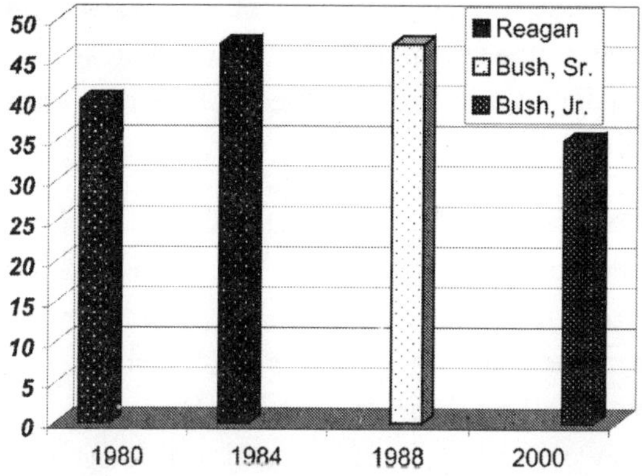

[DATA: James S. Marotta; TRPI; Matt Towery (see text)]

Fig. 16. Republican Presidential Winners And The Latino Vote 1980, 1984, 1988, 2000

Cultural pluralism as a theory of assimilation has challenged the very concept of assimilation as never before. Arguing that assimilation was not always a positive experience—either for society or for immigrants—and that the Melting Pot was nothing but Anglo-conformity (there cannot be a bigger attempt at theoretical confusion, because the Melting Pot and Anglo-conformity are different models of assimilation) and by emphasizing diversity and ethnicity, it has enabled immigrants to avoid assimilation entirely. The result: rather than American society transforming immigrants, immigrants are transforming American society. As Linda Chavez has rightly pointed out, in the ideology of cultural pluralism, an individual's worldview was determined by race, ethnicity, gender and class; no one was really capable to escape his or her cultural determinants.[74] In their zeal to preserve cultural diversity, cultural pluralists have created an environment in which political correctness reigns supreme; nothing can be done that might hurt a group. In terms of assimilation, this can be easily translated: society should show tolerance toward various immigrant groups and cultures, and even if they show intolerance toward the culture of the society they live in and refuse to assimilate, the host society should take it in its stride.

Though the United States as a nation promotes diversity increasingly and unfailingly, there are underlying concerns that the more emphasis there was on the factors that set people apart, the more likely it was that society will end up divided. The late Samuel P. Huntington voiced his concern about "a major potential threat" to America's "cultural and political integrity", pointing out that the "single most immediate and most serious challenge to America's traditional identity" came "from the immense and continuing immigration from Latin America, especially Mexico, and the fertility rates of these immigrants."[75] He was peeved with Hispanics for their refusal to assimilate; the reason, Huntington said, was that Hispanics were "comfortable with their own culture and often contemptuous of American culture."[76] The professor warned that the result will be a polarized America composed of "two peoples with two cultures".[77]

Not that Huntington's is an emotional outburst. The great majority of the nation's 29 million Hispanics are from Mexico, and they, more than any other group, are redefining the concept of assimilation; they have become the main focus for questions about how the United States was assimilating immigrants or how it was being transformed by immigrants. Huntington did have a word of caution: "The assimilation successes of the past are unlikely to be duplicated with the contemporary flood of immigrants from Latin America."[78]

True, it is very easy for Mexicans to get into the

United States: by either swimming across the Rio Grande or trudging through the Arizona desert, dodging the Border Patrol. Never before have so many immigrants come from a single country (Mexico) or from a single linguistic source (Spanish-speaking Latin America). This is also the first time that such large numbers of immigrants are coming from a contiguous country.

True again that Hispanics—the new immigrants especially—tend to cluster in "niche" occupations, live in segregated neighborhoods, and worship in separate churches. They congregate heavily in the American Southwest and consequently develop much greater cohesion than earlier immigrant groups. All of these impede the process of assimilation.

True again that Hispanics have a high birth rate: 106 births per 1000 women of child-bearing age yearly, compared to only 68 of the total population.[79] Huntington drew notice to this high fertility rate among Latinos, something that Dr. John Tanton did nearly two decades ago and brought upon himself a hail of violent protests that forced him to quit the chairmanship of U.S. English. In fact the Hispanic population itself has leaped 58% between 1990 and 2000, whereas the nation as a whole showed a 13% increase in population during the same time.

And, it is true that many Mexican Americans of the second or third generation who were brought up speaking English learned Spanish as adults. This despite the fact that more than 90% of second-generation Mexican Americans speak fluent English, triggering a fear among many Hispanic parents that their children may or may not choose to preserve their ancestors' language and cultural traditions. Parents who see language as the most important symbol of living culture, converse with children in Spanish at home, even if they were fluent English-speakers themselves.[80] Latino families generally cook Spanish food at home, celebrate traditional Hispanic domestic ritualistic parties (like the *quinceañera*, a 15-year old girl's passage into adulthood) and Hispanic holidays (like the *Cinco de Mayo*), and maintain the kind of close family ties typical of Latino culture.[81] As Maria Jacinto, a 32 year-old Hispanic housewife residing in Omaha (NE) said,

> It's difficult to adapt to the culture here. In the Hispanic tradition, the family comes first, not money. It's important for our children not to be influenced too much by the *gueros* (a derogatory term for "blondies," denoting all white English-speaking Americans).[82]

Many Latino parents fear that their cultural traditions were threatened by the Americanization of their children.

But just as there are many Latino children who learn English quickly and adopt American habits, there are many who insist on the performance of Latino rituals like the *quinceañera*.[83] In fact, Latinos are said to follow different paths to incorporation into American society, a process known as "segmented" assimilation. This ranges from blending into the vast American middle class (and becoming ethnically anonymous), to a sort of "downward assimilation" into an adversarial underclass, to a buffered integration into "immigrant enclaves" (and then fail to assimilate). Interestingly, members of the same family do take divergent paths to assimilation.[84]

Since the purpose of the U.S. immigration system

was the creation of new Americans, admission criteria should be revamped to prefer only those who wished to become American and naturalization should aim only at Americanization and nothing else, says one expert on assimilation.[85] There is no doubt that unassimilated immigrants were being reinforced by large numbers of immigrants from their own countries rather than getting absorbed into the culture and society of America. Since America had a history of intermittent immigration wherein large immigrant waves were later assimilated during pauses in immigration, immigration reduction and assimilation should be regarded complementary. The goal of Americanization can only be facilitated by smaller numbers of immigrants.[86]

However, the immigration reform bill introduced of late in the 111th Congress, is expected to make matters worse by seeking to legalize nearly 12 million illegal immigrants (mostly from Latin America) once it became law.

Not only are immigrants no longer expected to assimilate, federal and state governments pursue public policies that impede, even reverse, the process of Americanization. The problem is compounded by the fact that both cultural pluralists in the United States and officials and opinion makers in countries which send hordes of immigrants (like Mexico) are encouraging those immigrants to become not Americans (or at least hyphenated Americans) but *ampersand* Americans (Mexican and American, for example), citizens who maintained a dual identity and did not get transformed but transformed their host country after immigration. No doubt, then, that El Cenizo Mayor Rafael Rodriguez, an illegal immigrant himself, displayed both American and

Mexican flags in his office. This, despite the fact that immigrants in the United States were under no obligation to preserve their native cultures – something that even pluralist philosopher Michael Walzer admits:

> They (immigrants) are not... bound to the remembrance (of their past). Just as their ancestors escaped the old country, so they can if they choose escape their old identities.... He (the immigrant) may become an American simply, an American and nothing else, freeing himself from the hyphenation.... But, free from hyphenation, he seems also free from ethnicity: "American" is not one of the ethnic groups recognized in the United States census.[87]

If complete dissolution of ethnic identities was the hallmark of Americanism, attempts at ethnic revival were un-American—even anti-American—by the same logic.

John J. Miller, a leading opponent of multiculturalism but a supporter of mass immigration nevertheless, admitted in a recent article in the *National Review* that demographic changes in Texas fueled largely by Mexican immigration is reinforcing the ranks of Democrats, the "party of immigrants".[88] Prospective immigrants, even before migrating to the United States, now seem to know about the Democratic Party and its multiculturalist inclinations. There is enough evidence that reinforcing immigrants with new immigrants increases political pressure on Americans to conform to them rather than the other way round. The pressure is so great that even Republican politicians (like former President George W. Bush) are forced to learn Spanish and address their constituents in that language. Here lies the success of the anti-assimilationist, radically multiculturalist, *ampersand* philosophy.

Putting a stop to mass immigration, and amending the federal Constitution to make English the official language of the United States can help reverse this trend. Republican administrations of late have not been very successful with the first, but Republicans for more than two decades are trying relentlessly to achieve the second. The Senate's killing of H.R. 123—the Bill Emerson English Language Empowerment Act of 1996, passed by the U.S. House of Representatives in the 104th Congress—could not dampen their spirits.

In the 107th Congress was introduced two bills—the English Language Unity Act of 2001 (H.R. 1984) by Representative Bob Barr (R-GA) and the National Language Act of 2001 (H.R. 931) by Representative Peter King (R-NY)—to make English the official language of the United States. Forty-nine of H.R. 931's fifty-one co-sponsors were Republicans. H.R. 1984 was also overwhelmingly Republican-sponsored. In fact, H.R. 931 was revolutionary. It sought to repeal the Bilingual Education Act (1968) and the 1975 amendments to the Voting Rights Act (1965) requiring multilingual ballots and voter assistance, apart from requiring that all public ceremonies be conducted and the oath of allegiance to the Constitution be administered by the Immigration and Naturalization Service to new immigrants in English.

After H.R. 1984 was introduced in the U.S. House of Representatives in the 107th Congress on May 24, 2001, Representative Steve King (R-IA) tabled an identical bill (H.R. 997) — the English Language Unity Act of 2003—in the 108th Congress on February 27, 2003. Elected to the

House from Iowa's 5th congressional district in 2002, Representative King, a former state senator, had drafted the Iowa English Language Reaffirmation Act of 2001 that made English the official language of Iowa the following year. A longtime supporter of Official English, Representative King's objectives in establishing English as the official language of the United States—as it was in Iowa—was to encourage the assimilation of immigrants and prevent the growth of linguistic enclaves.[89] Not surprisingly, then, 100 of H.R. 997's 105 sponsors were Republicans.

H.R. 1984 wanted "to reaffirm" and H.R. 997 wanted "to declare" English as "the official language of the United States" and "to establish a uniform English language rule for naturalization and to avoid misconstructions of the English language texts of the Laws of the United States." H.R. 997—and interestingly, H.R. 1984—resembled the Iowa Act of 2001 to a great extent in their findings. According to the two English Language Unity Acts, "Throughout the history of the United States, the common thread binding individuals of differing backgrounds has been the English language" and "Among the powers reserved to the States respectively is the power to establish the English language as the official language of the respective States, and otherwise to promote the English language within the respective States." [H.R. 1984 and H.R. 997, Section 2 (2) & (3)]. Both declared that "The official language of the United States is English" [H.R. 1984 and H.R. 997, Section 161] and also that "The official functions of the Government of the United States shall be conducted in English" [H.R. 1984, Section 162(a) and H.R. 997, Section 163 (a)]. Most importantly, both sought to establish a uniform English language rule for naturalization: "All citizens should be able to read and understand generally the English language text of the *Declaration of Independence*, the Constitution, and the Laws of the United States made in pursuance of the Constitution" and that "All naturalization ceremonies shall be conducted in English" [H.R. 1984, Section 163 (a) & (b), H.R. 997, Section 164 (a) & (b)]. Only that H.R. 997 puts an additional obligation on federal government officials in preserving and enhancing the role of English as the official language of the United States which would "include encouraging greater opportunities to learn the English language" [H.R. 997, Section 162].[90] Both H.R 1984 and H.R. 997 were referred to the U.S. House Committee on Education and the Workforce and the U.S. House Committee on the Judiciary. Both H.R. 1984 and H.R. 997 met inglorious ends. This made James Crawford feel that the "Congressional Republican leadership has abandoned the cause" of Official English and that he did not "expect them to embrace it again anytime soon".[91]

Rep. King reintroduced H.R. 997 (the English Language Unity Act of 2005) in the 109th Congress on March 1, 2005. Out of its 164 co-sponsors, 5 were Democrats, 3 were unattached, and the rest of them were Republicans. It was referred to the House Committee on Education and Workforce (Subcommittee on Education Reform) and the House Committee on Judiciary (Subcommittee on Constitution). The purpose of this proposed legislation, based on findings similar to the earlier bills, was

> To declare English as the official language of the United States, to establish a uniform English language rule for naturalization, and to avoid misconstructions of the English language texts of the laws of the United States, pursuant to

> Congress' powers to provide for the general welfare of the United States and to establish a uniform rule of naturalization under article I, section 8, of the Constitution.

Needless to say, this bill also never became law. Rep. Peter King (R-NY) introduced H.R. 4408 (the National Language Act of 2005) in the 109th Congress on November 18, 2005. Sponsored by 18 other Republicans and 1 Democrat, the bill was referred to the same committees as H.R. 997. A simple bill to "declare English as the official language of the Government of the United States", it was killed in committee.

Rep Steve King had introduced H.R. 997 (the English Language Unity Act of 2007) once more, this time in the Democratic-controlled 110th Congress on February 12, 2007. Co-sponsored by 141 Republicans, 8 Democrats, 4 unattached, and 1 Independent, the bill was referred to the same committees as its dead predecessors and never saw the light of the day again. What is noteworthy is that even though their party was now in a majority in the U.S. House of Representatives, the number of Democrats sponsoring an English Language Amendment (ELA) had risen; in fact, it was more than when the House was Republican-controlled.

After the passage of H.R. 123 in 1996 and the failure of the U.S. Senate to ratify it subsequently, the introduction of ELAs in Congress had become a largely symbolic gesture for Republicans. Since Republican efforts in the states to declare English as their official language were met with one success after another, Republicans in Congress could not have sat idle. They continued to introduce ELAs in Congress with religious regularity.

Accordingly, Rep. Steve King has tabled a fresh H.R. 997 (the English Language Unity Act of 2009) on February 11 this year (111th Congress). Referred to the usual committees, its future is pretty evident. Interestingly, starting 2001 five English Language Unity Acts have been introduced in Congress, one every two years. Every year since 2003, Rep. Steve King was the chief sponsor. And every time he was the chief sponsor, the bill was numbered H.R. 997.

The 1996 legislation passed by the U.S. House of Representatives marked the first victory of the Official English movement at the federal level. The Inhofe Amendment of 2006 was the second.

Oklahoma's Republican Senator James M. Inhofe's National Language Amendment to the immigration reform bill—the Comprehensive Immigration Reform Act of 2006—in the United States Senate marked the culmination of a movement that began exactly 25 years ago. The Inhofe Amendment, apart from declaring English as America's "national language", relieved the federal government from any obligation to provide services to citizens and immigrants in any language other than English and required every immigrant legally entering the United States to learn English. It also recognized the pre-eminence of the English language in American society. The amendment was passed with overwhelming support (62-35) on May 18, 2006. Even though it was a bipartisan measure, more Republicans than Democrats voted for it.[92] Since the U.S. House of Representatives failed to ratify it with matching legislation, Sen. Inhofe has introduced S. 991 (the English language Unity Act of 2009) in the U.S. Senate on May 6 this year. It has been referred to the Senate Committee on Homeland Security and

Governmental Affairs. What will happen to it in a Democratic-controlled Senate is not difficult to guess.

Though the U.S. House of Representatives passed an Official English bill only once (in 1996), Republicans since 1981 have regularly moved ELAs to the federal Constitution. By these actions stretching over two decades, Republicans have identified themselves with the Official English cause. There has been no hesitation on their part in admitting that English was the language of Americans and it was the tie that bound all Americans into a single nation. Till the time the goal of complete assimilation of immigrants into American society was achieved, more ELAs would be proposed. Because Republicans know—so do others, even if they do not admit it—that assimilation was the end, Official English was the means.

Not surprising, then, that even though the Republican Party has officially refrained from endorsing Official English, party supporters and sympathizers embraced it with open arms. A survey authorized by Linda Chavez, when she took over as president of U.S. English, showed that 71% of the organization members identified themselves as Republican. That was in 1987. Another 1992 survey demonstrated that in California and Texas, the two states with the largest Hispanic populations, a little more than 78% of English-speaking voters who favored Official English legislation were staunch Republicans; also among Hispanic voters more Republicans (40%) than Democrats (20%) favored such legislation.[93] In voters' minds, then, Official English was Republican policy.

The revolutionary election of 2004

It was after 12 years that a Republican president was seeking re-election. In 1992, it was President George H.W.

Bush. This time his son—George W. Bush, 43rd president of the United States—was running for a second term. The father, an opponent of English *Only* measures,[94]lost to an avowed multiculturalist, then Arkansas Governor Bill Clinton. The son, a more vocal opponent of Official English and champion of English *Plus*, won re-election, beating another multiculturalist, Senator John F. Kerry (D-MA).

But what is most remarkable about the Bush victory is that he managed to substantially improve his share of the Hispanic vote: from 35% in 2000, it rose to 45% in 2004.[95] Even though it is still less than his father's Latino vote share in 1988 (47%) and Ronald Reagan's in 1984 (47%), this 10 percentage point increase is a groundbreaking achievement considering that Reagan could increase his share of Latino votes by only 7 percentage points when he sought re-election in 1984.

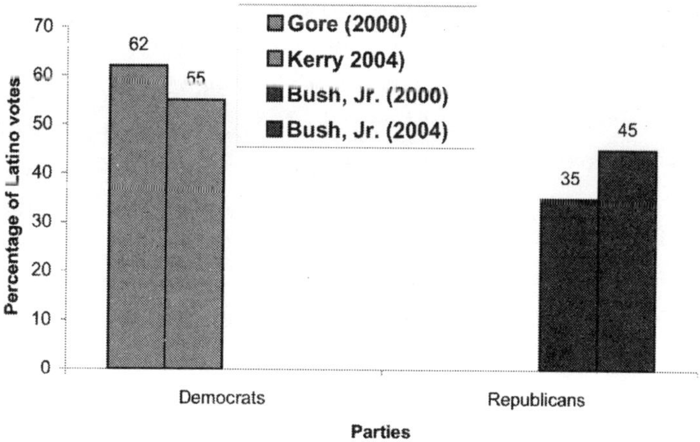

[DATA: *The Washington Post, www.newsmax.com*]

Fig. 17. Latino Voter Support for Democrats and Republicans in Presidential Elections, 2000 & 2004

How George W. Bush had endeared himself to

Hispanics has already been discussed. He had worked very hard to win Hispanics over by not only endorsing bilingual education and proposing English *Plus* but also distancing himself from his fellow Republicans who supported Official English and wanted strict control of illegal immigration from across the Mexican border. As president, he did not withdraw Executive Order 13166, signed by President William Jefferson Clinton on August 11, 2000 to improve access to federally assisted programs and services for persons with limited English proficiency (LEP)[96], much to the chagrin of pro-Official English Republicans. If his opposition to benefit cuts to documented aliens and rejection of the idea that children of undocumented workers should be denied public education—gestures that made him hugely popular among Latinos—was not enough, there was another reason behind his success with the Latino vote in 2004: his emphasis on traditional social values—faith and family—and particularly his opposition to gay marriage; Latinos, themselves devout Catholics deeply committed to traditional values, could not ignore Bush.[97] That the Republican ideal of economic opportunity and upward mobility had caught the imagination of the Latinos was evident from the fact that native-born, English-speaking, middle class Latinos had responded to Bush's appeal with their solid electoral support. Surely, Hispanics were no longer a secure constituency—a base vote—for Democrats.[98]

REFERENCES

1 *The United States Statistical Yearbook, 1999-2000*, p. 169-201

2 ibid. Also "Toward a United America", US English, *www.us-english. org /inc/official/ states.asp* (accessed on 09/21/09)

3 Charles V. Dale and Mark Gurevitz, "Legal Analysis of Proposals to Make English the Official Language of the United States" (Washington, DC), October 7, 1995.

4 See Chapter 1 (B) of this book.

5 Karen L. Adams and Daniel T. Brink (Ed.), *Perspectives on Official English: The Campaign for English as the Official Language of the USA* (New York, NY, 1990), p. 197

6 Dale and Gurevitz, op. cit.

7 ibid.

8 "Census 2000; Bilingual Education", *Migration News*, Volume 6, No. 2, April 2000. Also, Kenneth J. Cooper, "Riley Endorses Two-Way Bilingual Education", *Washington Post*, March 16, 2000

9 Dale and Gurevitz, op. cit.

10 ibid.

11 ibid.

12 ibid.

13 For details about *Meyer V Nebraska,* see Chapter 2 (B) of this book.

14 Dennis Baron, *The English Only Question: An Official Language for Americans?* (New Haven, CT, 1990), p. 10 & 107

15 Dale and Gurevitz, op.cit.

16 For New Mexico's English Plus Resolution, see Chapter 1 (A) of this book.

17 Jamie B. Draper and Martha Jimenez, "Language Debates in the United States: A Decade in Review", in *EPIC Events 2,* no.5 (1990)

18 George Skelton, "Deukmejian Opposes 3 Controversial Propositions", *Los Angeles Times*, September 03, 1986

19 ibid.

20 Erik P. Bucy and Michael J. Ensley, "Issue Benefactors or Issue Victims? Ballot Initiative Influence on the Vote for California Governor, 1982-1998", *The California Journal of Politics & Policy*, Volume 1, Issue 2, Article 12, 2009

21 Dale and Gurevitz, op.cit.

22 ibid.

23 ibid.

24 Gov. Richard D. Lamm and Gary Imhoff, *The Immigration Time Bomb: The Fragmenting of America* (New York, NY, 1985), p.115

25 Personal correspondence with former governor Richard D. Lamm of Colorado through e-mail dated February 7, 2004.

26 Raymond Tatalovich, *Nativism Reborn? The Official English Language Movement and the American States* (Lexington, KY, 1995), p. 247

27 Dale and Gurevitz, op.cit.

28 Quoted in Tatalovich, op. cit. p. 99

29 "Martinez, rights leaders meet about English rule", *The Gainesville Sun*, November 24, 1988, p. 4B

30 Dale and Gurevitz, op.cit.

31 ibid.

32 ibid.

33 ibid.

34 ibid.

35 *Puerto Rico Organization for Political Action (PROPA) V. Kusper*, 490F. 2nd 575 (7th Cir. 1973)

36 Dale and Gurevitz, op.cit.

37 ibid.

38 Tatalovich, op. cit. pp. 204-5

39 Dale and Gurevitz, op. cit

40 ibid.

41 For President Clinton's objections to H.R. 123, see Chapter 3 (B) of this book.

42 Robert D. King, "Should English Be The Law?", *The Atlantic Monthly*, Vol. 279, No. 4, April 1997, pp. 55-64

43 Dale and Gurevitz, op.cit.

44 ibid.

45 For details regarding *Lau v. Nichols*, see Chapter 2 (B) of this book.

46 "Arizona Report: Bilingual Ed. Less Likely To Produce English Proficiency", *http://www.proenglish.org/issues/education/azresults.html* (accessed on 10/06/09)

47 Dale and Gurevitz, op. cit

48 ibid.

49 ibid.

50 ibid.

51 ibid.

52 Heather May and Judy Fahys, "Its Official: English Only", *The Salt Lake Tribune*, November 8, 2000

53 "Iowa Passes English-Only Measure", *Newsmax.com Wires*, February 27, 2002.

54 Dale and Gurevitz, op. cit.

55 "Governor's Signature Makes English the Official Language of Kansas", *Business Wire*, May 11, 2007

56 Louisiana, 1864, *Proceedings*, 47. Cited in Baron, op.cit., p. 85

57 House Republican Policy Committee Statement on Official English, "Welcoming Immigrants to a Diverse America: English as our Common Language of Mutual Understanding" (Issued June 5, 1996), *www.englishfirst.org.*

58 For a detailed discussion on H.R. 123, please turn to Chapter 4 (B) of this book.

59 *www. rnc.org*

60 ibid.

61 ibid.

62 ibid.

63 "Texas Governor Bush Steps away from GOP Attacks on Bilingual Education", *www.Allpolitics.com.,* July 2, 1998

64 Madeline Baro Diaz, "Border City Goes All-Spanish", *Associated Press,* August 19, 1999. For a detailed discussion, turn to chapter 2 (B) of this book.

65 Governor George W. Bush, "Hardball With Chris Mathews", *www.foreign policy2000.org.*, May 31, 2000

66 William Booth, "A Key Constituency Defies Easy Labeling" *The Washington Post*, February 14, 2000.

67 Donald Lambro, "Republicans draw Hispanic voters from Democrats", *The Washington Times*, July 13, 2003.

68 Cited in ibid.

69 Booth, op.cit.

70 Quoted in Lambro, op.cit.

71 Matt Towery, "Inside the numbers: The Latino Vote", *www.townhall.com*, January 13, 2004

72 A Critique of "Impossible Dream or Distant Reality?", Latinos and Party Alignment in the 21st century: A Policy Statement by the Tomás Rivera Policy Institute, *www.trpi.org,* August 22, 2001.

73 James S. Marotta, "The Republican Party and the Hispanic Voter", *www.voterzview.com,* July 30, 1999

74 Linda Chavez, "Cultural Diversity," *Letter to the Editor of 'The Chronicle of Higher Education',* July 18, 1990.

75 Samuel P. Huntington, "The Hispanic Challenge", *Foreign Policy*, March/April, 2004. Quoted in Peter Carlson, "Hey, Professor, Assimilate This", *The Washington Post,* March 9, 2004

76 ibid.

77 ibid.

78 ibid.

79 Kathie Neff Ragsdale, "Becoming American, staying Latino", *The Eagle-Tribune,* August 18, 2001

80 ibid.

81 ibid.

82 William Branigin, "Immigrants Shunning Idea of Assimilation," *The Washington Post*, May 25, 1998

83 Ragsdale, op.cit.

84 Branigin, op.cit.

85 W. James Antle III, "Americanizing Newcomers Again: Immigration Reforms Promote Americanization", *Ether Zone*, November 5, 2002

86 ibid.

87 Michael Walzer, *What it means to be an American: Essays on the American Experience* (New York, NY, 1992), p. 28

88 John J. Miller, "The Hispanic Republic of Texas: Its coming. Soon," *National Review*, Vol. 54, No. 19, October 14, 2002, pp. 32-35

89 Interview to U.S. English, *www.us-english.org*

90 ibid.

91 James Crawford, personal correspondence with the author, February 2, 2004

92 Saumyajit Ray, "Official, at last: Bush and immigration", *Central Chronicle* (Bhopal), June 5, 2006

93 Carol Schmid, "The English Only Movement: Social Bases of Support and Opposition Among Anglos and Latinos" in James Crawford (ed.), *Language Loyalties: A Source Book on the Official English Controversy* (Chicago, 1992), p. 205

94 Huntington, *Who Are We? America's Great Debate* (London, 2004), p. 168

95 Dick Morris, "The Hispanic Vote Elects Bush", *www.newsmax.com.*, November 5, 2004

96 "Executive Order 13166: Improving access to Services for Persons with Limited English Proficiency", United States Department of Justice, Civil Rights Division, Coordination and Review Section, *http://www.usdoj.gov/crt/cor/13166.php*

97 Morris, op cit.

98 Martin Kasindorf, "Hispanic Voters paint and a new picture," *USA TODAY*, November 10, 2004. However, Sen. Barack H. Obama (D-IL) managed 67% of the Hispanic vote in the 2008 presidential election, compared to only 32% for Sen. John McCain (R-AZ).

6

A Nation of Immigrants, Not A Multilingual Boarding House

"We have room for but one language here and that is the English language, for we intend to see that the crucible turn our people out as Americans, of American nationality, and not as dwellers in a polyglot boarding house."
– **Theodore Roosevelt**

(A) *AMERO-CONFORMITY* : TOWARD A NEW THEORY OF ASSIMILATION

America is a nation of immigrants, but it is a nation nevertheless. It is not a *lebensraum* (a living space) where people from different parts of the world come, use it for their own benefit during the time they stay there, and ultimately leave without developing any emotional attachment or a sense of political loyalty toward the land. No immigrant—legal or illegal—to the United States arrives with the intention of leaving. For an immigrant, the old country is a closed chapter, politically if not always emotionally. For subsequent generations, the old country is not even a memory and it ceases to provide any sense of identity. Some know and love to talk of their origins—with curiosity, not nostalgia—whereas most simply could not have cared less. A child born in the United States to Indian American parents would be more likely to celebrate Halloween and not Holi because that is what children in America usually do. Even if the native culture is maintained and the native language spoken at home, the child knows and grows up knowing that they have no use in the world outside. If he/she has to stay, live and work in the United States, he/she has to conform to Americans and their public way of life.

Since almost all of the original European immigrants who founded the American republic were of British descent, subsequent entrants to the United States from Europe were expected and required to conform to the culture of the English- speaking population, accepting the desirability of preserving Anglo-American political institutions, the English language, and English-oriented cultural patterns as dominant and standard in American life. This type of assimilation refers to an ideological tendency commonly known as "Anglo-conformity," a phrase introduced by Stewart G. Cole and Mildred Wiese Cole in their Work *Minorities and the American Promise* (1954).

But assimilation in the United States worked differently, resulting in the forging of a new American cultural type out of the diverse heritages of Europe. Anglicization did not touch all spheres of American life, only the English language became the language of all Americans. Newcomers from Europe did give up the cultural forms of their native lands and adopt the behavior and attitudes of the dominant Anglo-Saxon mold of their new country, but they also made substantial contributions to American life and society ranging from political philosophy and practice to food and beverages. This required a fresh look at the nature of American assimilation.

The requirement was fulfilled to a great extent by J. Hector St. John Crevecoeur, an American of French descent, in his *Letters from an American Farmer* (1782). In that work, Crevecoeur described an American as "either an European, or the descendant of an European...who leaving behind him all his ancient prejudices and manners, receives new ones from the new mode of life he has embraced, the new government he obeys, and the new rank he holds". The Frenchman found that in America there was a "strange mixture of blood" which made it a country where "individuals of all nations are melted into a new race of men." For him, the blood-mixture of Europeans had given rise to a new race of Americans. But then, Crevecoeur's melting pot only melted diverse European peoples into a single race; it did not melt different cultures into a single American culture.

This loophole in the "Melting Pot" theory—the term was popularized by Israel Zangwill's 1908 play of the same name—was plugged by Ralph Waldo Emerson in 1845, Fredrick Jackson Turner in 1893, and Oscar Handlin in 1959. All three referred to a unique blending of cultures in America where all immigrant groups, based on their novel experiences, contributed to the emergence of a new national character.

The New Immigration that spanned the last two decades of the 19th century and continued into the next brought hordes of South and East Europeans to American shores. That this immigration necessitated and spawned the Americanization movement has already been talked about earlier in this book. But what has not been talked about is that though the leaders of the Americanization movement turned the melting pot into a pressure cooker, they would not like the new ingredients to add new color and/or taste to the broth. They feared that the new ingredients may take a long time to melt—which, under the prevailing political and diplomatic circumstances they were unwilling to spare—and, in any case, there was no guarantee that they would melt under normal circumstances. More importantly, they believed that the American national character that had emerged as a result of "melting" of cultures of people who belonged to the Old Immigration was irrevocable and immutable, and should not be altered whatever the provocation; all new immigrants should Americanize themselves by abandoning their native cultures and loyalties. This theory of assimilation—different from "Anglo-conformity" and the "Melting Pot", yet a combination of the two—is what I call *Amero-conformity*, relevant to the present situation.

It is in the aftermath of the New Immigration that Horace M. Kallen developed his theory of "cultural pluralism" in his 1915 essay in *The Nation*, "Democracy Versus the Melting Pot". As is evident from the title, Kallen had evolved a critic of the Melting Pot theory. Not only that, he saw in each group in America a tendency to preserve its own language, religion, communal institutions, and ancestral culture while at the same time learning to speak English as the language of general communication and participating in the overall political and economic life of the nation. What Kallen saw is still true for many ethnic groups—nay families—in the United States, but this tendency cannot be regarded as a model of assimilation under any stretch of imagination; in fact, it is an evidence of the refusal to assimilate by certain groups of immigrants. These unassimilated sections of the American population have most unfortunately not completed their journey from immigrant to American; they have transformed themselves from immigrants to ethnics under the disruptive influence of Cultural Pluralism and governmental policies based on it.

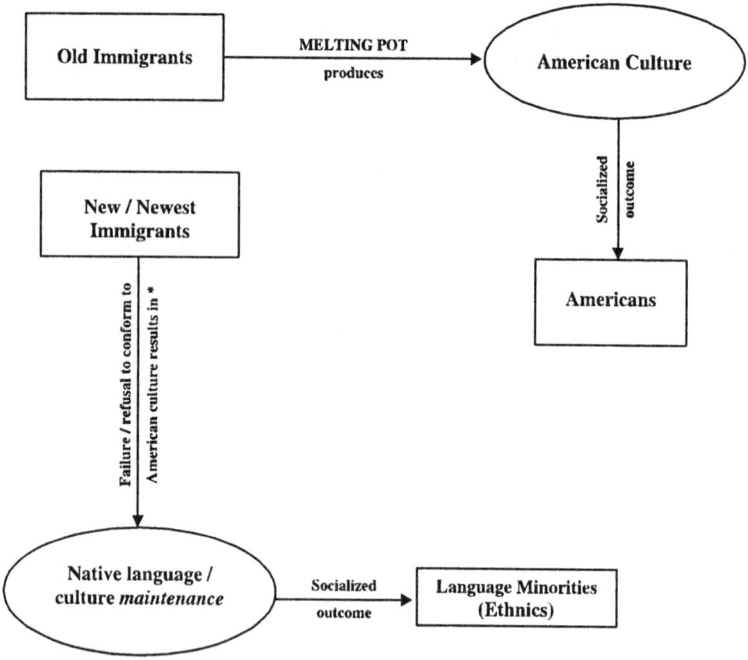

* Refusal to conform to American culture is a direct consequence of Cultural Pluralism and governmental programs based on it, like bilingual education and multilingual ballots.

Fig. 18. Cultural Pluralism Invariably Leads to Ethnic Segregation

As far as Americanization is concerned, it would be wrong then to consider it to be Anglo-conformity. '100%

Americanizers' believed in the pot that melted Euro-Americans of the Old Immigration into one national whole, racially and culturally. For them, the American national character that had evolved as a result of this melting was final, irrevocable, and immutable. Any effort to change it in any way by subsequent immigrants from southern and eastern Europe was blasphemous. Instead, Euro-Americans of the New Immigration were expected to undergo a process of supplanting completely their particular national characteristics with elements from the American national character: a love of individual liberty, free enterprise, limited and efficient government, freedom of worship, the English language. Even if none of these were found—and they were not—in the national characteristics of South and East European immigrants, they were required to acquire them as soon as possible (the sooner the better).

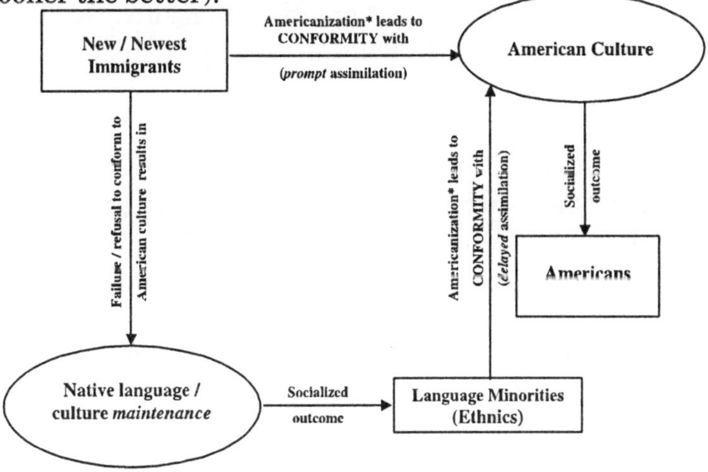

* Americanization efforts comprise the transition of language minorities from native languages to English, their rejection of bilingual education and multilingual ballots and inculcation of the assimilationist ideology.

Fig. 19. The Success of Americanization—Aimed at *Amero-conformity*—Consists in Weaning Language/Ethnic Minorities from the Influence of Cultural Pluralism

This principle of *Amero-conformity* was to apply to Americans of the Newest Immigration—those from Asia and Latin America—who came in after the Immigration and Nationality Act of 1965 became operational in 1968. If Slavs, Greeks, Poles, and Jews of the New Immigration had to abide by the rules of *Amero-conformity*, Asian-Indians, Arabs, Chinese, Koreans, Japanese, Vietnamese, Laotians, Cambodians, Filipinos, and Hispanics had to so as well. The American national character that had evolved as a result of the melting of Europeans of the Old Immigration—English, Welsh, Irish, Scot, Scotch-Irish, German, Dutch, and Huguenot—was to be regarded as the standard to be followed by subsequent generations of immigrants regardless of where they came from.

Seen in this light, Cultural Pluralism does not appear to be a model of assimilation, but a depiction of the failure to assimilate by certain sections of immigrants. Needless to say, Cultural Pluralism encourages hyphenism among immigrants, their ethnic identity becoming equally—sometimes more—important than the American identity. Theodore Roosevelt said "A hyphenated American is not an American at all." Accordingly, I consider the late president to be the chief proponent of the theory of *Amero-conformity*. He recognized that language was the most important ingredient of national character; if there was to be one nation, there had to be one language on which to base it: "We have room for but one language here, and that is the English language, for we intend to see that the crucible turn our people out as Americans, of American nationality, and not as dwellers in a polyglot boarding house."

Cultural Pluralism depicts a sad reality harmful to American society and polity. It does not believe in any wall of separation between public and private and acts as an impediment to the complete merger of ethnic communities with the American national whole. In fact, the highlighting of ethnic backgrounds that the theory engages in, in the name of democracy, tends to create ethnic enclaves and leads to the emergence of ethnic politics which is dangerous to democracy itself. Cultural Pluralism perpetuates cultural plurality which, in turn, sustains Cultural Pluralism as a political philosophy. Celebration of ethnic diversity produces a sense of ethnic and language separateness feared by the Founding Fathers and detested by subsequent generations of patriots. A *lebensraum* was not what the Founding Fathers had envisioned. Along with the establishment of the republic in 1776 the process of evolving a new nationality had begun. America has renewed itself through subsequent waves of immigration, but what was new was the composition of the population and not elements of its national character; presidential form of government, federal polity, free market economy, individual liberties, and the English language were not replaced or supplanted in any way.

A change in the national character would lead to a change in the nation itself: the form of government, the type of economy, the rights and freedoms enjoyed by the people, the language commonly used, all would change. The foundations of the state would be fundamentally altered. As far as the United States is concerned, such a change is not only undesirable, but inconceivable as well. In fact, it is the American national character that has attracted generations of immigrants from across the world. Giving up old loyalties and attachments for realizing the American Dream should not be a big price to pay. If an immigrant finds it difficult to overcome loyalties associated with the old country, he has to make a hard choice: to live in America like Americans for the sake of becoming a successful

American himself, or to leave the shores of America for where he had come from. Cultural Pluralism manifested through native language and cultural maintenance is the biggest obstacle to immigrants becoming successful Americans. The problem gets complicated when the failure to conform, under the influence of ideologies and leaders, becomes the refusal to conform.

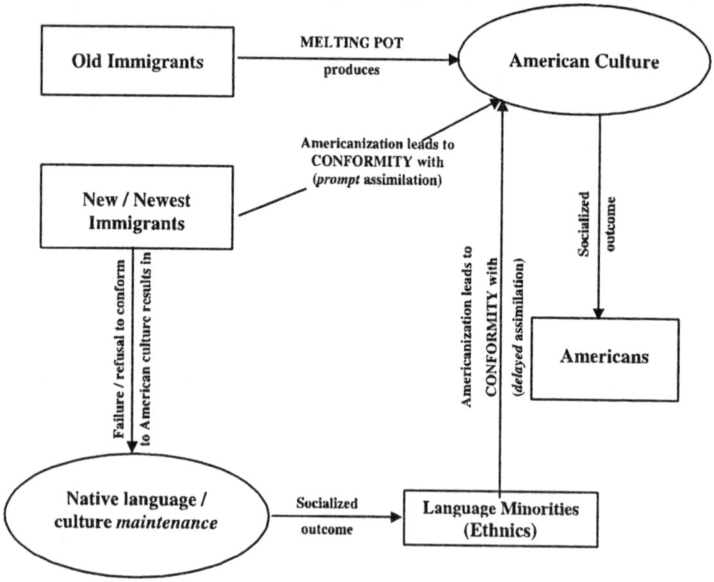

Fig. 20. The *Amero-conformity* Model Of Assimilation

But why isn't the Melting Pot an ideal for Americans of the New Immigration? Why is a complete renunciation of the immigrants' ancient cultures in favor of the values and behavior of Americans demanded from them? '100% Americanizers' believed that the Melting Pot would boil over if the national characteristics of the New Immigrants were added do it; for the ingredients in the Melting Pot to melt completely, they must have melting qualities. Otherwise, no amount of stirring would help. According to the Americanizers, the New Immigrants lacked those qualities. The best way to deal with them was to pressure-cook them so that they would dissolve without affecting its color, flavor, or odor. Greeks, Slavs Jews, and Poles were considered so different from the English, Scot, Scotch-Irish, and Germans of the Old Immigration that they were required to renounce completely their ancient cultures—so completely that nothing would be left of them—and take on the way of life of Americans of the Old Immigration as quickly as possible. This I call *prompt* assimilation. The cultures of southern and eastern Europe were treated with disdain—sometimes the people were too, by over-enthusiastic Americanizers—and the prescribed pattern of assimilation demanded their complete dissolution. The indigenous American culture that had developed as a result of the melting of various northern and western European cultural traditions was the set standard not to be violated under any circumstances. The duty of later immigrants was to abide by that standard. For *Amero conformity*, then, the Melting Pot had ceased to be functional once the Old Immigration had come to an end. The pot had melted the peoples and cultures of northern and western Europe in America into one American race and cultural type; no further addition was welcome. The fact that immigration from southern and eastern Europe could not be prevented necessitated Americanization in the late 19th and early 20th centuries. A fresh wave of immigration from Asia and Latin America in the late 60s and 80s necessitated another Americanization effort. But then, what was the immediate reason behind the latest Americanization movement, better known as the Official English Movement?

For one, the emergence of bilingual education was an important factor. The Bilingual Education Act (1968), which had the simple goal of teaching English to Limited

English Speaking Ability (LESA)—later renamed Limited English Proficient (LEP)—children of non-English speaking immigrant parents, somehow lost its purpose and direction and instead of remaining *transitional* bilingual education [using 'immersion' and/or English as a Second Language (ESL) methods] became *maintenance* bilingual education (using native language instruction). The various amendments to the Act of 1968, the *Lau V. Nichols* (1974) ruling of the U.S. Supreme Court, and the *Lau Remedies* (1975) of the Office for Civil Rights of the Department of Health, Education and Welfare were principally responsible for this loss of direction and purpose of bilingual education. Worse still, the 1975 amendments to the Voting Rights Act (1965) mandated multi-lingual ballots and voter assistance in electoral districts with substantial language-minority populations.

Bilingual education through native language instruction and multilingual ballots convinced many non-English-speaking immigrants that there was no need to learn English—let alone achieve fluency in that language—for living and working in America. Among these non-English speaking immigrants were many Asians and Hispanics. With time, Hispanics became the largest ethnic-minority group in the United States. This numerical strength, along with instigation from ethnic leaders and Cultural Pluralism-inspired politicians gave birth to a new reluctance—unheard of in earlier generations of immigrants—to learn English. This resistance to learning English—fanned by Cultural Pluralism—alarmed English-speaking Americans (many of them immigrants or children of recent non-English-speaking immigrants) of the growth of an un-American tendency opposed to assimilation. Let alone getting assimilated as quickly as they could, these Americans of the Newest Immigration—Asians and Hispanics, though not all of them—were refusing to assimilate at all. The need for a new Americanization movement was felt. And this time it was an urgent need.

This new Americanization movement—deridingly called the English *Only* movement by opponents—started with the formation in 1983 of the organization U.S. English by the late semanticist, Senator Samuel I. Hayakawa (R-CA), himself born to Canadian immigrant parents of Japanese descent and Dr John Tanton, a Michigan ophthalmologist. The most important objective of U.S. English was to amend the federal Constitution to declare English as the official language of the United States. Why? Because the English language is common to all Americans: it is the language of the Constitution and the laws, of the *Declaration of Independence*, of the Founding Fathers, of all Americans. Moreover, it is the language of the marketplace and of opportunity in the United States. It is not only the tie that binds Americans together but also the means to realize for every American his/her share of the American Dream.

U.S. English would also like multilingual ballots and voter assistance to be scrapped and funding only for *transitional* bilingual education (and not for *maintenance* bilingual education) to be retained by the federal government. It would also want government to control unbridled immigration which, along with bilingual education and multilingual ballots, has contributed to language segregation in the United States.

But nowhere does U.S. English propose the elimination of languages other than English. In none of the proposed amendments to the federal Constitution—the English Language Amendments (ELAs)—that it had helped prepare and in none of the Official English laws in the thirty states that it had backed did it suggest that the use of languages other than English be stopped altogether. In fact, it does not object to the private use of other languages at all. Accordingly, English *Only* Movement—spearheaded by U.S. English—is a misnomer. Official English Movement is the appropriate name for this new Americanization endeavor.

The chief concern of this movement is the total assimilation of non-English-speaking immigrants with the rest of the American population. Language is chosen as the instrument through which to assimilate because it has remained common to all Americans right from the initial days of the republic. No doubt that American society is plural, but any attempt to foster differences among people—and that is what Cultural Pluralism does—would divide the nation along ethic lines. In fact, the principal objective of the Official English Movement is to put an end to hyphenism among Americans. Hyphenism denotes ethnic identities and any attempt to perpetuate them would keep an American identity from developing among these immigrants, both Asian and Hispanic. In the tradition of Theodore Roosevelt, the Official English movement would want complete elimination of ethnic identities, if fostering them would mean undermining the American national identity.

But the Official English movement is a diluted version of the original Americanization movement: it accepts the private use of languages other than English, something neither '100% Americanizers' nor Theodore Roosevelt would have approved of. It is stringently opposed, though, to bilingual education through native language instruction. Public education is meant to prepare children for a successful public life; native language instruction ill-prepares language-minority children for life and work in the United States. If the American Dream eluded them, immigration for these children and their parents would be a bitter experience. And that may create a sense of alienation among them, a price they would have to pay for the lack of English proficiency.

There is no concrete evidence to prove that a child understood academic concepts better if taught in the native language. There are millions of non-English-speaking children in India who go to English-medium schools to be taught subject-matter courses in English. The native language is taught as a second language in Indian K-12 English medium schools. But college and university education is mostly in English, and that is what vernacular-medium schoolchildren find difficult. They have to labor hard to not only study their specialized academic disciplines but also master the English language. In the United States, where college and university education is wholly in English, it is not unusual for children taught through native language instruction to fare poorly and ultimately drop out. It is very difficult to attain an academic level of competence in two languages. In that case, English should be the language to be used for academic, professional, and public purposes; the native language can easily and, naturally, be the language used at home. The Official English movement's respect for the right of individuals to privately use languages other than English is an admission of this practical reality.

But why did this new Americanization movement have an Official English focus? During the old

Americanization movement, many restrictions were placed on the use of languages other than English (especially German) in the early years of the 20th century. Only one state, Illinois, passed a law declaring 'American' to be its official language. At that time in American history, no reluctance on the part of immigrants—those of the New Immigration, that is—to learn English was observed even by '100% Americanizers'. There were no federal laws mandating bilingual education and multilingual ballots. The need to declare English as the official language of the United States was not felt.

But the situation had changed in the 70s and the 80s. Not only were there federal laws that made bilingual education (through native language instruction) and multilingual ballots compulsory, latest immigrants—among them many Asians and Hispanics—were refusing to learn English, seriously disrupting the process of assimilation and jeopardizing the future of American society. Thus the Official English movement gave the battle-cry "One Nation, One Common Language" to enthuse not only its adherents but also common Americans.

But who was the battle against? Surely not against Asians and Hispanics, but against those who wanted to perpetuate bilingual education and multilingual ballots and were preventing non-English-speaking immigrants from assimilating into American society. Not only were these vested interests to be stopped in their tracks, their philosophy—Cultural Pluralism, that is—was to be eliminated as well. That would put an end to language and ethnic segregation forever, just as racial segregation had been abolished earlier. This I call *delayed* assimilation, because such assimilation can take place once language minorities are weaned away from the influence of Cultural Pluralism and made to realize the futility of bilingual education and multilingual ballots.

The Official English movement recognizes that in an ethnically plural society, Cultural Pluralism can never be allowed to become the reigning social philosophy because it would encourage ethnicity-based cultural diversity; more so, when ethnicities in the United States were themselves based on national origin. To build a culturally united nation out of an ethnically diverse society is the goal of all Americanization efforts, including that of the Official English movement. [In this context, it needs to be clarified that I use the term *ethnics* to mean national origin-based *language minorities* characterized by the *maintenance* of their native languages and cultures. Such *ethnics* are the result of the failure or refusal to assimilate. On the contrary, when I talk of *ethnic plurality*, I mean the whole gamut of ethnic communities—different from each other because of differences in national origin—that make up American society. Such *ethnic plurality* had seldom come in the way of evolving a common American culture (as with earlier immigrants from northern and western Europe) or of conforming to that culture (as with later immigrants from southern and eastern Europe and, to a much lesser degree, with latest entrants from Asia and Latin America).]

No doubt the United States has an ethnically plural society. But problem arises when that plurality is made synonymous with cultural diversity and sought to be perpetuated at the cost of national unity. Ethnic enclaves turn into voting blocs. Ethnic leaders are assured of bases of political and electoral support. And public polices are formulated with the purpose of acquiring and retaining such support. Divisive electoral campaigns tend to drive a permanent wedge between communities the effects of which are felt much after Election Day. Ethnic politics becomes an everyday affair. The great American Motto—*E Pluribus Unum* (From many, one)—stands thoroughly undermined.

The latest Americanization movement is nearly thirty years old. Thirty states—through statutes and constitutional amendments—have already declared English as their official language. There were many voter initiatives behind these statues and amendments, and most of them passed with huge majorities. Many Hispanics and other language–minority groups have supported these initiatives. The movement has made its presence felt in the other twenty states. An English Language Amendment (ELA) was proposed in every Congress since 1981. The Bill Emerson English Language Empowerment Act (H.R. 123) of 1996, passed by the 104th Congress, was a big victory for the Official English movement. That was the first time that the U.S. House of Representatives had approved of an ELA. The Inhofe Amendment of 2006, passed by the U.S. Senate in the 109th Congress, was a big victory too. It would not be imprudent to note that President Barack Obama and Vice President Joe Biden, then Senators from Illinois and Delaware respectively, had voted against the Inhofe Amendement. So did late Sen. Edward Moore "Ted" Kennedy (D-MA) and a certain Sen. Hillary R. Clinton (D-NY). If opponents of Official English—and of Americanization—have partisan interests to serve and have partisan support to fall back on, the Official English movement is not without partisan following either. In this, it is no different from the first Americanization movement.

(B) ONE CULTURE, ONE COMMON LANGUAGE : OFFICIAL ENGLISH AND THE FUTURE OF ASSIMILATION

Representative Norman Shumway (R-CA), testifying before the U.S. House Committee on the Judiciary, Subcommittee on Civil and Constitutional Rights, in favor of English Language Amendments (ELAs) in the 100th Congress on May 11, 1988 rejected arguments that he, as a sponsor of the amendments, believed in English *only*: "I do believe in English *primarily*". Protection of the primacy of the English language has always been a matter of highest concern for sponsors of ELAs in the U.S. Congress, from late Senator S.I. Hayakawa (R-CA) to Representative Tom Tancredo (R-CO). Almost all of these sponsors were Republicans.

But then, why did the Grand Old Party (GOP) not make Official English a plank in its party platform? There has been a Republican president—Ronald Wilson Reagan of California—known for his opposition to bilingual education; a presidential candidate—Bob Dole of Kansas—openly backing an ELA to the federal Constitution, that too during the campaign against multiculturalist president Bill Clinton in 1996; the US House of Representatives in the Republican 104th Congress did indeed pass an ELA in 1996 with House Speaker Newt Gingrich breaking convention to vote for H.R. 123 and supporting Official English in a moving speech; the Republican-controlled U.S. Senate repeated the feat in 2006 by declaring English as the "national language", but GOP party platforms have been traditionally silent on the issue.

On the contrary, state Republican committees—both in states with and without Official English laws—have since the 1980s, come out with statements expressing support to ELAs to the federal Constitution, and underlining the need to abolish bilingual education and multilingual ballots. In any case, party platforms are published during presidential nominating conventions once in four years. Only once did House Republicans bring out a platform—the conservative *Contract With* America—during an off year election in 1994. But even the *Contract*, which helped Republicans regain control of Congress after forty years, had no mention of an ELA to the federal Constitution. Interestingly again, it was in the 104th Congress, in which Republicans had a majority (thanks to their *Contract*), that the only ELA to the federal Constitution passed the U.S. House of Representatives till date. No doubt, then, that this Republican silence on Official English has met with curiosity, amazement, ridicule, disgust, impatience, even anger. Unfortunately, the party bosses have done little to address this range of sentiments.

Not only do Republicans believe in strong states, the nature of the American federal system has made state party committees more powerful than their national committees; in fact, national committees come alive only during election year. Seen in this context, the position taken by the various Republican state committees on Official English can be regarded as authoritative.

The GOP state committees have made no bones about supporting Official English and been categorical in their rejection of bilingual education. Even if the national party convention has shied away from raising—let alone debating—the issue, state party conventions have given opportunities to party leaders to speak on it. Hispanic Republicans have more than once rallied support for Official English during such conventions, though it would be wrong to say that all of them support the cause without reservations. In fact, prominent Hispanic Republicans are known to oppose Official English. Representative Ileana Ros-Lehtinen (R-FL) voted against H.R. 123 in 1996, despite being a Reagan Republican. Then Florida governor Bob Martinez called a ballot initiative to make English the official language of his state in 1988 "unnecessary". Perhaps Linda Chavez is the most famous Hispanic Republican to support Official English. Incidentally, a prominent Reagan Republican herself, she had been president of U.S. English between 1987 and 1988.

Accordingly, it would be wrong to say also that Republicans suffer from Hispanophobia. In both 1980 and 1984, Ronald Reagan got big chunks of the Latino vote, to be matched by Governor George W. Bush of Texas in 2000 (he was elected president of the United States that year and in 2004). Despite his opposition to bilingual education which became evident when he withdraw the *Lau Remedies* after becoming president, Reagan's conservative values endeared him to Hispanics. George W. Bush—who spoke fluent Spanish himself—was known to be opposed to the idea of Official English, supporting English *Plus* as a policy alternative. As Texas governor, Bush took no step to reverse El Cenizo's Official Spanish Law in 1999. Clearly, Bush's position on Official English—both as Texas governor and as U.S. president—was dictated by electoral compulsions.

There is evidence to show that Republicans had made inroads into the Democratic Party's Latino support base. A genuine need was felt among Republicans to expand its appeal to Hispanics beyond Cuban Americans, traditional GOP voters who support the party out of a loyalty rooted in its relentless opposition to the Castro regime.

Interestingly, Ros-Lehtinen, a Cuban-American herself, became the first from her community to be elected to the U.S. Congress in a special election in 1987 defeating a pro-Official English Democrat, Gerald Richman. Does that mean that to endear themselves to Hispanics—all Hispanics, not just Cuban Americans—Republicans have to give up Official English as a political cause?

Not really. For then, there would be no difference between them and Democrats. The GOP's politics of inclusion does not permit it to appeal to voters on ethnic lines. As the "party of Americans", it has always sent a message of unity between various ethnic groups in the United States. In fact, ethnicity has never been an electoral issue with Republicans; the party's conservative ideology of individual liberty, free enterprise, limited government, and strong national defense has always sufficed electorally. The GOP has always been judged on the basis of its ideology and not on the basis of ethnic support. On the contrary, as the "party of immigrants", the Democratic Party's appeal has generally been on ethnic lines, assuring immigrants of its commitment to protecting their rights to continue with their distinct ways of life, and its readiness to secure entitlements for them. It would not be wrong to say that Democrats have encashed Cultural Pluralism electorally. Seen in this light, the electoral battle between Republicans and Democrats is the manifestation of the ideological battle between *Amero-conformity* and Cultural Pluralism. But then, who has emerged winner in this battle?

The battle will not be won till the time Republicans continue publishing Spanish translations of party documents, including campaign materials, and the party platform; even the party website has a Spanish version.

Such translations tend to weaken the party's crusade—and that of its members who back Official English in Congress and outside—against bilingual education. In fact, Spanish translations of party documents belie an acceptance of the reality of the widespread use of that language. And there is not always much difference between acceptance and support.

The battle will not be won till the time Republican leaders continue to articulate positions contrary to Official English. If the party has officially kept quiet on Official English, its leaders—presidential candidates, presidents, governors, congressmen and senators—should refrain from the practice of opposing Official English in public. When most of the sponsors of proposed ELAs to the federal Constitution have been Republicans, opposition to Official English by national-level party leaders will send a wrong signal to rank and file activists. And that will ultimately undermine the cause.

The battle will not be won till Republicans fail to win Hispanics over ideologically. Many Hispanics, conservatives themselves, are finding Republicans to be a better electoral option because of the party's emphasis on faith and family values. The GOP has to now convince Latinos that prosperity lay in individual responsibility and free enterprise (along with limited government) and not in entitlements and government-dependence. Latinos have to be weaned from the Democratic Party's big government philosophy. Already, many Latinos have begun feeling that they are being taken for granted by Democrats. Republicans have to drive this point home. If African Americans, Jews, and Roman Catholics could veer toward the GOP, why not Latinos? Whenever immigrants had got over the immigrant mentality and assimilated with the rest of American society, socially and psychologically, they have switched loyalties from Democrats to Republicans. The Republican Party has given them a sense of belonging to the United States, whereas the farthest Democrats took them from being immigrants was to make them ethnics, separated from the rest of the nation by their peculiar languages, customs and mannerisms, and ways of life. Latinos who still vote Democratic have yet to free themselves from living life as ethnics.

And, the battle can never be won till the time Republicans as a party remain secretive about their position on Official English. The fact that most proponents of ELAs in Congress—almost all of them—have been Republicans, most Official English statues were passed in states with Republican-controlled Houses, the U.S. House of Representatives with a Republican majority passed an Official English bill (H.R. 123) in 1996, and the Republican U.S. Senate declared English as America's "national language" in 2006 have convinced many Latinos that the Republican party was behind the Official English movement. Worse, they believe that Republicans were nativists, even racists, and the Official English movement was a manifestation of such nativism and racism. It is high time Republicans disabused Latinos. If the GOP is apologetic about its philosophy of *Amero-conformity*, it will never be able to erase suspicions from Latino minds. It needs to convince Latinos that as a party it never launched the Official English movement, but because of its belief in the assimilationist ideology of *Amero-conformity*, individual party leaders had got involved with the movement because they shared that ideology. The fact that Republican leaders had led and still lead the Official English movement, coupled with the fact that many

Republicans have held leadership positions in U.S. English is not a coincidence, but there is nothing to be ashamed about that connection.

But then, is the Republican Party nativist? Attempts have been made to link the GOP with the Know Nothing Party, despite the fact that Know Nothings and Republicans had nothing in common. At a time when Know Nothings were opposing immigration and immigrants and rallying 'native' Americans as a political force, the Republican Party was born in opposition to the issue of slavery, something that had split the nation into two. In fact, the first presidential election fought by Republicans (in 1856) was also the last for Know Nothings. True that Republicans, in the early part of the twentieth century, were associated with moves to put various restrictions on the public use of languages other than English and to control unbridled immigration, but these actions can hardly be termed nativist. Republicans associated themselves with the first Americanization movement because of its own assimilationist inclinations. If nativism was tempered with hatred of immigrants, there was nothing to show that Republicans harbored such hatred. Republicans had indeed voted in Congress to control immigration, but they had never voted do isolate immigrants. By associating with the campaign for Official English, Republicans have affirmed their commitment to assimilationism a second time, the link with the earlier Americanization movement being the first. Accordingly it would be fallacious to brand Republicans as 20th century Know Nothings.

But is U.S. English a Republican grassroots organization? The answer is no. U.S. English is not a Republican grassroots organization, unlike the National

Rifle Association, the National Taxpayers' Union and the Christian Coalition; there are *no formal links* between U.S. English and the Republican Party. Grassroots organizations support the election efforts of their parent political parties in various ways, knowing that their causes find place as planks in the party platform. U.S. English, on the contrary, had opposed Republican election endeavors—as evident from the 1989 special election in Florida that elected Ileana Ros-Lehtinen to Congress for the first time—if the candidates were known not to favor Official English. In any case, Official English has never been a plank in any federal Republican platform and U.S. English has never got any official assurance from the party supporting the cause of Official English, relieving it of any obligation to endorse Republican candidates in elections. An overwhelming majority of Republicans support the campaign for Official English because they believe that English should be the official language of government of the United States as that was the easiest way to help assimilate immigrants. It is this belief that has made Republicans throw their lot behind the campaign endeavors of U.S. English.

U.S. English, on its part, has found in Republicans—though not in all Republicans—a platform from which to operate politically. Even though the cause—making English the official language of the United States through an amendment to the federal Constitution—is bipartisan, it has seldom found many takers among Democrats who have branded it divisive and anti-immigrant. The Democratic Party—though not all Democrats—has opposed the Official English campaign at both state and federal levels with a remarkable consistency. Since Democrats have almost always been unsympathetic to the Official English campaign, U.S. English has found it prudent to steer clear from them. The opposition of Democrats to and support of Republicans for an English Language Amendment to the federal Constitution have been responsible for identifying U.S. English as a Republican grassroots organization.

And this is where the difference between the two parties becomes glaring. The Democratic National Committee (DNC) opposes Official English as a matter of party policy. On the contrary, the Republican National Committee (RNC) is silent on the issue. A look at RNC policy papers would give the impression that the issue of Official English does not exist. This has helped cement the support of suspicious Latinos for the Democratic Party—who, otherwise, may not have voted for it—and also strengthened their suspicion about the "real" intentions and inclinations of the GOP. Platforms produced by the RNC, though affirming its support for funding *transitional* bilingual education only, have never spoken about the elimination of multilingual ballots and voter assistance. DNC policy papers, on the other hand, not only support bilingual education through native language instruction and promise more funds for such education, they also talk of continuing with multilingual ballots and voter assistance for the convenience of non-English-speaking residents and for ensuring their 'full' participation in American political life.

If more people who identity themselves as Republicans support Official English legislation than those who call themselves Democrats, the Republican leadership cannot be given the credit for it. In fact, some like former president George W. Bush may find this embarrassing. The credit for Republican grassroots support for Official English goes to party regulars who have relentlessly campaigned for the cause without direct help from the RNC. The GOP's support base of middle and upper-middle class English-speaking Americans is also readily receptive to the idea of Official English. U.S. English has successfully tapped this support base. But the overwhelming majorities with which Official English ballot initiatives have passed in several states prove that support for Official English goes beyond Republican sympathizers. Many working class voters with Democratic Party identification have said 'yes' to Official English. Middle class fear about being swamped by non-English-speaking immigrants in the neighborhood and labor apprehensions about the rising clout and numbers of non-English speakers in the workplace were primarily responsible for the support of these classes for Official English. That has been the case in every state with an Official English law.

If a threat perception among middle and working class voters is at the root of their support for Official English, how can that threat perception be removed? Surely, the idea is not to remove the threat perception in order to eliminate support for Official English. In fact, Official English itself can help remove the threat perception. Official English would give English-speaking Americans a sense of security in their own country. In towns with sizeable non-English-speaking populations—Hispanic, Chinese, whatever—native speakers of English feel threatened and alienated, and Official English gives them the feeling of having reclaimed their neighborhoods from outsiders. And what better way to assimilate outsiders than to teach them English? Official English, accordingly, would help eliminate a potential and potent source of social conflict in the United States. If suspicions and animosities between English and non-English-speakers have to come to an end, Official English should become federal law. An ELA to the federal Constitution can ensure that no state or local law mandates the official use of languages other than English; there would be no more El Cenizos. The Republican Party—called the "party of Americans" because of its assimilationist policy thrust—can help matters by supporting Official English openly.

But, then, what about the threat that Hispanics and other language minorities feel from Official English? True, many Hispanics are deeply concerned about the future of their culture and language in the United States. Democrats have convinced them that any attempt to "impose" English as the official language of the United States would mean the gradual elimination of the Spanish language and Hispanic culture. Though Hispanics are multiracial, all of them demonstrate a unique sensitivity toward the issue of language and culture and their protection and preservation. There is no party to tell them—barring, perhaps, U.S. English which is not a party—that Official English in no way threatens their language and distinctive way of life, that native culture and native language should direct the private sphere of life whereas the public sphere should be left to be governed by the English language. The Republican Party, though professing belief in this, has failed to articulate this position to Hispanics and other language minorities, giving rise to an ideological vacuum. Till the time the RNC fills up this vacuum at the federal level, language minorities would continue to perceive Official English as a threat and an imposition. More so, when organizations like the National Council of La Raza have demonized U.S. English as being that to Hispanics what the Ku Klux Klan was to Blacks.

The Ku Klux Klan as a white supremacist movement was not formally backed by any established political party.

If U.S. English is not formally backed by Republicans, Latinos will be convinced that it is indeed an Anglo-supremacist organization and the Official English movement aims to perpetuate that supremacy. In fact, as of today, many Latinos are already convinced about the racial nature of the Official English movement. Multiculturalists tell them day in and day out that they (Latinos)—more than their language and culture—are the real targets of the movement led by U.S. English, whereas the truth is that U.S. English is itself led by a Latino: Mauro E. Mujica. Another Latino—Linda Chavez, a prominent Reagan Republican—was president of the organization at one point of time. Can such an organization be Anglo-supremacist?

But is U.S. English striving for the supremacy of English? No, the Official English movement that it leads is striving for the *primacy* of English. Something that Representative Shumway (R-CA) affirmed way back in 1988. A categorical admission by the RNC that, as a party, it believed in the primacy of the English language would help remove the racist blemish on U.S. English and provide it with much-needed official partisan support.

If the Republican Party was born in opposition to slavery, the Klan was born to support and perpetuate that "peculiar institution" of the South. Many Republicans were regular targets of the wrath of the Klan. In fact, the Klan considered Republicans an anathema to American society, a Michigan-born delinquent with no understanding of how society operated in the South. The reason: Republicans had not only succeeded in undoing the secession of the South from the rest of the Union, but abolished slavery as well. Republicans had put an end to white supremacy; it is difficult to believe they would approve of a movement for

Anglo-supremacy. The *Amero-conformity* that they espouse is not aimed at establishing the supremacy of any language or language group. Supremacy of the English language would mean considering other languages to be inferior. There is no way that languages can be stratified, socially and academically. Of course a hierarchy of language groups can be constructed, but only on the basis of their populations. It is not the aim of the Official English movement to promote and ultimately establish the supremacy of either the English language or English speakers. Both Republicans and U.S. English aim at establishing the English language as primary in American public life—that includes education and voting, among other things—while respecting the right of individuals to use other languages in private situations. A formal association between the two organizations would help the early realization of this aim.

Nation-building is public activity, and the commonality that is necessary to build and sustain a nation can be supplied in the form of language, in this case English. But to make language minorities accept English as their own, they must be convinced that it is limited primarily to public life; any decision to use English in language-minority homes should be left entirely to individuals and families. Otherwise language-minorities would tend to regard English as a language "imposed" on them. There would be no difference, then, between teaching English to language-minorities in the United States and forcing Russian on non-Russian-speaking peoples in the various Soviet Republics of the erstwhile Soviet Union. Surely, language cannot be imposed on an unwilling people in a liberal democracy; Hindi, the official language of the Indian Republic, could never be forced on a reluctant Tamil population.

If individuals and families belonging to language-minority groups want to make a gradual transition to the use of English at home, the change would not only be voluntary but generational. This has been an American reality for people of the Old and New Immigrations; there is no reason to believe that those of the Newest Immigration cannot do likewise. The public life so influenced the private that second and third generation immigrants gradually, progressively, and ultimately took to using English at home. Children and young adults could not help using at home the language of the school, college, and workplace. When they had families of their own, they passed on the English language to their children and then to successive generations. That is how non-English-speaking immigrants had made the transition to English earlier, and completed their assimilation into American society. They ceased to belong to language-minority groups and became Americans. Till the time the present-day language-minorities make that transition, they would continue to be just that: language-minorities. Any attempt to treat them as ethnic communities—under the influence of Cultural Pluralism—would only impede the process of their assimilation. Language segregation and ethnic segregation would coexist, thus defeating the very purpose of their immigration to the United States. That would not augur well for the "nation of immigrants".

Since America is a nation of immigrants, the question of political loyalty of citizens to the dispensation—the government, the Constitution and the laws—becomes doubly important. Americans of German descent (though not all of them) supported the German war effort during World War I and brought upon themselves the wrath of other Americans. Indian Americans even run chapters of mainstream Indian political parties in the United States, instead of forming groups within the two major American parties (of late, though, Indian Americans have floated the Indian American Republican Council). These are two examples of incomplete assimilation. But Jews, while supporting Israel and determining to a great extent US policy in the Middle East, consider themselves Americans first. Being a nation of immigrants, the acquisition of nationality—different from the acquisition of citizenship—has a direct bearing on the question of assimilation in America.

The bestowing of American nationality demands the complete dissolution of past political loyalties. Immigrants generally arrive in the United States in search of a better life; their immigration does not necessarily involve enmity with the old country. The native land is fondly remembered, its culture cherished, a sense of belonging nurtured. On the other hand, refugees mostly flee persecution before ending up at Ellis Island; they certainly harbor animosity toward the old country. Accordingly, when one is an immigrant, like Indian Americans, the first generation almost never assimilates. Retention of food and dress habits, celebration of ethnic festivals, and repeated visits to the native land mark such immigrants; the old country is still 'home' to them. Though retention of language and culture is not uncommon among refugees like Iranians and Afghans, a visit to the old country is an absolute no-no for them (Cuban Americans are different: even though they never visit Castro's Cuba, they always had plans to go back to their native land after the communist dictator was overthrown).

As a result, refugees find it easier to assimilate, as ties with the old country are never renewed. Continued immigration, both legal and illegal, by Mexicans has reinforced cultural ties of Mexican Americans with their native land. Though cultural ties of immigrants with the old country decline in the second and third generations, to the point of becoming nil, such unbridled immigration needs to be controlled and finally stopped.

Only when old ties are forgotten and the old country becomes only a place on the map, does acquisition of American nationality become complete. The English language has an important role to play in this regard. English is a symbol of American nationality and no immigrant will become American till the time fluency in English eludes him. The sooner foreign accents perish the better it will be for the "nation of immigrants".

7

Postscript H.R. 4321

On December 15, 2009, Rep. Luis V. Gutierrez (D-IL), chairman of the Congressional Hispanic Caucus (CHC) Immigration Task Force, along with 90 of his party colleagues in the U.S. House of Representatives, introduced H.R. 4321, the Comprehensive Immigration Reform for America's Security And Prosperity (CIR ASAP) Act of 2009. It was described as a legislation "that secures our nation's economy, keeps families together and secures our borders while fixing our broken immigration system". The words have been carefully chosen, keeping in mind the "opponents of immigration reform" and the "immigant blame game" that they indulge in.

Addressing a press conference to introduce the bill, Rep. Gutierrez said "Our nation's immigration policy should be pro-family, pro-jobs and pro-security. Family, jobs and security. This bill accomplishes all three."[1] He added that these immigrants "want to be Americans". And H.R. 4321 was aimed at turning these immigrants "into Americans".

But the immigrants that the congressman from Illinois was talking about are those who have entered the United States illegally. Numbering around 12 million, most of them were from Latin America and had crossed over the Mexican–American border. Even though he admitted that "immigrants must learn English", in a situation where English was still not the official language of the United States, it would be very difficult to make them realize the importance of English. More so when Cultural Pluralists and Hispanic activists and organizations are ready to tell them that it was not necessary to learn English to become American, and that imposition of English was an Anglo-supremacist conspiracy to undermine and eliminate the culture and language of the Spanish-speaking population. The children of these immigrants will eventually attend bilingual schools, and we have seen how bilingual education produces "semi-lingual" students (those who end up mastering neither English nor Spanish).[2]

The opponents of immigration reform that Rep. Gutierrez talked about were those who wanted a check on unbridled immigration and demanded, among other things, that immigrants learn English. These people, branded nativists and Anglo-supremacists by Cultural Pluralists and bilingual education activists, would also want America not to become bilingual. James Crawford, that celebrated opponent of Official English, however admitted that the anti-bilingual current was a mainstream phenomenon.[3] In other words, most Americans would not like their nation to go the Canadian way. And that explains why Official English was such a popular issue among voters (it had passed with huge majorities in every state it was put on the ballot).

H.R. 4321, once it became law, will only complicate the situation. It will reinforce the sizable number of unassimilated limited-English-proficient Hispanics already residing in the United States as citizens. With 12 million more added to their ranks, Hispanics will continue to be the nation's largest ethnic minority. And, as an ethinc minority, they will continue to seek entitlements designed to keep them from assimilating into the American mainstream like bilingual education and multilingual ballots. How they will pursue their American Dream then is anybody's guess.

REFERENCES

1 To read Rep. Gutierrez's full statement, see *http://luisgutierrez.house.gov/PRArticle.aspx?NewsID=1407* (accessed on December 20, 2009).

2 Thomas Sowell, "The Failure of Bilingual Education", *The Social Contract*, Vol. 3, No. 3, Spring 1993, *http://www.thesocialcontract.com/artman2/publish/tsc0303/article_256.shtml* (accessed on December 26, 2009). See also Chapters 2 and 3 of this book.

3 James Crawford, *At War with Diversity: US Language Policy in an Age of Anxiety* (Clevedon, 2000), p. 5

8

Suggested Readings

ARTICLES

- "A Bilingual Prison", Editorial, *The New York Times*, September 21, 1995
- "A Critique of "Impossible Dream or Distant Reality?" Latinos and Party Alignment in the 21st Century", *A Policy Statement by the Tomas Rivera Policy Institute, August 22, 2001,* www.trpi.org *(accessed on March 14, 2003)*
- Antle III, W. James, "Americanizing Newcomers Again: Immigration Reform Promotes Americanization", *Ether Zone*, November 5, 2002
- Bane, Nancy, "Official English: Fear or Foresight?", *America*, December 17, 1988, pp. 515-16, 525
- Banks, Howard, "Bilingualism: A Wolf in Sheep's Clothing", *Forbes* 145, June 11, 1990
- Baro Diaz, Madeline, "Border City Goes All-Spanish", *AP Online,* August 20, 1999, http://www.highbeam.com/doc/1P1-23212867.html

(accessed on March 16, 2000)

- Baron, Dennis, "English in a Multicultural America", *Social Policy* 21, Spring 1991, pp. 5-14
- Bennett, William J., "The Bilingual Education Act: A Failed Path" in James Crawford, ed., *Language Loyalties: A Source Book on the Official English Controversy* (Chicago, IL: The University of Chicago Press, 1992), pp. 358-63
- Bikales, Gerda, "We Must Make English Our Official Language", *Washington Jewish Week*, March 19, 1987
- Bikales, Gerda and Gary Imhoff, "The Battle Over Preserving the English Language", *USA Today* 115, No. 2500, January 1987, pp. 63-65
- *"Bilingual Education", DNC Position Paper, Democratic National Committee,* http://www.democrats.org/record/positions/bilingualeducation.html (accessed on September 19, 2000)
- Booth, William, "A Key Constituency Defies Easy Labeling", *The Washington Post*, February 14, 2000
- Boxall, Bettina, "With gestures, but not chaos, Prop. 227 begins", *Los Angeles Times*, August 4, 1998
- Branigin, William, "Immigrants Shunning Idea of assimilation", *The Washington Post*, May 25, 1998, p. A1
- Broder, David S., "Dole Backs Official Language; English is Needed to Unify Nation, Presidential Hopeful Says", *The Washington Post*, September 5, 1995
- Bucy, Erik P. and Michael J. Ensley, "Issue Benefactors or Issue Victims? Ballot Initiative

Influence on the Vote for California Governor, 1982-1998", Article 12, *The California Journal of Politics & Policy, Volume 1, Issue 2, 2009,* http://www.bepress.com/cjpp/vol1/iss2/12/ (accessed on December 20, 2009)

- Burrell, Cassandra, "House Passes Official English Bill", *English Only Update EXTRA, August 2, 1996,* http://www.humnet.ucla.edu/humnet/linguistics/people/grads/macswan/updateex.htm (accessed on March 16, 2000)
- Bush, George W., "Hardball with Chris Matthews", *Council on Foreign Relations, May 31, 2000,* http://foreignpolicy2000.org/library/03_china/bush033100.html (accessed on August 31, 2000)
- Califa, Antonio J., "English-only laws would mean loss of rights", *Civil Liberties* 365, January 1989
- Came, Barry, "Accents of conflict: The melting pot menaces linguistic minorities", *MacLean's* 103, June 25, 1990
- Cárdenas, José A., "The Role of Native Language Instruction in Bilingual Education", *I.D.R.A. Newsletter*, January 1984
- Carlin, Jr., David R., "Outlawing Tongues: California's English Language Amendment", *Commonweal*, Vol. 113, No. 21, December 5, 1986, p. 648-49
- Carlson, Margaret, "Only English Spoken Here", *Time*, Vol. 132, No. 49, December 5, 1988, p. 29
- Carlson, Peter, "Hey, Professor, Assimilate This", *The Washington Post*, March 9, 2004, p. C01
- Carney, Jay, "English Spoken Here, O.K.?", *Time*, Vol. 128, No. 8, August 25, 1986, p. 27

- Cazden, Courtney B. and David K. Dickinson, "Language in education: standardization versus cultural pluralism" in Charles A. Ferguson and Shirley B. Heath (eds.), *Language in the USA* (Cambridge: Cambridge University Press, 1981), pp. 446-68
- Chavez, Linda, "One Nation, One Common Language", *Reader's Digest*, August, 1995, pp. 87-91
- Chen, Edward M. and Wade Henderson, " New 'English-Only' Movement Reflects Old Fear of Immigrants", *Civil Liberties*, Summer/Fall 1986
- Chetwynd, Lionel, "Are You Talkin' to Me?", *National Review*, Vol. 45, No. 15, August 9, 1993, p. 72
- Citrin, Jack, "Language Politics and American Identity", *The Public Interest*, Spring 1990
- Combs, Mary Carol and John Trasviña, "Legal Implications of the English Language Amendment" in *The English Only Movement: An Agenda for Discrimination* (Washington, D.C.: League of United Latin American Citizens, 1986)
- Contreras, Russell, "Dole attempts to out-right-wing other candidates", www.stp.uh.edu/vol61 (accessed on November 10, 2002)
- Cooper, Kenneth J., "Riley Endorses Two-Way Bilingual Education", *The Washington Post*, March 16, 2000
- Crawford, James, "Official English Isn't as Good as it Sounds", *The American School Board Journal* 176, March 1989
- Dale, Charles V. and Mark Gurevitz, "Legal Analysis of Proposals to Make English the Official Language of the United States", Congressional Research

Service, October 17, 1995, http://ourworld.compuserve.com/homepages/JWCRAWFORD/tenn.htm (accessed February 22, 2001)

- Davila, Alberto and Marie T. Mora, "English Fluency of Recent Hispanic Immigrants to the United States in 1989 and 1990", *Economic Development and Cultural Change*, Vol. 48, No. 2, January 2000, pp. 369-89
- Donahue, Thomas J., "U.S. English: Its Life and Works", *International Journal of the Sociology of Language* 56, 1985, pp. 99-112
- Draper, Jamie B. and Martha Jimenez, "Language Debates in the United States: A Decade in Review", *EPIC Events*, Vol. 2, No. 5, 1990, pp. 1,4,7
- Duignan, Peter, "Bilingual Education Advocates", *Hoover Essay*, Hoover Institution, www-hoover.stanford.edu (accessed on June 22, 2003)
- Duignan, Peter, "Bilingual Education: Yes or No?", *Hoover Essay*, Hoover Institution, www-hoover.stanford.edu (accessed on June 22, 2003)
- Ehrlich, Elizabeth, "Should English-Only be the law of the land?", *Business Week*, November 10, 1986, pp. 116, 120
- "English Only", *DNC Position Paper,* Democratic National Committee, http://www.democrats.org/record/positions/englishonly.html (accessed on September 19, 2000)
- Engwerson, Marshall, "A Tale of Two Languages: For Hispanic Immigrants, Shifts to English is Slow, but Sure", *Christian Science Monitor*, August 22, 1983
- Eskin, Leah, "Pro-Con: Should English Be Our Official Language", *Scholastic Update*, May 6, 1988

- Fallows, James, "Viva Bilingualism: English Has Nothing to Fear", *New Republic*, November 24, 1986
- Feder, Don, "An un-American act in a Texas Town", *The Washington Times*, September 1, 1999
- Fishman, Joshua A., "'English Only': Its Ghosts, Myths and Dangers", *International Journal of the Sociology of Language* 74, 1988, pp. 125-40
- Fishman, Joshua A., "Language policy: past, present, and future" in Charles A. Ferguson and Shirley B. Heath (eds.), *Language in the USA* (Cambridge: Cambridge University Press, 1981), pp. 516-26
- Fishman, Joshua A. and John E. Hofman, "Mother Tongue and Nativity in the American Population" in Joshua Fishman et. al., *Language Loyalty in the United States: The Maintenance and Perpetuation of Non-English Mother Tongues by American Ethnic and Religious Groups* (The Hague: Mouton and Co., 1966), pp. 34-50
- Fuchs, Lawrence H., "Immigration, Pluralism, and Public Policy: The Challenge of Pluribus to the Unum" in Mary M. Kritz (ed.), *US Immigration and Refugee Policy* (Lexington, MA: Lexington Books, 1983)
- Glazer, Nathan, "The Process and Problems of Language-Maintenance: An Integrative Review" in Joshua Fishman et. al., *Language Loyalty in the United States: The Maintenance and Perpetuation of Non-English Mother Tongues by American Ethnic and Religious Groups* (The Hague: Mouton and Co., 1966), pp. 358-68
- Gorov, Lynda, "Texas town makes Spanish official, stirs war of words", *The Boston Globe*, August 28, 1999, p. E08

- Guerra, Sandra, "Voting Rights and the Constitution: The Disenfranchisement of Non-English Speaking Citizens", *Yale Law Journal*, Vol. 97, No. 7, June 1988, pp. 1419-37
- Guthrie, Julian, "Language Barriers: Only the Beginning", *San Francisco Examiner*, May 15, 1997
- Halton, Mark R., "Legislating Assimilation: The English-Only Movement", *The Christian Century* 29, 1989
- Hayakawa, S.I., "Bilingualism in America: English Should Be the *Only* Language", *USA Today*, July 1989, pp. 32-34
- Hayakawa, S.I., "One Nation...Indivisible? The English Language Amendment", (Washington, DC: Washington Institute for Values in Public Policy, 1985), pp. 6-18
- Hayakawa, S.I., "Why English Should Be Our Official Language", *The Education Digest* 52, May 1987, pp. 36-37
- Headden, Susan, Linda Rodriguez Bernfield et. al., "One Nation, One Language? Would making English the nation's official language unite the country or divide it?", *U.S. News and World Report*, September 25, 1995, pp. 38-42
- Heath, Shirley Brice, "A National Language Academy? Debate in the New Nation", *International Journal of the Sociology of Language* 11, 1976, pp. 9-43
- Heath, Shirley Brice, "English in our language heritage" in Charles A. Ferguson and Shirley B. Heath (eds.), *Language in the USA* (Cambridge: Cambridge University Press, 1981), pp. 6-20

- Heath, Shirley Brice, "Language Policies", *Society*, Vol. 20, No. 4, May/June 1983, pp. 56-63
- Henry III, William A., "Against a Confusion of Tongues", *Time*, June 13, 1983, pp. 30-31
- Hornberger, Nancy H., "Bilingual Education and English-Only: A Language-Planning Framework", *The Annals of the American Academy of Political and Social Science*, Vol. 508, No. 1, March 1990, pp. 12-26
- "House Bill Would Declare English Official Language", *CNSnews.com,* May 29, 2001, http://archive.newsmax.com/archives/articles/2001/5/29/62653.shtml (accessed on October 24, 2003)
- Imhoff, Gary, "The Position of U.S. English on Bilingual Education", *The Annals of the American Academy of Political and Social Science*, Vol. 508, No. 1, March 1990, pp. 48-61
- "Immigrant Hispanic teens more likely to drop out", *CNN.com / EDUCATION*, June 13, 2003
- "Immigration and Official English Legislation", *Migration News,* Vol. 3, No. 9, September 1996, http://migration.ucdavis.edu/MN/comments.php?id=1023_0_2_0 (accessed on June 12, 2004)
- "Immigration Reform", *Congress and the Nation, Vol. II, 1965-1968, A Review of Government and Politics* (Washington, DC: Congressional Quarterly Service, 1969), pp. 57-61
- Jimenez, Martha, "The Educational Rights of Language-Minority Children" in James Crawford, ed., *Languages Loyalties: A Source Book on the Official English Controversy* (Chicago, IL: The University of Chicago Press, 1992), pp. 243-51.
- Joelson, J.R., "English: The language of liberty", *The*

Humanist 49, July/August 1989, pp. 35-36

- Judd, Elliot L., "The English Language Amendment: A Case Study on Language and Politics", *TESOL Quarterly*, Vol. 21, No. 1, March 1987, pp. 113-35
- Kasindorf, Martin, "Hispanic voters paint a new picture", *USA Today*, November 11, 2004, p. 04A
- King, Jack, "NMSU professors say votes of women, Hispanics should not be taken for granted", October 19, 2000, http://www.nmsu.edu/~ucomm/Releases/2000/october2000/votblocs.html (accessed on February 4, 2004)
- King, Robert D., "Should English Be The Law?", *The Atlantic Monthly*, Vol. 279, No. 4, April 1997, pp. 55-64
- Kjolseth, Rolf, "Cultural Politics of Bilingualism", *Society*, Vol. 20, No. 4, May/June 1983, pp. 40-48
- Krashen, Stephen D., "Bilingual Education, Acquiring English, and the Case of Richard Rodriguez", *California Association for Bilingual Education Newsletter*, May-June 1982
- Lambro, Donald, "Republicans draw Hispanic voters from Democrats", *The Washington Times*, July 12, 2003
- Lamm, Richard D. and John Love, "Apartheid, American Style: Growth of Minorities and Their Failure to Assimilate Result in Great Divide", *Rocky Mountain News*, September 18, 1988
- "Latinos", *DNC Position Paper,* Democratic National Committee, http://www.democrats.org/record/positions/latinos.html (accessed on September 19, 2000)
- Leibowicz, Joseph, "The Proposed English language

Amendment: Sword or Shield?", *Yale Law and Policy Review 3*, No. 2, Spring 1985, pp. 519-50

- Leibowitz, Arnold, "The official character of the English language in the United States", *Aztlan* 15, 1984
- Lexion, Valerie A., "Language Minority Voting Rights and the English Language Amendment", *Hastings Constitution Law Quarterly* 14, 1987, pp. 657-81
- Lyons, James J., "The Past and Future Directions of Federal Bilingual-Education Policy", *The Annals of the American Academy of Political and Social Science*, Vol. 508, No. 1, March 1990, pp. 66-80
- Mackaye, Susannah D.A., "California Proposition 63: Language Attitudes Reflected in the Public Debate", *The Annals of the American Academy of Political and Social Science*, Vol. 508, No. 1, March 1990, pp. 135-46
- Madrid, Arturo, "Official English: A False Policy Issue", *The Annals of the American Academy of Political and Social Science*, Vol. 508, No. 1, March 1990, pp. 62-65
- Mann, Arthur, "From Immigration to Acculturation" in Luther S. Luedtke, *The Society and Culture of the United States* (Chapel Hill, NC: The University of North Carolina Press, 1992), pp. 68-82
- Marotta, James S., "The Republican Party and the Hispanic Voter", July 30, 1999, www.voterzview.com (accessed on March 2, 2000)
- Marshall, David F., "The Question of an Official Language: Language Rights and the English Language Amendment", *International Journal of the Sociology of Language* 60, 1986, pp. 7-76

- "Martinez, rights leaders meet about English rule", *The Gainesville Sun*, November 24, 1988, p. 4B
- McBee, Susanna, "A war over words", *U.S. News and World Report*, Vol. 101, No. 14, October 6, 1986, p. 64
- Miller, John J., "The Hispanic Republic of Texas: Its Coming. Soon", *National Review*, October 14, 2002, http://www.thefreelibrary.com/The+Hispanic+Republic+of+Texas%3a+It's+coming.+Soon.-a092049019 (accessed on April 24, 2004)
- Morris, Dick, "The Hispanic Vote Elects Bush", *Newsmax.com,* November 5, *2004,* http://archive.newsmax.com/archives/articles/2004/11/4/203450.shtml (accessed on December 16, 2004)
- Murchison, Bill, "Bilingual nuttiness", *townhall.com,* February 26, 2002, http://townhall.com/columnists/BillMurchison/2002/02/26/bilingual_nuttiness (accessed on April 2, 2003)
- "Naturalization", *DNC Position Paper,* Democratic National Committee, http://www.democrats.org/record/positions/naturalization.html (accessed on September 19, 2000)
- "New US migrant reform bill", *Hindustan Times* (Delhi), December 17, 2009, p. 16
- "Official English", *Migration News,* Vol. 2, No. 9, September 1995, http://www.un.org/popin/popis/journals/migratn/mig9509.html (accessed on September 20, 2000)
- "Official English: Federal Limits on Efforts to Curtail Bilingual Services in the States", *Harvard Law Review*, Vol. 100, No. 6, April 1987, pp. 1345-62
- "People can't be pouring over border: Obama", *Hindustan Times* (Delhi), March 20, 2009, p. 17

- Porter, Rosalie Pedalino, "Introduction", *READ Perspectives*, Vol. V, No. 1, Spring 1998, p. 2
- Pratt, Larry, "English Should be Official Tongue", *Winter Haven News*, October 29, 1998
- "Proposition 227: The Future of Bilingual Education", *El Futuro Newsletter*, Summer 1997
- Ragsdale, Kathie Neff, "Becoming American, Staying Latino", *The Eagle-Tribune*, August 18, 2001
- Rodriguez, Richard, "Bilingualism, con: Outdated and Unrealistic", *The New York Times*, November 10, 1985
- Rotberg, Iris, "Some Legal and Research Considerations in Establishing Federal Policy in Bilingual Education", *Harvard Educational Review* Vol. 52, No. 2 (May 1982), pp. 149-68
- Roth, Bennett, "Survey Says Most Hispanics Support Bilingual Education", *Houston Chronicle*, April 23, 1998
- Salholz, Eloise, ct. al., "Say It in English", *Newsweek*, Vol. 113, February 20, 1989, p. 34-35
- Schlafly, Phyllis, "The Importance of Our English Language", *The Phyllis Schlafly Report*, Vol. 34, No. 10, May 2001, http://www.eagleforum.org/psr/2001/may01/psrmay01.shtml (accessed on November 30, 2002)
- Schmid, Carol, "The English Only Movement: Social Bases of Support and Opposition Among Anglos and Latinos" in James Crawford (ed.), *Language Loyalties: A Source Book on the Official English Controversy* (Chicago, IL: The University of Chicago Press, 1992), pp. 202-09
- Schmidt, Ronald J., "Language Policy Conflict in the

United States" in Crawford Young (ed.), *The Rising Tide of Cultural Pluralism: The Nation-State at Bay* (Madison, WI: The University of Wisconsin Press, 1993), pp. 73-92

- Schmitt, Eric, "House Panel Approves Bill Making English Official Language", *The New York Times*, July 25, 1996
- Skelton, George, "Deukmejian Opposes 3 Controversial Propositions", *Los Angeles Times*, September 03, 1986
- Sowell, Thomas, "The Failure of Bilingual Education", *The Social Contract,* Vol. 3, No. 3, Spring 1993, http://www.thesocialcontract.com/artman2/publish/tsc0303/article_256.shtml (accessed on July 21, 2005)
- Spener, David, "Transitional Bilingual Education and the Socialization of Immigrants", *Harvard Educational Review 58*, No. 2, May 1988, pp. 133-53
- Stalker, James C., "Official English or English Only", *English Journal* 77, March 1988, pp. 18-23
- Stevens, Gillian, "Immigration, Emigration, Language Acquisition, and the English Language Proficiency of Immigrants in the United States" in Barry Edmonston and Jeffrey S. Passel (ed.), *Immigration and Ethnicity: The Integration of America's Newest Arrivals* (Washington, DC: The Urban Institute Press, 1994), pp. 163-85
- Stewner-Manzanares, Gloria, "The Bilingual Education Act: Twenty Years later", *New Focus* (Washington, DC: The National Clearinghouse for Bilingual Education), No. 6. Fall 1988, pp. 1-11
- Tanton, John, "US English—Its Being Victimized by the 'Big Lie'", *Houston Chronicle*, October 30, 1988

- Tarver, Heidi, "Language and Politics in the 1980s: The Story of US English", *Politics and Society*, Vol. 17, No. 2, June 1989, pp. 225-45
- "Texas Governor Bush Steps Away from GOP Attacks on Bilingual Education", *AllPolitics.com*, July 2, 1998
- "Texas Town Declares Itself America's First "Spanish-only city"", (Washington, DC: U.S. English, August 13, 1999)
- "The New Apartheid", *National Review*, Vol. 42, No. 14, July 23, 1990, pp. 14-16
- "Toward a United America", *US English Brochure*, 1993
- Towery, Matt, "Inside the numbers: The Latino vote", January 13, 2004, http://townhall.com/columnists/MattTowery/2004/01/13/inside_the_numbers_the_latino_vote (accessed on May 22, 2005)
- Turbak, Gary, "Bilingualism: Terrible Time Bomb?", *Kiwanis Magazine*, Vol. 69, No. 6, June-July 1984, pp. 21-23, 27
- "Welcoming Immigrants to a Diverse America: English as our Common Language of Mutual Understanding", *House Republican Policy Committee Statement on Official English, June 5, 1996,* http://englishfirst.org/eff/GOPPOL.HTM (accessed on October 17, 2002)
- Whitworth, Damian, "Texas town bars English", *The Statesman* (Calcutta), August 15, 1999, p. 20
- Yang, John E., "House votes for official English language", *The Washington Post*, August 2, 1996
- Zall, Paul M., "The American Language: Follow the Founders?", *Freedom Review*, Vol. 26, No. 4, July-

August 1995, p. 2

- Zentella, Ana Celia, "Language Politics in the USA: The English-Only Movement" in Betty Jean Craige (ed.), *Literature, Language, and Politics* (Athens, GA: University of Georgia Press, 1988), pp. 39-53

BOOKS AND PAMPHLETS

- Adams, Karen L. and Daniel T. Brinks (eds.), *Perspectives on Official English: The Campaign for English as the Official Language of the USA* (New York, NY: Mouton de Gruyter, 1990)
- Archdeacon, Thomas J., *Becoming American: An Ethnic History* (New York, NY: The Free Press, 1983)
- Arias, M. Beatriz and Ursula Casanova, *Bilingual Education: Politics, Practice and Research* (Chicago, IL: The University of Chicago Press, 1993)
- Baker, Keith A. and Adrian A. de Kanter (eds.), *Bilingual Education: A Reappraisal of Federal Policy* (Lexington, MA: Lexington Books, 1983)
- Baron, Dennis E., *The English Language Amendment: Backgrounds and Prospects*, ERIC Document (Washington, DC: ERIC Clearinghouse on Languages and Linguistics, Center for Applied Linguistics, 1988)
- Baron, Dennis E., *The English-Only Question: An Official Language for Americans?* (New Haven, CT: Yale University Press, 1990)
- Bennett, David H., *The Party of Fear: From Nativist Movements to the New Right in American History* (Chapel Hill, NC: University of North Carolina Press, 1988)
- Bennett, William J., *Our Children and Our Country:*

Improving America's Schools and Affirming the Common Culture (New York, NY: Simon & Schuster, 1988)

- Bennett, William J., *The Condition of Bilingual Education in the Nation, 1988: A Report to Congress and the President* (Washington, DC: US Government Printing Office, 1988)
- Bikales, Gerda and Gary Imhoff, "A Kind of Discordant Harmony: Issues in Assimilation", Discussion Series, No. 2, (Washington, DC: US English, 1985)
- Bryson, Bill, *Made in America: An Informal History of the English Language in the United States* (New York, NY: William Morrow and Company, Inc., 1994)
- Cline, H.H., *Is there a Hidden Agenda? The English Language Amendment* (New York, NY: City College of the City University of New York, 1989)
- Conklin, N.F. and M.A. Lourie, *A Host of Tongues: Language Communities in the United States* (New York, NY: The Free Press, 1983)
- Cooper, R.L., *Language Planning and Social Change* (Cambridge: Cambridge University Press, 1989)
- Craige, Betty Jean, *American Patriotism in a Global Society* (Albany, NY: State University of New York Press, 1996)
- Crawford, James, *At War with Diversity: US Language Policy in an Age of Anxiety* (Clevedon: Multilingual Matters Ltd., 2000)
- Crawford, James, *Bilingual Education: History, Politics, Theory and Practice,* Second Edition (Los Angeles, CA: Bilingual Education Services, 1991)
- Crawford, James, *Hold Your Tongue: Bilingualism*

and the Politics of "English Only" (New York, NY: Addison-Wesley Publishing Company, 1992)

- Crawford, James (ed.), *Language Loyalties: A Source Book on the Official English Controversy* (Chicago, IL: The University of Chicago Press, 1992)
- Dallek, Robert, *Flawed Giant: Lyndon Johnson and His Times 1961-1973* (New York, NY: Oxford University Press, 1998)
- Daniels, Harvey A. (ed.), *Not Only English: Affirming America's Multilingual Heritage* (Urbana, IL: National Council of Teachers of English, 1990)
- Daniels, Roger, *Coming to America: A History of Immigration and Ethnicity in American Life* (New Delhi: Affiliated East-West Press Pvt. Ltd., 1992)
- Dharmadhikari, S., *The Official English Movement in New York and in the nation* (New York, NY: New York City Department of City Planning, 1989)
- Edmonston, Barry and Jeffrey S. Passel (ed.), *Immigration and Ethnicity: The Integration — of America's Newest Arrivals* (Washington, DC: The Urban Institute Press, 1994)
- Epstein, Noel, *Language, Ethnicity, and the Schools: Policy Alternatives for Bilingual-Bicultural Education* (Washington, DC: Institute for Educational Leadership, 1977)
- Fairchild, Henry Pratt, *The melting-pot mistake* (Boston, MA: Little, Brown & Co., 1926)
- Ferguson, Charles A. and Shirley Brice Heath (eds.), *Language in the USA* (Cambridge: Cambridge University Press, 1981)
- Fishman, Joshua A. et al, *Language Loyalty in the United States: The Maintenance and Perpetuation of*

Non-English Mother Tongues by American Ethnic and Religious Groups (The Hague: Mouton & Co., 1966)

- Fishman, Joshua A., Michael H. Gestner et al, *The Rise and Fall of the Ethnic Revival: Perspectives on Language and Ethnicity* (Berlin: Mouton Press, 1985)
- Foner, Eric: *Give Me Liberty! An American History* (New York, NY: W.W. Norton & Company, Inc., 2005)
- Ford, M.L., *One Language for the United States?* (Washington , DC: Council of State Governments, 1984)
- Gavit, John Palmer, *Americans by Choice* (New York, NY: Harper & Bros., 1922)
- Gingrich, Newt, *To Renew America* (New York, NY: HarperCollins Publishers, Inc., 1995)
- Glazer, Nathan, and Daniel P. Moynihan, *Beyond the Melting Pot: The Negroes, Puerto Ricans, Jews, Italians, and Irish of New York City*. Revised Second Edition. (Cambridge, MA: MIT Press, 1970)
- Glazer, Nathan, *Ethnic Dilemmas, 1964-82* (Cambridge, MA: Harvard University Press, 1983)
- Gordon, Milton M., *Assimilation in American Life: The Role of Race, Religion, and National Origins* (New York, NY: Oxford University Press, 1964)
- Graham, Hugh Davis, "American Liberalism and Language Policy: Should Liberals Support Official English?", (Washington, DC: US English, 1990), pp. 18, 20
- Grant, Lindsay and John H. Tanton, *Immigration and the American Conscience* (Washington, DC: The Environmental Fund, 1982)
- Grosjean, F., *Life with Two languages: An*

Introduction to Bilingualism (Cambridge, MA: Harvard University Press, 1982)

- Hakuta, Kenji, *Mirror of Language: The Debate on Bilingualism* (New York, NY: Basic Books, Inc., 1986)
- Handlin, Oscar, *Race and Nationality in American Life* (Garden City, NY: Anchor Books, 1957)
- Hartmann, Edward G., *The Movement to Americanize the Immigrant* (New York, NY: Columbia University Press, 1948)
- Higham, John, *Strangers in the Land: Patterns of American Nativism, 1860-1925*. Second Edition. (New Brunswick, NJ: Rutgers University Press, 1988)
- Hirsh, Jr., E.D., *Cultural literacy: What every American needs to know* (Boston, MA: Houghton Miffin, 1987)
- Hitchens, *Christopher, Blood, Class, and Nostalgia: Anglo-American Ironies* (New York, NY: Farrar, Straus, and Giroux, 1990)
- Hraba, Joseph, *American Ethnicity* (Itasca, IL: F.E. Peacock, 1979)
- Hudson, Winthrop S., *American Protestantism* (Chicago, IL: The University of Chicago Press, 1961)
- Huntington, Samuel P., *Who Are We? America's Great Debate* (New Delhi : Penguin Books, 2004)
- Imhoff, Gary (ed.), *Learning in Two Languages: From Conflict to Consensus in the Reorganization of Schools* (New York, NY: Transaction Books, 1990)
- Johnson, Donald Bruce (compiled), *National Party Platforms, Vol. 1, 1840-1956* (Urbana, IL: University of Illinois Press, 1978)

- Jones, Maldwyn Allen, *American Immigration.* Second Edition (Chicago, IL: The University of Chicago Press, 1992)
- Kachru, B.B. (ed.), *The Other Tongue: English Across Cultures.* Second Edition (Urbana, IL: University of Illinois Press, 1992)
- Kallen, Horace, *Cultural Pluralism and the American Idea* (Philadelphia, PA: University of Pennsylvania Press, 1956)
- Kloss, Heinz, *The American Bilingual Tradition* (Rowley, MA: Newbury House Publishers, 1977)
- Knobel, Dale T., *"America for the Americans": The Nativist Movement in the United States* (New York, NY: Twayne Publishers, 1996)
- Laird, Charlton, *Language in America* (Englewood Cliffs, NJ: Prentice-Hall, 1970)
- Lamm, Gov. Richard D. and Gary Imhoff, *The Immigration Time Bomb: The Fragmenting of America* (New York, NY: Truman Talley Books and E.P. Dutton, 1985)
- Laughlin, Harry H., *Conquest by Immigration: A Report of the Special Committee on Immigration and Naturalization* (New York, NY: Chamber of Commerce of the State of New York, 1939)
- Leibowitz, Arnold H., *The Bilingual Education Act: A Legislative Analysis* (Rosslyn, VA: National Clearinghouse for Bilingual Education, 1980)
- Luedtke, Luther S. (ed.), *Making America: The Society and Culture of the United States* (Chapel Hill, NC: The University of North Carolina Press, 1992)
- Macias, Reynaldo F. (ed.), *Are English Language Amendments in the National Interest? A Policy*

Analysis of Proposals to Establish English as the Official Language of the United States (Claremont, CA: Tomas Rivera Center, 1988)

- Mahoney, John J. and Charles M. Herlihy, *First Steps in Americanization: A Handbook for Teachers* (Boston, MA: Houghton Miffin, 1918)
- Mann, Arthur, *The One and the Many: Reflections on the American Identity* (Chicago, IL: The University of Chicago Press, 1979)
- Mencken, H.L., *The American Language* (New York, NY: Alfred A. Knopf, 1985)
- Miller, John J., *The Unmaking of Americans: How Multiculturalism Has Undermined America's Assimilation Ethic* (New York, NY: Simon & Schuster, 1998)
- Newman, Edwin, *Strictly speaking: Will America be the death of English?* (Indianapolis, IN: Bobbs-Merrill, 1974)
- O'Barr, W.M. and J.F. O'Barr (eds.), *Language and Politics* (Berlin: Mouton, 1976)
- Olsen, Laurie, *Made in America: Immigrant Students in Our Public Schools* (New York, NY: The New Press, 1997)
- Ovando, Carlos J. and Virginia P. Collier, *Bilingual and E.S.L. Classrooms: Teaching in Multicultural Contexts* (New York, NY: McGraw-Hill, 1985)
- Paral, R., *English Only: The Threat of Language Restrictions* (Washington, DC: National Association of Latino Elected and Appointed Officials, 1989)
- Piatt, Bill, *¿Only English? Law and Language Policy in the United States* (Albuquerque, NM: University of New Mexico Press, 1990)

- Portes, Alejandro and Rubén G. Rumbaut, *Immigrant America: A Portrait*. Second Edition (Berkeley, CA: University of California Press, 1996)
- Rodriguez, Richard, *Hunger of Memory* (Boston, MA: David R. Godine, 1982)
- Salazar, Rubén, *Stranger in One's Land* (Washington, DC: US Government Printing office, 1970)
- Simcox, David E. (ed.), *US Immigration in the 1980s: Reappraisal and Reform* (Boulder, CO and Washington, DC: Westview Press and Center for Immigration Studies, 1988)
- Simpson, David, *The Politics of American English, 1776-1850* (New York, NY: Oxford University Press, 1986)
- Skutnabb-Kangas, Tove, *Bilingualism or not: The Education of Minorities* (Clevedon: Multilingual Matters Ltd., 1984)
- Solomon, Barabara Miller, *Ancestors and Immigrants* (Cambridge, MA: Harvard University Press, 1956)
- Sowell, Thomas, *Ethnic America: A History* (New York, NY: Basic Books, Inc., 1981)
- Stein, Jr., Colman Brez, *Sink or Swim: The Politics of Bilingual Education* (New York, NY: Praeger, 1986)
- Steiner, Edward A., *From Alien to Citizen* (New York, NY: Fleming H. Revell, 1914)
- Tanton, John H., *Rethinking Immigration Policy* (Washington, DC: Federation for American Immigration Reform, 1979)
- Tatalovich, Raymond, *Nativism Reborn? The Official*

English Movement and the American States (Lexington, KY: The University Press of Kentucky, 1995)

- Tibbetts, Arnold and Charlene Tibbetts, *What's Happening to American English?* (New York, NY: Charles Scribner's Sons, 1978)
- Trasviña, John, *Official English / English Only: More Than Meets the Eye* (Washington, DC: National Education Association, 1988)
- Veltman, Calvin J., *Language Shift in the United States* (Berlin: Mouton Publishers, 1983)
- Walzer, Michael, *What it means to be an American: Essays on the American Experience* (New Delhi: Affiliated East-West Press, Pvt. Ltd., 1994)
- Webster, Noah, *Dissertation on the English Language: With Notes, Historical and Critical* (Meniston, Scolar Press, 1967)
- Weinstein, Brian, *The Civic Tongue: Political Consequences of Language Choices* (New York, NY: Longman, 1983)

WEBSITES (THIS LIST IS NOT EXHAUSTIVE)

Pro-Official English

- http://www.us-english.org/
- http://www.proenglish.org/
- http://englishfirst.org/
- http://www.fairus.org/
- http://workings.com/ELPAC.htm
- http://www.ceousa.org/
- http://www.eagleforum.org/

- http://www.gop.com/
- http://www.gopusa.com/
- http://www.buchanan.org/
- http://newt.org/

Anti-Official English

- http://www.nabe.org/
- http://www.tesol.org/
- http://www.lulac.org/
- http://www.maldef.org/
- http://www.nclr.org/
- http://larazaunida.tripod.com/
- http://www.naacp.org/home/index.htm
- http://www.democrats.org/
- http://www.languagepolicy.net/

U.S. Government sites

- http://www.hhs.gov/ocr/
- http://www.justice.gov/
- http://www.house.gov/
- http://www.senate.gov/

Index

Adams, John 5, 6, 8, 9, 183
Adams, John Quincy 18, 19
AFL-CIO 49
Alabama
  Official English law in 181, 194, 195
Alain, William A. "Bill" 199
Alaska
  Official English law in 181, 196, 197
Aldrich, Thomas Bailey 55
Alexander, Lamar 201
Allen, George F. 188
American Civil Liberties Union 120
American Dictionary of the English Language 7, 8
Americanization 33, 34, 220, 225, 245, 255
  not Anglo-conformity 244
Americanization movement 28-32, 92, 144, 243, 249, 252, 254, 256, 263
  Official English movement as new 249, 251-53, 256
American Republican Party 22, 23
American Revolution 2, 3, 5, 7
Americans for Border Control 141
Amero-conformity 240, 243, 245, 246, 249, 260, 269
  Republicans and 262, 269
ampersand phenomenon 34, 225, 227
Anglo-conformity 17-19, 221, 241, 243
  Official English projected as 144
Anglo-Protestant culture 11-13, 32
Ariyoshi, George R. 189
Arizona
  Official English law in 181, 202, 203
Arkansas
  Official English law in 181, 201, 202
Aztlan 122
Barr, Bob 227
Bell, T.H. 72
Bennett, William J. 74, 75, 91, 120
Biden, Joe 256
Bikales, Gerda 143, 160, 162
Bilingual education 63-65, 68-75, 89-129, 138, 140, 148, 151, 153, 156, 158, 169, 184-86, 188, 191, 196, 197, 200-04,

206-09, 213, 214, 244, 245, 250, 251, 253-55, 257-259, 265, 274
Bilingual Education Act (1968) 15, 63-65, 67, 68, 70, 90, 99, 101, 102, 104, 107, 129, 156, 227, 249, 250
Bilingual Education Act (1974) 68, 69
Bilingual Education Act (1978) 70
Bilingual Education Act (1984) 72-75
Bilingual Education Act (1988) 74
Bilingualism 98, 104, 105, 136, 148, 151, 153-56, 158, 164
Bill Emerson English Language Empowerment Act (1996) 162-74, 201, 213, 227, 230-32, 259
Boulet, Jim 80
Buchanan, James 25, 27
Buchanan, Patrick J. 155
Bush, George H.W. 220, 232, 233
Bush, George W. 187
and the Hispanic vote 215-18, 220, 221, 226, 232-34, 259
opposition to Official English 214, 215, 233, 259
silence on Spanish-only measure in El Cenizo 79-81, 213, 215, 259
Bush, Jeb 218
California 25, 39, 40, 66, 71, 109, 112, 113, 126, 168, 219, 232, 257
Official English law in 181, 190-92, 194, 195
bilingual education abolished in (Unz Initiative) 123-26, 213
California Teachers' Association 124
Cardeñas, José A. 93-96
Carnahan, Mel 205
Carter, James Earl "Jimmy" 136
Castañeda v Pickard 69
Center for Immigration Studies 141
Chavez, Linda 138, 140, 221, 232, 259, 268
Chinese American students 66, 67
Chinese Exclusion Act (1882) 40, 44
Cleveland, Grover 42
Clinton, Hillary R. 256
Clinton, William Jefferson "Bill" 184, 185
and H.R. 123 167, 201
and Official English law in Arkansas 167, 201
and the Hispanic vote 167, 201, 215, 216
and LEPs 234
as multiculturalist 107, 233, 257
silence on Spanish-only measure in El Cenizo 79
Collins, Martha Layne 199
Colorado 99
Official English law in 181, 192, 193
Contract with America 163, 166, 258
Crawford, James 78, 79, 82, 139-41, 229, 274
Cultural Pluralism 4, 63, 105, 144, 156, 221, 225, 243-48, 250, 252, 254, 255, 260, 270, 274

Cummins, Jim 97, 207
Cunningham, Randy "Duke" 163
Dade County "anti-bilingual" ordinance 135, 136, 193, 194
Daughters of the American Revolution 30
Declaration of Independence 2, 9, 16, 57, 148, 150, 229, 251
Democratic Party 21-25, 47, 49, 58, 70, 146, 163, 164, 166-68, 187, 207, 210, 215, 217-19, 226, 230-34, 259-62, 264-66, 274, 275
  as "party of immigrants" 21, 45, 117, 165, 226
  opposition to Official English 207, 264, 265
  position on bilingual education 117-19, 123, 184, 186, 265
Democrats *See* Democratic Party
Deukmejian, George 190, 191
Dillingham, William P. 39
Dole, Robert J. "Bob" 81, 82, 215, 257
Dukakis, Michael 183
El Cenizo
  Safe Haven Ordinance in 77, 80, 215
  Spanish-only measure in 14, 16, 77-83, 215, 259
English as a Second Language (ESL) approach/programs 68, 98, 101, 103, 111, 126, 188, 203, 250
English First 159, 160
English Language Amendment (ELA) 15, 137, 138, 141, 143-47, 151, 153, 162-64, 192, 213, 214, 230, 232, 256, 258, 261, 262, 265-67
English Language Unity Acts (2001, 2003, 2005, 2007, 2009) 227-31
English *Plus*
  as philosophy/policy 120, 122, 233, 259
  in New Mexico 13-16, 189
English Plus Information Clearinghouse (EPIC) 120, 121
English *Plus* Resolution 121, 122
English-speaking denominations 11
Epstein, Noel 107-09
Ervin, Sam 48
Federalist Papers 10
Federation of American Immigration Reform (FAIR) 139-41
Ferré, Maurice 136, 137, 145, 148, 149
Fillmore, Millard 25, 27
Fishman, Joshua A. 105, 117
Florida
  Official English law in 181, 192-94
Franklin, Benjamin 9, 10, 17
Gaarder, A. Bruce 97-98
Georgia
  Official English law in 181, 186, 187
Geringer, James Edward "Jim" 204
German Americans 2, 4, 9-11, 17, 20, 29, 39, 41-43, 58, 92, 189, 249, 270
Gingrich, Newt 163, 165-67, 172, 180, 219, 257
Gordon, Milton M. 17, 144
Gutierrez, Luis V. 174, 273, 274

Hamilton, Alexander 10
Hawaii
Official English law in 181, 189, 190
Hayakawa, S.I. 137, 149, 150, 153-55, 157, 164, 174, 192, 251, 257
Heath, Shirley Brice 3
Higham, John 29
Hispanics 45, 55, 58, 62, 76, 80-82, 104-06, 109-12, 115-17, 119, 122, 127, 129, 136, 138-40, 144, 153, 154, 157, 161, 165-67, 171, 175, 185, 190, 191, 194, 201, 214-20, 222-24, 232-34, 250, 252, 254, 259-62, 266-68, 274, 275
as LEP/LESA 62, 64-66, 93, 105, 109, 111, 113, 115-17, 124, 275
Hobbes, Thomas 8
H.R. 123 *See* Bill Emerson English Language Empowerment Act (1996)
Hunt, Guy 195
Huntington, Samuel P. 11, 33, 34, 109, 154, 155, 222, 223
Idaho
Official English law in 181, 208, 209
Illinois
Official English law in 181, 197, 198
Imhoff, Gary 95, 99, 104-06, 109, 128, 159, 192
"immersion" approach 99, 103, 118, 124-26, 202, 203, 250
Immigration Act (1903) 40
Immigration Act (1907) 41
Immigration Act (1917) 41, 42
Immigration Act (1924) 43, 57
Immigration and Nationality Act (1965) 48, 50-52, 54, 55, 246
Immigration Restriction League 42
Indiana
Official English law in 181, 198
Inhofe Amendment 231, 256
Inhofe, James M. 231
Intercultural Development Research Association (IDRA), Texas 93
Iowa
Official English law in 181, 207, 208, 228
Janklow, William John "Bill" 204
Jay, John 10
Jefferson, Thomas 2, 4-6, 8
Johnson, Lyndon B. 47-49, 51, 65, 167
Kallen, Horace 62, 63, 105, 243, 244
Kansas
Official English law in 181, 209, 210
Kennedy, Edward Moore "Ted" 256
Kennedy, John F. 44, 46, 167
Kentucky
Official English law in 181, 198, 199
Kerry, John F. 187
King, Peter 227, 230
King, Steve 227-31
Know Nothing movement/party 24-27, 42, 139, 194, 263
Krashen, Stephen 95-97, 125
Ku Klux Klan 194, 195, 171, 267, 268

Lamm, Richard D. 99, 104, 192, 193
La Raza Unida 122
Latinos *See* Hispanics
Lau Remedies (1975) 68, 70-72, 103, 202, 250, 259
Lau v Nichols (1974) 66-68, 71, 102, 103, 202, 250
League of United Latin American Citizens (LULAC) 104, 120, 214
Lebensraum 240, 247
Leibowicz, Joseph 143, 144
Limited English Proficient (LEP) students 62, 65, 70, 71, 73-75, 90, 94, 95, 98, 101, 102, 108, 111, 113, 117, 125, 126, 185, 186, 196, 197, 202-04, 206-08, 250
Limited English Speaking Ability (LESA) students 64, 65, 68-70, 90, 101, 103, 250
Louisiana
  Official English law in 10, 11, 180, 181
Lyons, James J. 98
  Madison, James 10, 11
Maintenance bilingual education *See* Native language instruction
Mann, Arthur 156
Mann, Horace 129
Martin, James G. 184
Martinez, Robert "Bob" 193, 194, 259
Massachusetts
  Official English law in 181-83, 188
McCarran, Patrick A. 45, 47
McCarran-Walter Act (1952) 44, 45, 47, 48
McCormick, Washington J. 8
Melting pot theory 8, 62, 63, 146, 152, 153, 165, 171, 221, 242, 243, 248, 249
Merrill, Steve 186
Mexican-American Legal Defense and Educational Fund (MALDEF) 104, 120, 124, 125
Meyer v Nebraska (1923) 59-63, 189
Miller, John J. 226
Miller, Zell B. 187
Mississippi
  Official English law in 181, 199
Missouri
  Official English law in 181, 205
Monroe, James 18
Montana
  Official English law in 181, 206
Montgomery Guards 22
Movimiento Estudiante Chicano de Aztlan (MECHA) 122, 123
Muhlenberg, Frederick Augustus 10
Mujica, Mauro E. 81, 138, 268
Multilingual ballots 76, 140, 151, 158, 163, 166, 168, 182, 187, 191, 197, 198, 200, 244, 250, 251, 254, 265, 275
  Also see Voting Rights Act (1965)
National Americanization Committee 30
National Association for Bilingual Education (NABE) 98, 120, 124
National Association for Latino Elected Officials (NALEO) 124

National Association for the Advancement of Colored People (NAACP) 125
National Council of *La Raza* 120, 123, 171
National Language Acts (2001 & 2005) 227, 230
National Origins Quota System 43, 44, 46, 47, 49, 51, 55, 57
Native American Democratic Association (NADA) 21-23
Native language instruction 56, 63-65, 67-74, 90, 94-98, 100-03, 107-12, 115, 119, 124, 127, 156, 184, 186,188, 196, 197, 200-02, 204, 206, 209, 250, 251, 253, 265
Naturalization Act (1906) 40, 41
Nebraska
  Official English law in 59, 181, 188, 189, 214
New Hampshire
  Official English law in 181, 185-87
Nixon, Richard M. 67
North American Civic League 30
North Carolina
  Official English law in 181, 183, 184
North Dakota
  Official English law in 181, 199
Numberg, Geoffrey 174
Obama, Barack 58, 256
Official English 137, 138, 142, 144-47, 160, 164, 165, 168, 170, 171, 173, 174, 180, 181, 187, 192, 194, 195, 210, 211, 213, 232, 234, 257-62, 264-67, 274
Official English movement 77, 135, 137, 139-45, 151, 153, 156, 157, 159, 160, 162, 194, 231, 252-56, 262, 268
Ogilvie, Richard B. 198
Order of the Star-Spangled Banner (OSSB) 24
Order of United American Mechanics (OUAM) 23, 24
Order of United Americans (OUA) 24
Orr, Robert D. 198
Otter, C.L. "Butch" 208
Patriotic Daughters of America 23
Pickering, Jesse 19
Pioneer Fund 141
Porter, Rosalie Pedalino 126
Portes, Alejandro 128, 129
Primary or Home Language Other Than English (PHLOTE) 71, 126
ProEnglish 160, 161
PROPA v Kusper (1973) 197
Quota Act (1921) 42
Racicot, Marc F. 206
Reagan, Ronald W. 71-73, 91, 120, 136, 164, 220, 233, 257, 259
Republican Party 27, 91, 123, 136, 163-66, 168, 171, 186, 187, 207, 210, 211, 213, 214, 216-20, 226, 227, 231, 232, 234, 257-69
Republicans *See* Republican Party
Research in English Acquisition and Development (READ) 126
Riley, Richard W. 123, 124, 184, 185
Rodriguez, Rafael 14, 78, 225 *Also see* El Cenizo
Romer, Roy 193
Roosevelt, Theodore 57, 58, 89, 92, 157, 240, 246, 252

Ros-Lehtinen, Ileana 168, 259, 260, 264
Rumbaut, Ruben G. 128, 129
Schmidt, Ronald J. 127, 128
Sebelius, Kathleen 209
Shumway, Norman 150-52, 164, 257, 268
"Sink-or-swim" approach 93, 99
Sinner, George 199
Solarz, Stephen 145-47
South Carolina
  Official English law in 181, 184, 185, 187
South Dakota
  Official English law in 182, 204
Spanish American League Against Discrimination (SALAD) 120
Taft, William Howard 42
Tanton, John 137, 139, 140, 162, 223, 251
Teachers of English to Speakers of Other Languages (TESOL) 120
Tennessee
  Official English law in 182, 199-201
Transitional bilingual education 63, 70, 73-75, 90, 94, 98, 100, 102, 106, 107, 109, 110, 140, 158, 159, 184, 185, 188, 197, 250, 251, 265
Truman, Harry S. 44, 45, 47
Unz Initiative *See* California (bilingual education abolished in)
Unz, Ron 123
United Daughters of America 24
United Sons of America 24
U.S. English 137-41, 143, 148, 152, 157-62, 170, 171, 173, 251, 252, 263-69
Utah
  Official English law in 182, 206, 207
Vilsack, Tom 207
Virginia
  Official English law in 181, 188
Voting Rights Act (1965)
  1975 amendments to 15, 75, 76, 162, 163, 166, 168, 187, 197, 198, 200, 227, 250
Walter, Francis E. 47
Walzer, Michael 27, 34, 226
Washington, George 4
Webster, Noah 7, 8, 183
Wilson, Pete 219
Wilson, Woodrow 29, 42
Wyoming
  Official English law in 182, 204, 205
Yarborough, Ralph 63-65, 89, 90, 99, 107, 129
Zangwill, Israel 8, 242